DARK HEART

A True Story of
Sex, Manipulation,
and Murder

KEVIN FLYNN
AND
REBECCA LAVOIE

BERKLEY BOOKS, NEW YORK

BERKLEY

An imprint of Penguin Random House LLC
375 Hudson Street, New York, New York 10014

DARK HEART

A Berkley Book / published by arrangement with the authors

ISBN: 978-0-425-28110-9

PUBLISHING HISTORY
Berkley premium edition / March 2016

PRINTED IN THE UNITED STATES OF AMERICA

10   9   8   7   6   5   4   3   2   1

Cover art: Leather whip in heart shape © michelaubryphoto/Shutterstock.
Cover design by Jane Hammer.

Some names and identifying characteristics have been changed to protect the privacy
of the individuals involved.

Penguin
Random
House

DARK HEART

"Flynn and Lavoie expertly layer on stunning, devastating detail to explain the inexplicable—a case that had the media stumped for months. I couldn't stop reading, and neither will you." —Robert Kolker, author of *Lost Girls*

"*Dark Heart* is a twisted and intriguing true story dripping with sex, lies, and the terrifying manipulation of an innocent young woman. Kevin Flynn and Rebecca Lavoie do a masterful job tackling a disturbing case of a murdered New Hampshire coed. The book is a riveting suspense thriller that paints a ghastly portrait of one couple's perverse sexual relationship that led to a shocking murder. *Dark Heart* exposes the truly horrific side of the BDSM world and will make *Fifty Shades of Grey* seem tame."

—Shanna Hogan, *New York Times* bestselling author of
Picture Perfect: The Jodi Arias Story

**PRAISE FOR OTHER BOOKS
BY KEVIN FLYNN AND REBECCA LAVOIE**

"Harrowing and haunting . . . [A] story not only filled with twists and suspense but also rich with heartbreak and humanity."

—Megan Abbott, Edgar Award–winning author of
The End of Everything

continued . . .

DEDICATION

To all those working to keep her memory alive
through the Lizzi Marriott Intrepid Explorer Fund.
rememberlizzi.org

CONTENTS

Prologue   ix

PART ONE Bondage   1

1. Lizzi   3
2. Kat   15
3. Wild Card   31
4. Skarlet   49
5. The Sacrifice   61

PART TWO Pain   83

6. Mother Dragon   85
7. Akasia   101
8. The Lair   113
9. Camp   135
10. The Punishment   147

PART THREE Submission   163

11. Missing   165
12. Good Cop   179
13. Peirce Island   195
14. Current Events   207
15. "Take Care of This"   223
16. Bishop's Vacation   243

PART FOUR Discipline   **255**

17. Gross Injustice   257
18. The Gauntlet   271
19. Star Witness   285
20. Without Tears   303
21. Closing Act   321
22. Until the Tides Bring You Back to Me   337

    Authors' Note   349
    Acknowledgments   355

The air on the morning of October 10, 2012, was brisk, a light breeze shuffling the latest batch of leaves to have given up their grip on nearly bare branches. As the sun was rising, Randy Bolduc left his house in Portsmouth, New Hampshire, to take his dog to Peirce Island, a little piece of land in the Piscataqua River tethered to the riverbank by two hundred feet and two lanes of asphalt. The snap of the morning wind always made for a hearty walk, but the view from the island is breathtaking in the morning, dawn breaking orange in duplicate, the sky reflecting off the waves of the Piscataqua's current.

The islet is the size of a decent city park, and that's what the city has made out of it, with a public swimming pool, walking trails, boat landings, and a dog park—a popular attraction for residents who don't have large backyards of their own. From Peirce Island, one can follow the winding path carved by the Piscataqua, one of the strongest tidal currents on the continent. It dumps into the sea only three miles farther downstream and, when the tide is rising, flows briskly in the opposite direction. The river, brackish with salt water, marks the border between New Hampshire and Maine, and while it's mostly rest and recreation on the south side of the water, on the Maine side, Kittery's shore bustles with workers at the naval shipyard repairing and maintaining nuclear submarines.

Randy Bolduc walked his dog on the island's trails, picking his path mostly by habit. But on that morning, when he came upon an intersection at which he normally turned left—later saying he'd gone that way at least a hundred times before—Bolduc changed it up and took the path less traveled.

The path to the right dead-ended at a scenic overlook about twenty feet above an outcropping of rocks and the water line. Following the dirt trail, he spotted strange tracks in the ground that varied in depth. The marks were thin, like they'd been made by smooth wheels, but in some places there were two tracks and in others only one. At some points along the path, the marks disappeared altogether, only to start again several feet away.

Bolduc knew bicycles weren't allowed on this path, but these didn't seem like bike tracks anyway. It looked more to him like something had been dragged. What he saw on the ground was unusual enough to pique his curiosity. His first thought was that someone had illegally dumped trash in the underbrush, but there wasn't any trash that he could see.

He walked his dog along the drag marks, following them all the way to the end of the dirt path, where they disappeared and the gravel surface of the scenic overlook, a semicircle ringed with granite block benches and an iron-rod railing, began. The tracks may have vanished when they reached this point, but it was easy for Bolduc to trace their invisible trajectory: a straight line past the railing, down into the Piscataqua River, and into the mouth of the Atlantic Ocean.

PART ONE

BONDAGE

"Will you walk into my parlour?"
said the Spider to the Fly.

—MARY HOWITT,
"THE SPIDER AND THE FLY"

CHAPTER ONE

Lizzi

On October 2, 2012, Elizabeth Marriott slowed down to make the final turn toward her aunt and uncle's house. She had clocked nearly a hundred miles in her eleven-year-old Mazda Tribute that day alone—driving first to a full day of school at the University of New Hampshire campus in Durham, then to a friend's house in Dover to hang out, and, finally, now home to bed. The fog was thickening, the dashboard thermometer number falling a degree at a time as her tires crunched over wind-drifted leaves.

As Lizzi reached the driveway, her foot instinctively hit the brake before she could make the turn, her heart jumping into her throat. Standing in the front yard was a large man wearing dark clothes. He was completely still, his arms hanging at his sides, his feet planted slightly apart. It was as if he had been waiting for her.

The man was facing Lizzi's car and stood in silhouette, the front porch light glowing behind him. She couldn't make out his face as she inched the SUV forward, and she soon realized why—the man was wearing a mask. And in his hand he held what appeared to be a large hook.

———

Lizzi Marriott had seen many unusual things along New Hampshire's rural back roads since she'd moved in with her aunt and uncle to save on costs while she attended college nearby. Two days earlier, she'd spotted a Great Dane sticking its enormous head out the front window of a car Lizzi was passing, making it look like the dog itself was doing the driving. Three weeks before that, she'd encountered an endangered species, a Blanding's turtle that had decided to quit crossing the road halfway across. Lizzi had pulled over, run to the rare turtle, and picked it up, snapping an iPhone photo of its leathery head tucked inside the shell before releasing it on the side of the road.

"Poor little muffin," she wrote when she posted the photo on Facebook. "Now it's safe to continue on its journey."

Lizzi's aunt and uncle, Tony and Becky Hanna, lived in the tiny town of Chester, an hour closer to campus than her parents' house in central Massachusetts. Her hometown of Westborough, a classic New England town of just eighteen thousand within commuting distance of Boston, was small but distinctly modern and suburban, while Chester, a village established fifty years before the American Revolution, was the epitome of bucolic New

England—merrily stuck in an era gone by. Residents still gathered at town meetings, where everyone voted on the local budget and decided whether the town's part-time fire department should buy a new pumper truck.

Lizzi slept in a small, drafty attic bedroom with a crooked door and liked to complain that the room was haunted, blaming every bump in the night on some otherworldly presence (but never on any of the thriller/horror paperbacks she read under the covers for fun). The *tap tap* outside her window was likely water dripping onto the air conditioner; scratches at the door were probably the family's tiger cat, and a scratch found on her cheek upon waking was also likely from the cat. "But let's be serious," she told her friends jokingly. "It's far more likely to be a ghost."

If there was anyone in the house Lizzi didn't get along with, it probably was that cat, who could often be found hiding under Lizzi's laundry or deep under the duvet on her bed. She was allergic to cats but couldn't bring herself to shove it off her schoolbooks or even out of her room. Lizzi posted one time on Facebook that the cat had pounced from a hidden corner like a ninja, sending her running down the stairs spouting "a string of expletives that would make even sailor/rap artist hybrid blush."

Rural life bemused and befuddled Lizzi. Growing up, she'd never had to stop her car for cows loitering in the middle of the road. She added a blaze orange vest and hat to her running gear after going for a jog in the woods, only to hear gunshots from hunters echoing around her; she hoped they would be enough to distinguish her from the deer. But even that wasn't a traumatic turn, just another fun story to share with her friends.

"Have you ever had venison?" the Hannas asked their niece, cooking up the meat from someone's deer hunt. Ever the risk-taker, Lizzi filled her plate.

"Don't eat anything out of *that* pan," they warned her. "That's the heart."

Lizzi stifled a shriek at the prospect of eating the dubious delicacy of deer heart and continued her meal like a good sport.

As they later related on the television show *48 Hours*, it was important to the Hannas for Lizzi to feel like their rural house and its backyard menagerie of chickens and cows was her home too.

"I'm ho-ome!" Lizzi would announce each time she arrived at her aunt and uncle's house. The Hannas made sure Lizzi was included in everything they did as a family. She went with them to the state fair and binged on fried food. They took her along to help them pick out the family Christmas tree and gave her a turn at the hacksaw while they cut it down. She rode a motorcycle and drove her uncle's Dodge Ram 1500, the kind of muscle truck you might need for errands in Chester but never in Westborough. Her cousin showed her how to go four-wheeling through the woods on an ATV. The lesson consisted of: "This is the gas. These are the brakes. Now go!"

"Lizzi, come here," her uncle called to her from the barn one afternoon.

He was welding a piece of metal and stopped to show her the molten seam he'd made.

"Put this on."

She put the welder's mask he handed her over her face and followed his directions as she guided the torch. The mark she left was serviceable enough, and she handed the tools back to Tony.

"I guess I'm a welder now," she said chipperly as she walked off. It was simply another happy moment in the continuing adventure of her life.

Lizzi Marriott was born on June 10, 1993, and grew up to be a fresh-faced and undeniably beautiful girl with sandy shoulder-length hair, a broad smile, and wide-set light blue eyes. Her eyes were usually the first thing people noticed, and "ocean" was the color often ascribed to them, mostly because Lizzi herself had always loved the ocean.

Her mother would take the family to Hampton Beach, New Hampshire, for summer vacations, and while her younger brother played in the sand, Lizzi played in the tide, spending hours examining the shells and seaweed deposited by the Atlantic surf.

Before Lizzi was old enough to read books herself, one of the adults in her life would read aloud to her while she sat beside them, a finger on her nose and a thumb in her mouth. According to the *MetroWest Daily News*, her aunt tried to get her to stop sucking her thumb, reminding her that she was almost old enough to go to school, but young Lizzi would just laugh and turn on the charm that would become the hallmark of her personality.

In high school, Lizzi had a tight group of friends and was popular with everyone. She stood out in a way that was endearing and sweet, never using being well liked to her advantage the way teenage girls are wont to do.

Lizzi was cheerful, loving, and affably ditzy. She loved Harry Potter and all things magical and embraced fantasy literature, sci-fi, and so-called "nerd" culture. She also had a great voice, which won her a music scholarship. Students remembered how, during workouts in the school gym, with music blasting and students running laps, Lizzi would always jog in the opposite direction of everyone else singing a completely different song out loud. For the junior prom, she made up her mind to sew her own dress. She looked stunning in it, and was crowned junior prom queen.

Her funny stories and winning personality drew people to her like a magnet. People found Lizzi Marriott lovable, witty, and trusting. Very trusting. It may have been that she was too eager to look on the bright side of life and see the best in people, making it hard for her to detect when she was being taken advantage of. But there are worse Achilles' heels to have.

Lizzi never lost her interest in the ocean and marine life. On the dashboard of her car, she kept a collection of thumb-sized toy animals: dolphins, penguins, sea lions, and whales. Wherever she went, her aquatic friends came with her.

As often as she could in high school, Lizzi would

volunteer at Boston's New England Aquarium. A premier research facility and metropolitan tourist destination, the aquarium was the perfect place for a young adult to feed her curiosity about marine biology. The aquarium's signature feature is an immense cylindrical tank, forty feet wide and four stories tall with a walkway that corkscrews around it where visitors can take in marine life at various depths and watch human divers plunging in to check on or feed certain specimens—or spot clean the Plexiglas.

Lizzi's duty was working at the aquarium's Edge of the Sea Touchtank exhibit, the oceanic equivalent of a petting zoo. She'd stand at a shallow, man-made coral pool and answer questions about the creatures crawling around. Visitors were encouraged to touch the hermit crabs and the patchwork collection of starfish, but even many adults were hesitant to reach in and stroke a moon snail or try to handle a sea urchin. Lizzi would joyfully lead the way, reaching into the water past her elbow and plucking out a horseshoe crab and showing that it was nothing to be afraid of.

According to her college application, visitors' questions varied from "What does this creature eat?" and "How old is it?" to (her personal favorite) "Are clams alive?" Visitors were often surprised to hear she wasn't a trained marine biologist, just a high school kid with a passion for the ocean.

Lizzi's best-loved visitors were children, whose reactions to scaly, snappy, or hidden creatures suddenly crawling out of the rocks were priceless. Even when tiny hands inadvertently splashed poor Lizzi, salt water mottling her clothes and dripping from her bangs, it was impossible to dampen her spirit. She was even charmed by the rambunctious kids who preferred to attack her with their souvenir squid puppets than to try petting one of the Touchtank's lobsters.

It may have been at the aquarium where Lizzi first fell in love with cephalopods, those gelatinous multilegged swimmers like cuttlefish, squid, and octopi. It was definitely where she made her mind up that she wanted to become a marine biologist.

Lizzi had her eye on the University of New Hampshire, a top-notch school for marine science with a laboratory on the shore of the Great Bay Estuary. But attending the University of New Hampshire isn't cheap. Lizzi decided that for her freshman year, she would instead attend the nearby small Manchester Community College, where her uncle Tony Hanna taught welding technology. He vouched that it was a good place to earn some required credits at a fraction of the cost. If accepted to UNH, Lizzi could transfer there later and graduate with significantly less debt.

It was settled. There were no dorms at the community college, so Lizzi would move in with the Hannas in Chester during the school year. She would live in the "haunted" bedroom in the attic, the room with the crooked door. Lizzi kept in constant touch with her parents in Massachusetts on the phone and through social media. Bob and Melissa Marriott knew their daughter was in good hands with Bob's sister's family.

On school breaks, Lizzi would return to Westborough

to spend time with family and friends. While at home, she got a part-time job at a grocery store, where she clicked right away with a kind girl behind thick glasses. Brittany Atwood loved everything about the radiant Lizzi.

Displaying an extraordinary level of self-assuredness, Lizzi "came out" to her friends and family as bisexual and felt ready to have a relationship with a woman. Her family was supportive, and Brittany quickly became a fixture at family gatherings. When it was time to return to New Hampshire, Lizzi and Brittany agreed to keep their long-distance relationship going.

After completing her freshman year at community college, Lizzi applied to the UNH marine science program. In her application essay, she described her role interacting with the public at the New England Aquarium and how the volunteer job helped her work toward her goals.

"My visitors don't see me as some teenage girl," she wrote. "Instead they see me as an intrepid ocean explorer. They see an adventurer who plunges fearlessly into the unexplored depths of the tank, bringing bizarre new animals into the light of day!"

She continued, "Some day, I'm determined to be a prominent figure when it comes to protecting our oceans. I want to help everyone when it comes to learning the wonders of our surrounding waters. But until then, I'm more than happy to be the intrepid ocean explorer, arm deep in the tank."

Lizzi was accepted into the program and began her studies at UNH in the fall of 2012.

But even with financial aid and a free place to live, she still needed to make extra money, so in the summer of 2012, Lizzi had taken a job at a Target store in Greenland, New Hampshire, not far from the UNH campus in Durham.

Lizzi quickly entranced her new coworkers with her bubbly personality. She was the sort of person who turned even the mundane tasks of work into play, and it was impossible to bring her down. Just as splashing children had been a source of joy at the aquarium, Lizzi also found her department store customers a never-ending source of amusement.

One day, a man asked Lizzi where the exit to the store was. She bit her tongue and pointed that he was standing directly in front of it. A family who apparently spoke only French wandered in to browse the store's merchandise. Lizzi couldn't discern what they were saying until they stumbled onto a *Big Bang Theory* T-shirt. They kept yelling "Bazinga!" at one another and giggling. Lizzi giggled too.

While she was working at the checkout one night, an old man in a fedora took his change, looked Lizzi square in the eye, and said, "Behave yourself, now," before walking away, muttering under his breath. Lizzi was nonplussed. Perhaps she seemed so pleasant that people thought she must be up to no good.

One night, a mother with a screaming baby rolled into the section where Lizzi was folding shirts. The woman, probably immune by now to the sound of her son's cries, ignored the child while she browsed the racks. Instead of pitching her own fit about this reversal of fortune, Lizzi played peekaboo with the child across the shelving and made funny faces. The boy settled down and the mother never knew why. Writing about the incident on her Facebook page, Lizzi said "Cry-sis (Hah! Puns!) averted!"

———

Soon, between school and work and stealing the occasional trip back to Massachusetts, Lizzi's life was a controlled blur, but after her first month at UNH, she got into a groove. She was racking up the miles on her Tribute, accompanied on her hour-plus commutes only by the plastic marine life resting on her dashboard. She needed to post her schedule in the Hannas' kitchen to keep things straight and to let them know whether to expect her for dinner on any given night.

Her drive home to Chester the night of October 2, 2012, was the end of another marathon day—Lizzi had finished her evening chemistry lab, then gone to a new friend's apartment to watch *The Avengers*. She'd briefly met her friend's boyfriend, who seemed to want her to come back again. They'd made plans to watch movies again the following week.

It was at the end of that late-night drive when she pulled into the Hannas' driveway to find a threatening man waiting for her in the front yard. He wore a mask over his face and brandished some kind of hook or weapon in his hand. The intruder was broad shouldered and sinister, standing still in the fog.

As the circle of her headlights crawled up the man's

body, Lizzi widened her eyes in disbelief and let out a bark of nervous laughter.

The man wasn't a man at all, but a scarecrow, a straw man wearing her uncle's welding gear. The family had done some early Halloween decorating, the front porch of the house full of pumpkins and buckets of mums.

"Thank you, Mr. Scarecrow, for not limiting your scare tactics to crows," Lizzi wrote in sharing the whole incident on Facebook after she flopped into bed that night. "I'm really feeling the love."

The scarecrow, the "ghost" in her room, the noises in the night: None of those things could hurt her. Loving her life and living every day to the fullest, she was safe with her family in New Hampshire with no boogeyman in sight.

A week later, Lizzi Marriott disappeared.

CHAPTER TWO

Kat

Kathryn McDonough sat in one of the many empty seats in the theater and faced the half-lit stage. Her teenage eyes were upturned, large as saucers, watching the adult actors pace through their blocking. Some were still not off-script, carrying their pages with them as they spun from stage left to stage right, but *she* knew all the lines in the play and mouthed them along with the actors from her spot in the seventh row.

If this were her life story, as Kat imagined it, it would be a musical that followed the tropes of her favorite Disney movies. This part, where she sat alone watching the grown-ups rehearse, would be the opening number, the "I want" song that every ingénue sings to tell the audience her hopes and desires.

She would rise from her seat and walk blithely through

the maze of milling minor characters, prima donnas, and closet queens. There would be a clever cut, and she'd suddenly be backstage skipping past the makeup artists and set designers and dancing around the lighted mirrors. She would harmonize with a chorus of half-costumed actors and stagehands, declaring—as the key shifted ominously from major to minor—that something big was coming her way.

The end of the number would find her alone on the now-empty stage, captured by a spotlight, singing that someday her prince was sure to come. She'd finish by belting out a triumphant high note, pointing back at the audience while the orchestra reached a crescendo and the stage plunged back into darkness.

But this wasn't a Disney musical. Kat was just sitting there by herself in row seven watching another community theater production come together. Just sitting there with her own copy of the script, her five or six lines highlighted in yellow as if she hadn't memorized them the same night she got the part. Just sitting there, waiting for her scene. Waiting for her turn in the spotlight.

If it had been a Disney musical, her castmates' thoughts would have been expressed in rhythm and rhyme, not told in hindsight to police and reporters. They would say Kathryn was indeed a nice girl, but she often seemed lost, like someone waiting to be discovered, waiting to escape.

"I never met anyone," one fellow actor would later remark about Kat, "so looking for help, or to start her life."

But Kat wasn't just waiting for something big to come

her way. She was waiting for *anything* to happen. Anything at all.

———

Kathryn McDonough practically grew up in the auditoriums and amphitheaters dotting New Hampshire's Seacoast Region. The oldest of three children and the only girl, she would often accompany her mother, Denise, to play rehearsals. She wore the title of "theater brat" proudly.

Denise McDonough was a set builder and a performer, and she had both the artist's eye and the saint's patience needed for costuming, which meant the area's amateur and semiprofessional troupes would often call on her talents. Denise could sing and dance and was an expressive actress. She was the total package, and local producers fought over her time and time again.

There was steady theater work—union work—an hour south in Boston. But Denise didn't make her living off of costuming or performing. In fact, very few people on the Seacoast can make a career at any of the region's theater companies; some, despite being high quality, are simply too small, while some of the larger productions only run seasonally, catering to outdoor audiences at city parks. The thespian population in New Hampshire can be divided into two groups: those cutting their teeth before intending to go to Boston or New York or L.A., and those who live in the area and work day jobs in between and during productions. With very few exceptions, the people in the first group eventually migrate into the second.

Denise was one of those in the latter group. Costuming for the Garrison Players or the Seacoast Repertory Theatre was milk money for Kat's mother, who owned and operated a successful paint-your-own-pottery shop in Portsmouth, where customers selected unfinished ceramic plates, platters, or coffee mugs from shelves, then slathered them in acrylic colors. The staff then fired the work in a kiln and the motley tableware was ready for pickup in a week.

Birthday parties, camps, and grown-up "girls' nights" were big business at the shop. As a young teenager, Kat would help her mother herd the paint-stained children to the sink to wash their hands or collect the dripping sets of cups, which would never match anything, and line them up for the kiln.

When Kat was growing up, she and Denise were close. But on the evenings when Denise would work late, Kat was outnumbered at home by her father and two younger brothers.

Peter McDonough got along well with his boys. His daughter, on the other hand, was harder for him to decipher. Peter worked in the information technology field and was most at ease in front of a computer screen. A devout Catholic, he was often described as uncomfortable in his own skin, a trait that hampered his ability to express affection for others. Long before the typical teenage awkwardness set in for Kat, the pair was out of step with each other. If her father tried to be helpful or made some sideways comment, Kat would bristle and give it right back to him.

When Peter tried to quarrel with his wife, Denise would brush him off and not engage. But Kat always took the bait. The father and daughter would bicker like little children, neither having the good sense to let anything lie or to concede the last cutting word.

Denise tried to act as a translator between her husband and daughter, tried to get Peter to appreciate their daughter's creative side, but it was a battle in which she could never gain any ground. In virtually every way, Kat reminded Peter of her mother. Denise often told friends her husband wasn't supportive of her own artistic endeavors, and art was Denise's life. Their impasse ran so deep that the couple slept in separate bedrooms, but they never discussed a divorce.

When Peter was in charge of the house, Kat would retreat to her room with her cat, Merlin. It was part nervous capitulation, part escape from the blanket of tension she felt smothered by when her mother wasn't home. It didn't help that the family's house, which sat in a tree-lined neighborhood called Elwyn Park, was tiny. The ranch was 1400 square feet and had just one bathroom for the family of five to share and only a basement to which one could escape for any semblance of real privacy.

Kat would pretend her room was a fortress of solitude, though, and would text, chat on Facebook with friends, or watch videos on YouTube in order to escape the inevitable confrontations with her father. At an hour he designated as bedtime, Peter would yell for everyone to turn off the lights and go to sleep, but Kat's room glowed cool blue as she surfed the web from her bed. More than once,

Peter would unplug the family's router and turn off the Internet connection in the house.

Dinnertime was another battle of wills. Kat was famously picky about her father's cooking.

"I don't like this," she would say at the table, pushing her plate away. "This spaghetti sauce is too salty."

"Your brothers don't mind it."

Now muscular teenagers, Kat's brothers would wolf down virtually anything that was put in front of them.

"I don't care. I'm not going to eat this," she would insist.

Peter refused to be a short-order cook for his kids. Kat was free to make herself a can of soup or heat up leftovers, but he drew the line at making separate entrees for her. When she'd refuse to eat and complain instead of feeding herself, he'd lose it.

"Fine," Peter would tell her time and time again. "You'll stay at that table until you clean your plate!"

The boys would finish and ask to be excused, and Peter would follow, clearing the table of everything save Kat's plate. Different lights would turn on and off, the din of the television swelling from the other room, as Kat remained at the table, staring at the plate but refusing to eat a bite. She would stew, feeling as if she'd been sentenced. She felt there would never be any reprieve from her father, and as she sat there, she fantasized about someday getting out of the house and escaping his control.

One afternoon, Kat and one of her brothers found themselves in a screaming, giggling chase through the house. How it started had been forgotten, only that one sibling had zinged another—a harmless insult tossed like a ball across a room. Kathryn fled first, then the chase reversed itself. Her brother bolted up the basement stairs and vanished before she could make it to the main floor. The bedroom doors were all open, so she assumed he was hiding in the locked bathroom. She began banging her fists on the closed door.

"Come out of there," she demanded playfully. There was no response from inside, so she kept pounding and pounding. "Come on, you little shit. Come out."

She only stopped when the knob clicked to spring the bolt and her father whipped open the door. He had been using the bathroom the entire time, choosing to let Kat continue her tantrum while he fumed on the other side of the door. Her eyes widened in surprise and her tongue tripped over an apology. Peter grabbed Kat by the shoulders and shoved his daughter out of the doorway and into the opposite wall, then stomped away.

Denise was upset when she heard about the incident. Later, when she quizzed her family separately, they gave identical stories. Peter admitted to laying hands on Kat. He had never done it before and he never did it again. Kat admitted pounding on the door and swearing at her father. She had a sore back but was otherwise unhurt. Denise scolded them both for acting like children; they apologized to each other and agreed to put the mess behind them.

Kat asked if she could start sleeping in Denise's bedroom, a place Peter wouldn't enter. In every way, she felt unloved by her father and felt the absence of his love like a hole in her heart. She didn't long for him to change, though. She longed for someone else to come along and love her instead.

———

Kat shared the details of her teenage love life with her mother. Her first boyfriend was a typical high school crush. There was handholding and deep kissing, but not much else. The relationship with her second boyfriend was more physical. He convinced her to perform oral sex on him—which she didn't particularly care for—and she lost her virginity with him. As she grew older, Kat was also learning more about her own desires. She described herself as "bi-curious," but was primarily drawn to men.

Denise was there to help Kat through the broken hearts, assuring her there *was* someone special for her— someone worth waiting for. Despite the complications of her own marriage, Denise told her daughter again and again that true love awaited her.

By seventeen, Kat was a petite size three juniors and, if not for her exploding squiggle of curly dark hair, could have been taken for a boy. But on stage, in her impossibly feminine costumes, she became somebody else, somebody bold or sexy or mysterious.

Kat had always had a vivid imagination, and her mother's many roles all seemed like a fantastic game of make-believe. As a child, Kat's fantasies flourished from wanting to hold a sword or wear a hat to trying on dresses and playing with makeup as a pre-teen. She loved pirates and princesses, and loved pirate princesses most of all.

As a teenager, Kat's own talents emerged. Like her mother, she could act, sing, and dance, making her a budding triple threat. The theater pulled her in because it gave her the chance to play against type, proving that she wasn't the unsure and shy kid her mother's friends thought she was. On stage, Kat finally had the chance to reinvent herself. On stage, she was big and brash and fearless. Everyone in the theater community agreed it would be impossible to keep her from becoming an actress.

She'd been part of shows as long as she could remember. Her first public performance was in the chorus for a teen production of *Once Upon a Mattress*, the musical comedy inspired by "The Princess and the Pea" that launched the career of Carol Burnett. There were two other girls named Kathryn in the cast, so she'd taken to calling herself "Kat" instead. It started as a stage name, but soon everyone was calling her Kat McDonough.

Kat had been a full two years younger than the rest of the teens in the cast, too young to gossip about the boys. Still, she longed to make an impression on stage. "How do you want to look?" her mother, the show's seamstress, had asked.

The girl smiled. "Pretty."

Denise set out to assemble the dress, a pink-and-white flowing number. Topped by a crown of fake flowers, Kat looked every bit the lady-in-waiting.

Her mother's costume-making forte was medieval/fantasy wear, like that worn by the lords and ladies in *Mattress*. Kat, running her hands along the racks, developed her own affinity for the aesthetics of the period.

While any costume tempted her, it was the fantasy-genre dresses she loved the most.

Theater literally *is* role -playing, but many stage actors also enjoy games of Live Action Role-Play (LARP). But Kat wasn't into suiting up between performances just to play a game of medieval capture the flag. Fantasy provided a spiritual rabbit hole for the troubled teen to slide into when things didn't go her way.

When she was a junior at Portsmouth High School, Kat decided to create an alter ego—a persona she could channel when she needed to be someone else. Born from the avatars and characters she fabricated playing video games online, Kat created an inner character she named "Scarlet."

Scarlet was stronger than Kat, more self-assured. When faced with adversity, Kat often thought about what Scarlet would do. Scarlet became something of a spirit guide. As she would later discuss in public, sometimes Kat would imagine stepping into Scarlet's body—the way an actress stepped into a character—and facing her problems head-on. One can imagine Kat at the kitchen table pondering what Scarlet would do, what lengths she'd go to to escape the situation.

To Kat, Scarlet was just a person she would pretend to be. Kat wasn't hallucinating or hearing voices. She didn't have a split personality, nor was she living in a Walter Mitty–type alternate reality. Scarlet was not *real* in that sense. The idea of Scarlet was a coping mechanism, a tool; she wasn't like an imaginary friend dreamed up by a child.

Kat was a good student, but she only connected with

a handful of the teachers. She confided her secret about summoning Scarlet when she needed strength to a science teacher she thought of as a role model. He told her there was no shame in channeling Scarlet when she needed to. In the teacher's estimation, Kat's belief in Scarlet's power was a normal, positive behavior, no different from people believing the Lord walks alongside them in their hours of need.

Kat shared everything with her mother, including the nature of her alter ego, Scarlet. Denise wasn't surprised. A strong believer in intuition, she'd always felt Kat had her own attuned sense.

Denise's own love of fairies and fantasy was common knowledge. Medieval costumes had always been her favorite to make, and she frequently posted her own original illustrations of warrior princesses and steampunk heroines on social media. Like her daughter, she was equally as fascinated with fire-breathing dragons as she was with butterflies, sharing art of both the mighty and the delicate on her Facebook page. Denise enjoyed wearing her own creations to Renaissance fairs; her costumed persona was named "Violet."

At the same time Kat's Scarlet persona was developing, her interest in otherworldly fantasy began to express itself through her art. She posted her drawings, short stories, and photography on a community website under the username of "vampirate-actress" (*vampirate* a likely portmanteau of "vampire" and "pirate," two of her fascinations).

The photographs were often moody self-portraits, some in which she hid behind a drama mask, others treated in oversaturated black-and-white filters to give her a Goth appearance, that of a pale-skinned vampire with curly ebony hair.

Kat was able to transfer her years of experience painting ceramics to computer art and photo manipulation. Some works depicted angelic cherubs bound by iron chains. Others were of dragons and ghosts.

Kat also posted some of her early attempts at poetry and short stories. She began with a piece of Harry Potter fan fiction, a story about a fellow student at Hogwarts named Scarlet whose mother was an infamous witch named Violet. Kat posted her intention to expand the story into a full-length book in which Scarlet might be led down the same nefarious path as her mother. By pulling in her mother's persona, Kat demonstrated a belief that these "other" personas could coexist.

Harry Potter was one of the greatest influences on Kat's adolescence. From a young age she loved the books and the movies, which were full of witches, wizards, and dragons. She imagined being like Harry, rescued from the home in which he was unwanted only to discover he was no ordinary person.

Harry wasn't the only character in the Potter universe she could identify with. For a midnight release of the sixth Harry Potter movie, Kat and her friends—and her mother—arrived at five P.M., all wearing costumes inspired by the books. Kat dressed as one of the book's villainous witches. When the seventh Harry Potter movie premiered, Kat arrived at three P.M. for the midnight showing dressed as a different witch and carrying an official-looking magic wand.

Kat next tried her hand at original fiction. Her longest story was about a girl—again named Scarlet—trapped in a stalled elevator with a mysterious, handsome man named James. While "Scarlet" was usually the imaginary version of a braver Kat, this story's Scarlet sounded more like the real teen. In the story, Scarlet's parents nagged her about the smallest things, but she didn't have the strength to stand up for herself.

"Most people saw her as the sweet, shy little girl . . . now all she wanted to do was live, and live her life to the fullest."

As more short stories were written, "James" appeared again and again as Scarlet's partner. It seemed, as with Scarlet, the idea of a "James" was important to Kat's coping mechanisms.

More darkly, Kat wrote a poem in which she described a fight between a husband and wife.

"From behind his back, silver appears, propelling itself through my chest."

Kat described blood on the tile floor, red drops piled like rubies.

"This is how you will find us," it ended. "Till death do us part."

———

For all of her darker interests, Kat had a paradoxical infatuation with Disney. As a child she watched all of the studio's movies, all of the princess cartoons. She grew up singing the songs from *The Little Mermaid* and *Beauty and the Beast.* Full of costumes, music, and fantastical endings, the Disney films dovetailed with her love of theater. In fact, Kat hoped that after high school she could move to Florida and get a job as a performer at Walt Disney World. Her plan was to work there for a year and then to go to college in New York City to study drama. She hoped this would lead to a career in acting or costuming on Broadway.

Eager to beef up her theater resumé, Kat wanted to get into as many community theater productions as she could. Summer shows were the easiest, but she had to work rehearsals around her part-time job at Target and the two-week theater camp she attended.

The summer between her sophomore and junior years, Kat landed a part in the chorus for *Oliver!* at the Rochester Opera House. The following summer she got a speaking role in a dark comedy called *Last Rites* at the Players' Ring. The play was essentially a one-man show about a burned-out psychologist looking back at his chaotic life, but four other characters moved in and out of the action during the protagonist's alcohol-fueled rant.

The play's supporting cast comprised two men and two women. The other actors were in their late twenties and thirties, and—though age-appropriate for her role—the addition of seventeen-year-old Kat was in stark contrast to the more seasoned actors in the show.

Rehearsals revolved around the lead actor, so the other

four clustered in different combinations waiting for their scenes. Unlike the mammoth production of a musical, in which it's easy for people to be drawn into cliques or to wander off alone and unnoticed, downtime with the tiny cast was much more intimate. The supporting players had no mutual scenes, so they had no lines to run with one another. Instead they would chat about past theater experiences, news of the day, and eventually, their love lives.

Leading up to the July performances, Kat and one of the men started breaking away from the pack. His name was Lex, and he was not only an actor but also a fight choreographer who was originally drawn into the show to craft a stage fight. Lex had black hair and an intense face. Though he was around twenty-eight, there was something about him that made him seem younger.

The other actors found Lex to be a bit odd—and these were folks who were used to the quirky personalities of "theater people." While trying to make small talk, Lex would practice his fight choreography in an exaggerated slow motion that made him seem awkward, almost comical. He also revealed that "Lex" was a stage name, something almost no one used in the Seacoast theater scene. His real name was Seth.

———

Kat began looking forward to rehearsal so she could spend time with Seth. She told him about her mother's costume designs and hobby of making outfits for renaissance fairs. Seth said he enjoyed dressing up for LARPing, acting as a knight or wizard in "reenactments" of magic-infused medieval wars. He confessed that when play acting he felt as if he embodied other people, spirit versions of himself.

Kat found herself telling Seth about Scarlet, her alter ego. Seth said he could sense the presence of another being within Kat. He said he too had a psychic alter ego named Card, short for "Wild Card." Seth told Kat that Card was the bold one, just like Scarlet.

For Kat, it seemed her prince had finally come.

CHAPTER THREE

Wild Card

While instant messaging with her friends on Facebook on her black laptop, a new IM popped open on Kat McDonough's screen. It was from "Seth J Mazzaglia."

"Our conversations the last couple of shows have been extremely interesting—when would you like to continue them?"

He then asked if there was a good time to talk away from the prying ears of the *Last Rites* cast.

Kat thought about it for a minute. It was late July 2011, and the play's run would end the following week. She would soon be leaving for two weeks to train as a counselor at theater camp, and then she'd be back to start her senior year of high school.

She liked this guy, though, and decided she wanted to spend more time with him. Kat enjoyed pretending to be

Scarlet. She thought it made her more interesting in twenty-eight-year-old Seth's eyes. He seemed to understand Scarlet better than she did. Most intriguing of all, he seemed extremely interested in her, like he was willing to chase her. It felt good to be wanted.

As they prepped for the final performance of *Last Rites* backstage, Kat agreed to go to a movie with Lex. They settled on *Captain America*. Kat's mom dropped her off at the Regal Cinemas on a Tuesday afternoon. Kat usually told Denise everything, but this time she had simply said that she was going to meet some friends, not revealing that the matinee was a date.

"Did you have any trouble sleeping?" Seth asked Kat on Facebook after the date.

"No. Why?"

"I felt Scarlet invading my astral space last night," he said. "Just noting it in case there was a blackout on your end."

Kat felt exhilarated. Was this for real? Could her Scarlet persona be something more than just a pretend personality? Might she be some psychic manifestation of a real woman? And could the man she knew as Lex interact with Scarlet on an otherworldly plane?

Seth Mazzaglia (his last name rhymed with "azalea") lived in Dover, about twenty-five minutes north of Portsmouth, in a studio apartment in a converted nineteenth-century woolen mill. The complex, called Sawyer Mill, sat astride the Bellamy River, which had powered Dover's textile looms for a century.

Seth's parents had divorced when he was young. He confessed to Kat that hearing about her family troubles brought him back to his own childhood. Seth claimed he had more self-control than his parents ever had, but what he described made it sound more like they'd walked on eggshells around him.

"If they lose their tempers, I take it as permission to lose my own temper. The whole family learned very quickly to keep civil tongues during arguments."

His mother, Heather Mazzaglia, was an educator in a local school district and had been on the library's board of trustees. Seth appeared to have a strong bond with his mother and talked on the phone or visited for dinner often.

Heather Mazzaglia's home sat in a little neighborhood that abutted the beginning of the runway for what had been a major U.S. Air Force base, until hundreds of military facilities like it were decommissioned after the Cold War. The base remained partly in the hands of the New Hampshire Air National Guard (whose KC-135s were flying midair refueling missions for the War on Terror) and partly in the hands of port authority officials seeking to build commercial and cargo flight routes out of Portsmouth. As a result, the house was frequently bombarded with the noise of planes coming in for a landing.

It was hard for friends and acquaintances to get a handle on what Seth's relationship with his father, Joseph, was like. No one believed he had a *bad* relationship with him. The older Mazzaglia seemed perfectly nice to all, and no one could recall Seth publically bad-mouthing his dad.

Joe Mazzaglia was a karate instructor, and Seth, who was a third-degree black belt himself, also taught self-defense to children and adults at the same dojo in Dover.

Seth was known for his patience as a teacher. At least one adult student described him as quiet and unremarkable, though disciplined. Seth told them his father had been his sensei.

Seth's father also lived at the Sawyer Mill apartments in another part of the complex. Despite their physical proximity, acquaintances couldn't recall either of them spending any considerable time in the other's apartment—certainly not the same amount of time Seth spent visiting his mother. Whatever the quality of their emotional relationship was, it seemed to be known only to the two of them.

———

Unlike Kat McDonough, Seth hadn't started out seeking a career in the theater. In high school, he developed an interest in computers and in graphic design, and in 2001, was accepted to Rensselaer Polytechnic Institute in Troy, New York. Admission to the engineering school is competitive, and Seth's acceptance implied a considerable level of academic promise. He never lived up to it.

In his freshman year, Seth signed up for a course that seemed tailor-made for him: Cyberlore and Science Visions, a writing and literature class that focused on science fiction. For the class project, the students were tasked to work in groups to create websites tying their work to larger themes. On the site Seth worked on, he identified himself as a certified web designer "working on a dual major in Electrical Engineering and Computer science while maintaining his interests in Medieval reinactment [*sic*]."

According to a classmate, however, Seth wasn't good about keeping in contact with his project group, and the others found the icon graphics he created for the site to be subpar, so they made new ones without his knowledge.

————————

When people would ask Seth to tell them something about himself, he eventually would tell them an incredible story about his first love. If one were to compare notes, there would be variations in details, though it was always tragic and simultaneously dubious.

While attending RPI, Seth said, he met the woman he thought was the love of his life. Her name was Natasha. Seth said she was beautiful and had liked to highlight her natural platinum-blond hair with bright pink and amber accents.

Seth claimed that as he and Natasha walked alone through a Troy park one night, a mugger jumped from the bushes intending to rob them. The man pulled out a gun, pointed it at them both, and made threatening demands. Seth said the mugger then turned the gun on Seth and pulled the trigger, but Natasha threw herself in front of the speeding bullet. It caught her in the chest and she stumbled back into Seth's arms. The mugger ran off into the darkness as Seth slumped to the ground, holding the love of his life as blood seeped from her chest wound. He said Natasha died in his arms that night.

The story always struck Seth's friends as peculiar. Even his best friend, Andy, wasn't sure he believed it. But it was one of Seth's go-to personal tales. In some versions, Natasha woke up in the hospital before dying. He often worked the Natasha story into icebreaker conversations, as he did with a community theater husband and wife who were told a version in which Natasha was actually Seth's fiancée. The couple assumed it was just another overdramatic anecdote from another eccentric actor.

While the truth is easy to prove, a lie is surprisingly difficult to confirm, as there's no way to say for sure that something *didn't* happen. That being said, the story didn't pass even a cursory sniff test. Not only was no one in Troy ever arrested in that time frame for a shooting like the one Seth described, the Troy police have no reports of the incident. No news clippings exist that mention a homicide in a public park, a murderous mugger at large, or any similar crime committed against a person named Natasha. There are no records at all of a shooting involving an RPI student during the brief time Seth was enrolled there, from September 2001 to January 2002, nor do his RPI classmates remember hearing about a girlfriend who got shot. And while administrators at the school agree that such an event would be remarkable, there's no institutional memory of it having happened.

But Troy, New York, seemed a million miles away from the New Hampshire Seacoast. Perhaps that was what Seth counted on when he told the Natasha story. For him, it wasn't just an anecdote about a tragic thing that happened in his life. It was part of a mythology he was creating.

Natasha's "death" would be the source of a darkness inside him, a motivation for wanting to destroy the world and rebuild it anew.

Seth left RPI weeks into his second semester, returning to Dover in January 2002 with a different girlfriend he'd met while in Troy, and the two of them moved into an apartment at Sawyer Mill. The girlfriend stuck around for about a year before breaking it off.

Free from his academic pursuits, Seth's other interests blossomed. He began socializing with student groups at the neighboring University of New Hampshire, including the school's "pagan circle." Seth's obsession with video games and role-playing games like Dungeons & Dragons deepened. He was a part of a "nerd culture" that hadn't yet reached the mainstream.

At social gatherings (which he preferred to avoid), he spoke to as few people as possible. When Seth did engage, others found his manner affected. He spoke and even dressed with an ill-placed formality, and whatever effect he was trying to achieve missed the mark. Seth came across as someone with no natural social graces stiffly trying to exert artificial ones.

Seth applied for full-time admission to the University of New Hampshire. After taking night-school classes to complete some prerequisites, he was accepted into UNH's drama program. He studied ballroom dancing and eventually graduated at age twenty-four with a degree in theater, and a minor in dance.

After leaving high school with dreams of being an engineer, Seth finally left college as an out-of-work actor.

———————

Even eight years postgraduation, Seth's apartment at Sawyer Mill retained the distinct feel of a dorm room. He didn't drink or do drugs, so there were no empty cans or smoking paraphernalia left around, but there were always clothes on the floor, strewn across seats, or hanging from doorknobs. Plastic cases for DVDs and Xbox 360 games were piled on the stained gray carpet. Extension cords and overtaxed power strips begged to trip someone. Dishes piled up in the sink, dust gathered beneath the appliances. The apartment also bore the telltale odor of Raven, Seth's black cat. He owned almost no furniture. His couch was an inexpensive futon that doubled as his bed. There were a couple of wooden chairs but there was no table in the apartment's small kitchen, so he ate his meals on folding tray tables he could move around the apartment. There was no cable TV plugged into his small flat-screen monitor, just a video game console. The only things that might have passed for grown-up furniture were a particleboard computer desk and a black office swivel chair. It was at this workstation that Seth spent hours each day on his desktop computer, writing bits of novels and plays and lengthy online missives.

Seth did have a bookcase, packed top to bottom, which served as an indicator of his interests: a smattering of books on drama and one-act plays; a couple of classics like *The Odyssey* and *The Art of War*, and two copies of Bram Stoker's *Dracula*; hardbound editions of Batman and Superman graphic novels; and mainstream horror from Edgar Allan Poe to Stephen King. There were also more obscure selections in Seth's library. He owned every book in a sword-and-sorcery series that was labeled ultraviolent by critics, as well as a copy of the Egyptian *Book of the Dead*.

Instead of a traditional bookend, he used a life-sized ceramic skull on one of his sagging shelves, and around the room were several prop skulls serving as decoration on windowsills, footlockers, and stereo speakers. His decorating style leaned toward faux Halloween-esque candelabras, dragon statuettes, and figurines of wizards and warriors. Affixed to the walls were a four-foot-long battle sword meant to look as if it had been forged during the Dark Ages, a framed poster from the vampires vs. werewolves movie *Underworld*, and a pair of Native American dream catchers.

Overall, the place gave the impression that its occupant was stunted, like an overgrown man-child—someone with a preoccupation with the occult and the supernatural.

At the time he met Kat, Seth didn't have a full-time job. He'd obtained a certification as a basic emergency medical technician (EMT-B) and was seeking work with local ambulance companies. He'd held several retail jobs, but his steadiest gig was teaching karate. The kind of self-defense he excelled in was not a discipline in which one protects oneself by deflecting an attacker's jabs. His karate was the study of pressure points used to immobilize a foe with crippling pain.

Seth's proficiencies in both hand-to-hand combat and with weapons were skills he tried to leverage in the local theater scene. Occasionally Seth would find work as a stage combat choreographer for local theater companies, and he made sure those involved with the productions also knew he was a trained actor.

He needed the edge. In the subjective world of talent evaluation, local directors later said they thought Seth Mazzaglia did not audition well. His awkward personality traits often showed through whether he was delivering a memorized monologue or cold-reading lines from a script. One director called him "off-putting." Another saw him as one of the "regulars," someone who would continue to audition despite rejection, to whom it was easier to grant a small part after the principal characters were cast.

Seth had a reputation for attempting to flirt with actresses during tryouts and rehearsals. He was not smooth, though, and while too polite to say so to his face, many women shared junior high school–like "*ick* factor" stories about him.

One of the few people who thought Seth was a good performer was Kat's mother, Denise McDonough. She'd only worked with him at a script-reading workshop, but she thought he had a strong voice and a good presence.

Seth was neither tall nor short. His hair was dark and full, and he almost always sported facial hair. He was broad-shouldered and had a solid build, but his body type didn't carry weight well. In a matter of a couple of months, Seth could easily transform from fit to doughy if he didn't keep up a strict diet and exercise regimen. It didn't help that his cooking skills were as stunted as his other domestic skills and were limited to boiling macaroni and cooking variations of stir-fry.

Seth was keenly aware of how he was typecast. With his deep, close-set eyes and average build, he knew he would never be seen as a leading man. He did think he was sinister-looking, however, and saw that as a potential advantage. He thought he could get bigger roles as villains or their henchmen. Sometimes he would fashion his whiskers with wax to make himself look like an archetypal silent-film villain, the sort who'd tie a damsel to the railroad tracks.

Though he won no big theater roles, Seth still believed he could have a starring turn somewhere. He eventually landed a bit part playing a stickup man in a low-budget indie film shot on the Seacoast. On set, he talked to the stunt coordinator about what it would take to break into that field, but the stuntman was discouraging, telling Seth that the training was long, the pay bad, and that a stuntman was finished the first time he fractured a bone.

For a *Christmas Carol*–inspired show in which he'd been cast, the costumer asked for Seth's input on his Victorian-era wardrobe. Standing in front of the dressing-room mirror, Seth said he was fine wearing the assigned black suit and cravat, but his eyes lit up when the seamstress slipped a blue vest on him. He liked the way it felt and thought it made his torso appear slim.

In every show he was cast in from that point on, Seth would wear a vest if he could get away with it, even if his costume didn't require a jacket. He thought the look was dapper. To most everyone else, he looked like a bartender.

At home, Seth dabbled in writing plays and films. *Write what you know*, he'd heard, so his stories were primarily horror and fantasy, the genres he read most avidly. Theater had scores of whodunit mysteries but few truly scary horror stories had ever been staged, and Seth thought he could create a niche: shows that would terrify the audience, perhaps even spray them with fake blood. (It apparently hadn't occurred to him that such an experience might be unpleasant for those who'd dressed up for a night at the theater.)

On the page, his characters were powerful, untamed. They were warriors and ghosts who lived on a spiritual plane, on the other side of the mystical "Veil of Separation" that divided our world from theirs. Some of these characters were heroes; others were motivated only by laying waste to their universe.

Seth seemed to believe there were other entities on other spiritual planes—perhaps from past lives—that were tethered to his current existence. He told Kat that he had not one, but many of these personas, and he sometimes held them responsible for his life's difficulties. He'd turn to the more reliable ones for direction on major decisions. The personas offered him guidance as well as excuses for his failures.

Like Kat's "Scarlet," there's no indication Seth's personas were the manifestation of a clinical mental illness—delusions or hallucinations. In this own imagination, his alter egos gave him comfort and satisfaction, and were

wish-fulfillment fantasies of a certain sort. And Seth Mazzaglia and his fantasies had big plans for one another.

––––––––

Aware that their ten-year age difference would necessitate
some secrecy, Seth and Kat developed their relationship
largely online. Most notably, they used Facebook's instant
message feature to communicate when Kat wasn't in
school, often late into the night.

As a cautionary move to avoid detection, Seth urged
Kat to regularly delete the chat log on her computer. Seth
did the same on his end, but before emptying the log he
would copy and paste their conversations into a separate
text file. Left behind were more than eight hundred pages
of instant messages between the two of them, document-
ing a rare, intimate look at the course of their courtship.

This historical record would be incredibly valuable
source material for investigators and writers reconstruct-
ing what would become a most unusual relationship. It
was a relationship that lived in two worlds: one bizarrely
spiritual, one dangerously sexual.

Communicating remotely had its obstacles in the Mc-
Donough home. Kat had complained to Denise that her
father's habit of unplugging the family's Wi-Fi at night
was keeping her from chatting with friends, so Denise
agreed to get Kat a smartphone so she could use its 3G
signal to connect directly to the Internet instead of rely-
ing on the house's router.

The phone was an LG model called Optimus and
Kat named it "Optimus Prime," after the robot in the hit

movie *Transformers.* She customized the phone's sounds so that every time she received a text, the phone said, "Incoming transmission from Autobot headquarters!"

Age difference aside, Kat and Seth found that they had much in common. They were both fans of superheroes and science fiction. Kat had a purple belt in karate. Seth was tickled he'd met a girl who could geek out on science fiction along with him. She was intrigued by his interest in Live Action Role-Playing, in which large groups of people in Tolkeinesque costumes would wage mock combat with foam swords. They both liked video games, fantasy adventures in which players use magic to survive in a world of monsters, evil wizards, and dragons.

Each Monday night Seth would play Xbox games with his friend Andy. The two had met as seventh graders at a summer camp, then had attended Berwick Academy, a private school in Maine. Seth also had a platonic female friend, Peggy,[1] who sometimes came to game night. He told these friends little about Kat other than he was seeing someone younger. They nicknamed her the "mysterious disappearing dragon."

————

In the intimacy of their private online conversations, Seth aggressively drew Kat into his fantasy world, telling her all about his alter egos who thrived there.

Seth said his Wild Card persona lived in another spiri-

————

1 Denotes pseudonym.

tual dimension beyond the Veil of Separation between our corporal world and a magical one. The barrier created by the Veil, however, is thin. The powerful entities there can see into our world, predict our futures, even change our destinies. Likewise, we on Earth can sometimes take actions that affect the fates of these beings.

Teaching his new student, Seth said he was psychically "tethered" to Wild Card. He said Scarlet also resided beyond the Veil and was tethered to Kat. He was trying to convince her that the persona that had been in her head, the one she'd used as an emotional escape, was a real spirit living alongside other spirits.

"There is another being with Scarlet, isn't there?" he asked her.

Though Kat had never previously mentioned any personas except for Scarlet, she told Seth that all of his talk about other spirits had indeed put her in touch with another persona within her. Her name was "Charlotte," Kat said, and her personality was different from Scarlet's. Scarlet was a fighter. But Charlotte was more mature, someone who knew how to handle herself without resorting to combat. Seth responded as if he were already aware of this.

"She [Charlotte] has begun invading my astral space too," he said knowingly. His plan to mingle their personas had begun.

————

After their first date, they made plans the following weekend to see another movie.

"Let me know if something goes wonky with three P.M.," he typed on his desktop computer in Dover. In her bedroom in Portsmouth, Kat began composing her response. Earlier in the day she had mentioned her deepening friendship with Seth to Denise, a trial balloon designed to gauge her mother's reaction. It didn't go as she hoped.

"I'm not sure if I'm even gonna be able to go now. My mum is kinda freaked about the age difference."

"I'm willing to jump through a hoop or two if it'll calm her mind," he wrote.

Seth said he "didn't do well" in large gatherings because he felt he couldn't speak freely, but he suggested Kat hang out with some of her friends at an agreed-upon place so they could "cross paths." Afterward, she could mention bumping into Seth and get her mother used to the idea of him hanging around.

Kat tried it and lied to her mother about how innocently random the meeting was, but Denise's opinion didn't improve. Kat was still only seventeen, she wouldn't be turning eighteen for another three months, Denise said, and she wasn't comfortable with her daughter dating a twenty-eight-year-old man.

The following Saturday, Kat asked Denise to drop her off at the Bowl-O-Rama in Portsmouth so she could spend the afternoon with her friends. Denise pulled up to the front door, kissed her daughter good-bye, and watched her enter the bowling alley. Inside, Seth loitered by the bowling alley's arcade games. After waiting until the coast was clear, the pair walked out the building's side door and resumed dating in secret.

When Kat went away for two weeks to Camp CenterStage in Maine, the couple tried to stay in touch. It was Kat's third year, and she was a "counselor in training," which meant she could work at the camp the following year as a summer job. While she was away, Seth made some demo reels with the hope of landing parts in more indie films.

Kat waited until lights were out in the camp's cabins before instant messaging with Seth. When IMing, Seth would greet "Kat and Skar" as if he were chatting with two people simultaneously. Kat always played along.

Seth decided that "Scarlet" should instead be spelled "Skarlett." That made it more of a warrior's name. Kat agreed to the "k" but insisted on one "t" when writing out her whole name. From then on, Kat's alter ego went by "Skarlet" or "Skar" for short.

This name change was not an insignificant suggestion. Scarlet had been Kat's personal creation. Seth was attempting to put his own stamp on her persona, to in a way make it his own. It was the first of many actions he would take to control the narrative of the Veil and—by extension—control Kat.

After theater camp and a brief family vacation, Kat returned to Portsmouth and readied herself for her senior year. She told her friends she was excited about school starting, especially because both of her younger brothers would be attending Portsmouth High along with her. She said she planned to take pictures of everything and make a scrapbook of all her high school memories.

Kat and Seth kept up the charade that they weren't

seeing each other. When Kat worked her after-school shifts at Target in neighboring Greenland, Seth would park in the store's lot and wait for her to come out on break. If the night got too chilly, Seth would go inside and pretend to shop in men's apparel or the video game section. After her shift, they'd retreat to his car and make out. Seth urged Kat to devise plausible excuses for getting out of the house so they could spend even more time together.

Knowing the kind of reaction it would get from Seth, Kat told him how her father had once shoved her in the bathroom doorway; however, she greatly exaggerated the story's outcome. Instead of the family hugging it out, Kat said the confrontation ended with her nose being broken by the flying door. Seth was furious. Kat got what she wanted out of the lie: the display of a hero wanting to rescue a damsel in distress. Seth chivalrously offered to swoop in and rescue her from her dungeon, just like a knight would.

It's not clear reading the chat transcripts whether Seth worked to debunk the story, whether he'd asked why no one at school took note of such an obvious injury, whether the doctor's office notified the police, whether her father was arrested, or why the door swung *into* the hallway when doors usually swing into rooms. It didn't matter. Seth got what he wanted too: a clear path for convincing Kat to leave home and move in with him.

CHAPTER FOUR

Skarlet

Seth Mazzaglia took Kat McDonough under his wing, shepherding her through the "astral plane" and showing her how to use her powers in real life.

Seth said he helped himself make contact with the other world by keeping a dream journal within reach of his futon. The book was green and leather-bound, embossed with a Celtic cross.

Every morning when he awoke, he turned to the next page, put down the date, and wrote whatever he could remember.

"Sometimes it's a list of names, places, descriptions," Seth told her. "Sometimes it's half a novel."

He told Kat her abilities would take time to develop. He suggested she attempt to channel them when she wasn't asleep. Seth claimed to be a very experienced "dreamwalker," but he also used tarot cards to map his future. He said using waking visions or meditations could put Kat in touch with her past lives.

"What you'll find," he said, "is that you've done all of these things before."

It was clear that Kat believed the things he told her, believed that his reports from beyond the Veil were true.

Seth told Kat that he had a long game: These spirit personas were going to guide not only his life, but hers as well. The tarot cards told him that he and Kat were soul mates who had been with each other in past lives and were destined to be together in this one. The psychic purpose for joining Seth and Kat was not merely for love. It would be together, he said, that their combined strength would allow them to achieve the ultimate goal.

Seth then said he believed that within four years he and Kat would lay waste to the world and then rule it together.

————

The cast of characters Seth claimed to have living beyond the Veil of Separation was numerous. In addition to Wild Card, there was "Cyrus." He was a benevolent enforcer, something like a knight. There was "The Nameless One," an evil, brooding persona—one who emerged when Seth became angry or depressed. "The Hollow One" was even *more* evil than the Nameless One. There were others, like "Rune," "Black Knight," "Powered Achron," "Scourge," "Kushira," "the Arbitor," "Old Evil Brain," "Dark Kaiser," and "the Horror of all Nightmares." There was even the female spirit, a woman with ebony hair and black eyes named "Eve," who Seth said was his unborn daughter caught in the Veil. Each had different characteristics, but all sounded menacing. Some posed threats to other personas. Some could foresce the future. Others could affect what happened in the real world on this side of the Veil.

The persona Seth most often took was called "Darkheart." He was the spirit of a dragon who lived inside of Seth's mortal coil. Darkheart, explained Seth, was largely in control of his body and his fate.

Darkheart had one important job: to control "the Darkness." This was the wicked, doleful cloud that would sometimes overcome him psychically and emotionally. It could make him do terrible things. The Darkness was sent by the Nameless One, and Darkheart would have to take any measure to stop it. Any measure. Seth said that Darkheart would often make requests of him and others—all so the Darkness would not consume him.

If Kat were ever to fully believe in the existence of the Veil of Separation and its inhabitants, then she would have to accept Seth as Darkheart. Doing so would give Seth wide latitude to make demands of her, all in the name of keeping the Darkness in check. It would give him a means of control.

There was one more persona Seth cautioned Kat about. He was called "Doomsday." This was the most powerful of all his personas. Doomsday lurked in the depths of the Veil. Seth said he could unleash Doomsday only once. It would be on the day he would launch his plan to destroy the world.

———

Seth said there was another persona—not his—that was circling him from the Veil. It was a female persona he called "Anay," a redheaded spirit who he said had followed him through many of his lives, and who had the power to inhabit women's bodies and become his lover. But Anay never stuck around. She was forever visiting then abandoning Seth. He told Kat that Anay had inhabited his slain love, Natasha. Anay, Seth explained, was the love who had slipped through his fingers for all eternity.

"I think the one you know as Charlotte," he told Kat, "is actually Anay."

Seth was co-opting Kat's persona to make it his own, to further drive the point home that they were psychically tethered. He was creating another way to control her.

After all of Seth's talk about his different personas, Kat revealed that she too had detected more personas. One was "Kitty." Simply put, Kitty was Kat's normal high school self, the antithesis of the mighty warrior Skarlet. She described this persona in terms that implied she found Kitty to be annoying.

One was named "Violet." She was a healer, Kat said, someone who was good at defending her. Violet had strong powers but she used them only for good, only for protection. Violet was the name Kat's mother, Denise, had used as her own fantasy persona, as well as the name of Scarlet's witch mother in her Harry Potter fan fiction. It's possible Violet's creation served a real-life purpose for Kat, an emotional projection of something she was missing in her relationship with Denise, or Kat's way of letting her mother into the secret world she shared with Seth.

Another figure was male, someone Kat said was tied to Skarlet in past lives. He was a brother-figure named "James Sweeten." James (another name from Kat's fiction) was not Skarlet's lover, Kat said, nor did she believe he was Seth in some other form. Rather, James was Skarlet's partner in mayhem.

In one life, Kat said, Skarlet was captain of a pirate ship and James was her first mate. In another, they were robbers together. In the ethereal world, Kat could sense James was nearby, always watching out for Skarlet and ready to take up arms in a fight.

When she was ten years old, Kat said, she'd had a dream she was walking around colonial Portsmouth and then setting fire to the city. (Such a dream could very easily have been inspired by real-life local history lessons, as the port city burned three times between 1802 and 1813. The worst fire was the final one, a conflagration that destroyed virtually every wooden structure in Portsmouth.)

Though Kat said she'd had the dream seven years earlier, Seth declared that *he too* remembered having the same dream seven years ago on the same night. They compared notes.

Kat said in her dream, she was Skarlet but was dressed in little boy's clothes, James by her side.

Seth elbowed in on this too, claiming that he was there in some form as well, and was certain he'd seen Skarlet through the flames. When Kat said she was burned during the fire, Seth insisted he had saved her from the flames, but was himself killed during the rescue. Because of his sacrifice, Seth said, he'd become a kind of guardian angel, who watched over Skarlet and protected her whenever she was in mortal danger.

Kat seemed to believe Seth's vivid description of the role he'd played in her own dream. She never protested how he inserted himself into every story she told.

The night wore on, and Kat's Facebook responses took longer and longer to transmit. Seth recognized his young girlfriend was nodding off. He had a standard sign-off he used each night.

"Until the tides bring you back to me . . ."

———

Given the tensions she felt at home, Kat was always happy to be out of the house during the week, either at work or a rehearsal for another play. Seth, who had no steady job or schoolwork to occupy his own time, was persistent when Kat would counter there wasn't enough time to see each other. He wanted to see her, even if it was only for half an hour.

On the weekends, the plan was always the same. Denise would drop Kat off at Bowl-O-Rama, believing her daughter was spending the afternoon with friends who would give her a ride to work later. (Though she was nearly eighteen, Kat still did not have a driver's license herself.) Instead, Kat would meet Seth inside the bowling alley, then the two of them would emerge from the side door and begin their date.

Often they chanced detection by walking around Portsmouth's downtown Market Square, browsing in shops and people watching. They frequented coffee shops, but because neither liked the bitter taste of java, they sipped mugs of hot chocolate al fresco.

Less than a mile's walk away, beyond the docks where commercial fishermen set off each morning in search of lobster, was the bridge leading to Peirce Island, twenty-seven acres of green grass, boat launches, dog parks, and tree-lined walking paths. Seth liked taking Kat to Peirce Island because it felt far away from the Market Square crowds. On the island, they could spend a Saturday afternoon feeling safely hidden, pretending their fantasy world was real.

Once, while walking along a trail, Kat stopped and stepped off the path. She leaned against a tree and waited for Seth to follow. He approached her and kissed her deeply on the mouth.

"There's magic in this tree," he said.

Kat smiled. "Yes, I think so. This is our magic tree."

The island's scenic overlook offered 270-degree views of the river and of Kittery, Maine, on the opposite bank. There was a trio of granite benches at the overlook, each just wide enough for the two of them to share. If they timed it right, they'd see a commercial freighter making its way up the river, being nudged around the bends by tugboats, and eventually spurring the alarm to sound on the river's drawbridge.

New Hampshire's coastline is the shortest of any coastal state, just thirteen miles along the Atlantic, pinched between Maine and Massachusetts like a finger stuck in a door. Portsmouth's linkage to the Atlantic is three miles down the Piscataqua River. The body of water is less like a river and more like a vein to the sea. Its brackish waters run upstream when the tides are in, raising water levels by eight feet when the daily surge sends the river in reverse. When the tides ebb, the Piscataqua returns its brine to the Atlantic, leaving behind fresher waters tinged with green, brown, and red seaweed. For centuries, sea captains sailing for Portsmouth have navigated around inconvenient isles with colorful names: Four Tree Island, Pest Island, Smuttynose Island, and the Devil's Dance Floor.

"My mother said the tides on this river are really fast," Kat told Seth. "Like the fastest in North America. That's why there's never any ice."

"I know."

"I love Halloween. It's my birthday," Kat said. "Well, not actually. My birthday is November first, but I always considered Halloween to be my birthday."

"It's your strong psychic ability. You have a connection to Ol' Hallows Eve."

"I sometimes have nightmares that I miss it, that I miss Halloween and my birthday."

Seth raised a knowing eyebrow. "You'll be eighteen in a couple of weeks. An adult."

———

Seth announced to Kat that he planned to change his career path. He'd decided to become a police officer, and he wanted to do all he could to prepare himself for any upcoming department entrance exams. Seth believed his EMT experience gave him an edge, and he began working out —lifting weights and running on a regular basis—to stay trim.

Seth told Kat he wanted to sign up for a local Citizens Police Academy. This wasn't a formal police academy; it was a nine-week public outreach program demonstrating various aspects of law enforcement to curious residents and business owners. Participants got a behind-the-scenes look at everything from constitutional law and restraining orders to crime-scene investigation and defensive tactics. A ride-along in a patrol car was usually the highlight of the course.

"This is the first step to making it all happen," he instant messaged Kat.

"The Plan," as Seth referred to it, was both elaborate and far-fetched. It called for Seth to cut his teeth in law enforcement, where he would join a SWAT team. When the time was right, he'd use his reputation as a "veteran police officer who has seen the dark side of life" to start a private security firm. The people he'd hire would serve as Seth's private army, and among their ranks, he would plant those he called "minions."

To Seth, minions were men and women who would do his bidding without question. The men would follow his orders with a cultlike discipline. The women would serve as sexual playthings. Minions were to be collected and groomed. Seth thought college protest groups, their minds open to influence, would be a source to find potential minions. They'd be more reliable in the revolution, he explained, than "allies from overseas."

The beauty of collecting minions, Seth wickedly told Kat over Facebook, was that they were expendable— particularly the ones used for sex.

Seth would release Doomsday from the Veil, along with his army of bone rippers, to raze the world. What would rise after Doomsday's campaign of destruction would be a far better world. In his vision, the "outsiders" would inherit the Earth. His visions said that Skarlet would be fighting alongside him.

"It should be a world where people can be who they want to be, without having to deal with abuse and misery and aggravation."

To someone older and more experienced, Seth's words would have been more than a red flag, they would have sounded like an alarm screaming, "RUN AWAY!" But when she heard about Doomsday and the Plan and the role Seth wanted her to play, Kat McDonough was ensorcelled.

———

As fall progressed and Seth focused on passing police department tests, Kat had her own exams to worry about. The SATs were administered the first weekend in November, and how she scored on the test would likely determine what college she could get into. Kat still hoped to take a year off after graduation to work at Walt Disney World before going to school in New York, but Seth was skeptical of her plans.

"Darkheart doesn't see Florida in our future."

Seth promised to lay down tarot cards to seek an answer as to whether he would follow Kat to an out-of-state college, or whether she should abandon her plans altogether.

"It's probably out of the question," typed Kat, with one short sentence letting go of her dreams of Florida, college, and Broadway. She was going to let Seth determine her future now.

One evening, Kat messaged Seth that there was a boy at school who had psychic powers of his own, someone who could talk to Skarlet. Kat called the boy "Mr. Valentine," although it wasn't his true name.

"Even his dark ones knew how to talk to Charlotte," she wanted Seth to know. "Oh, and he wanted me badly."

Here was a flip of the script. Seth had been testing her, looking to see whether Kat could be influenced by what he said was happening beyond the Veil of Separation. This time, it appeared Kat was testing him. It could have been a simple teenage ploy to make her boyfriend jealous. Or was she doing to Seth what he'd been doing to her: measuring how seriously he took this talk of a spiritual world?

Seth downplayed this boy's psychic abilities. He explained that people with his and Kat's aptitude would always attract those who could sense their power and try to prey upon it. Seth even suggested that "Mr. Valentine" might really be temporarily possessed by one of Seth's own personas trying to reach out to Skarlet and Charlotte from beyond the Veil. As he had with the Portsmouth fire story, Seth was taking something Kat had claimed as hers and trying to convince her it was his.

As the nightly messages continued past midnight, Kat's IMs got shorter and slower in coming. It was time to say good night. Over the weeks in which he'd been drawn more deeply into talking about the Plan, Seth's once romantic sign-offs had devolved considerably.

"Sleep well," he wrote. "Dream of dark, bloody, and psychotic things."

CHAPTER FIVE

The Sacrifice

While Seth's friends only knew his girl was the "mysterious disappearing dragon," Kat let it slip at school she was seeing somebody named "Lex," but the name was meaningless outside of community-theater circles.

Not long after school started in September, the relationship began to get physical. Seth always wore a condom, and Kat assumed his furious thrusts were part of his excitement to be with her. He told her over and over again how much she turned him on. His seemingly uncontrollable devotion turned *her* on.

At the start of each week, he'd ask her to detail her schedule. When he could identify a potential hole in her calendar, he threw out excuses for her to give, cover stories about double shifts at Target or additional show rehearsals. Kat wanted to be with Seth so, invoking her best community-theater performances, she repeated the lies to her parents.

"Dream not of madness and doubt," Seth would tell her as she tried to go to sleep, "but rather of a future with castles and wonder and fantasy and love. Because that future *is* yours, yours and Darkheart's."

One night, they made love on the futon while it was folded into a couch. Kat was on top and found that position to be the most pleasurable. Facing her, his hands free, Seth tried some things he hadn't before. There was some pinching and twisting. He then moved his hands up to her throat and gently squeezed on and off until it was over. Afterward, Kat admitted the sex game had turned her on.

Seth asked her then what she knew about BDSM. Kat would later say she knew some rudimentary things because her ex-boyfriend had talked about it, but nothing had ever come of it. Seth offered to teach her about a sexual world that few ventured into, just as he had guided her through the mysterious world beyond the Veil.

BDSM is shorthand for "bondage, discipline [although some substitute the word "dominance"], and sadomasochism." The mega-bestselling *Fifty Shades of Grey* novels brought BDSM into the mainstream. Originally conceived as fan fiction inspired by the Twilight series of vampire novels, the books were equal parts cultural scandal and cultural sensation, normalizing a brand of fantasy that had previously been largely dismissed as "perversion." *Fifty Shades* was not everyone's cup of tea, but millions of readers were curious why their friends and neighbors were reading a "whips and chains" book, and got a healthy lesson on kink as a reward.

People have long dabbled in minor variations of BDSM by giving in to urges to spank a partner or turn dirty talk into filthy talk, or allowing a lover to tie their hands and have their way with them. It's not unusual for loving, committed couples to experiment in bed, to learn what turns each other on.

Actual BDSM goes well beyond these suburban fantasies. Participants—many of whom are loving, committed couples themselves—enjoy more hard-core versions of these games.

Instead of a necktie knotted to the headboard, a woman might allow herself to be fully bound with soft rope or belted to the corners of a bed and rendered completely immobile. Instead of an open palm, a spank on the buttocks might be delivered repeatedly with a paddle or leather flogger, leaving the skin red or bruised. One lover might so totally submit to the other that they allow themselves to be slapped or struck, or ordered to crawl around as if in humiliation.

The science behind it, like many sexual studies, is largely conjecture. The part of the brain activated by pain is very close to its pleasure center. One theory says that if pain is not in response to fear or a threat, the pleasure centers are stimulated and counteract that pain. Some believe the level of pleasure is equal to the corresponding level of pain.

Perhaps for some consensual couples, the act is not the attraction. It's what the act signifies. Following bondage there is freedom. Following discipline there is absolution. Following humiliation there is respect. Following injury there is healing.

Whatever the flavor or intensity, most people who enjoy BDSM agree on its basic tenet: complete trust in one's partner, the ability to give up control or to take it absolutely without fear. Trusting one's lover to know one's limits is essential. Knowing that one's partner will stop when asked (or will ask to stop) if the contact is no longer pleasing is essential.

Because some consensual partners pretend to beg "no . . . stop" as part of the sex game, couples who practice BDSM agree on "safe words" in advance to indicate when things must come to a halt. These are code words that wouldn't be confused with dirty talk; safe words are phrases like "lollipop" or "red" (as in "stop").

The safe word is the ultimate expression of trust.

———

Seth had honed his interest and practice of BDSM as a young adult. When Seth left RPI after completing only one semester, he returned to New Hampshire with a long-distance girlfriend. She was a high school senior from Pennsylvania named Catherine Fish, who called herself "Cat" for short.

Catherine's best friend, Barbara[1], attended RPI, and Catherine often made the trip to upstate New York to visit

———

1 Denotes pseudonym.

her. All Catherine originally knew of Seth Mazzaglia was he had just gotten out of a rocky relationship with Barbara. But Barbara was not "Natasha," the girl who had allegedly died in his arms. Never during their relationship did Seth mention Natasha or someone who died in a similar manner.

Catherine was a pretty girl with a round face who wore neon streaks in her delicate blond hair, giving her the look of an approachable Goth-next-door. (Noteworthy is that Seth's physical description of Natasha was similar.)

Like Kat, Catherine's home life wasn't happy. Years later, Catherine would describe her parents' relationship as extremely volatile, and at seventeen she was looking for a way to get out of the house once and for all. She'd planned on joining the military after graduation, but September 11, 2001, made her reconsider. She was also still exploring her sexual identity and had just ended a relationship with another girl on bad terms.

Although Catherine knew hooking up on the rebound wasn't a good idea, she found herself attracted to the college freshman she'd met while visiting RPI, despite his having dated her best friend.

Catherine got together with Seth the long weekend of Martin Luther King Day in 2002, about a week into his second semester. She was there when Seth received a letter from the college saying he was being expelled for unspecified "violence issues." After reading the letter, Seth reacted by repeatedly kicking the porch of the off-campus house he was living in.

He never told Catherine the specifics of what led to his

expulsion, and she didn't ask. Years later, Catherine learned from Barbara that Seth had been rough with her. Barbara was a virgin, and when she'd refused Seth's advances, she said he'd thrown her across the room.

It was possible that this incident was what led to Seth's expulsion. The school could have learned of these allegations through Barbara, through an eyewitness, or from someone connected to a completely different incident. The college would not comment on Seth's apparent expulsion.

After getting kicked out of RPI, Seth moved back to Dover and into a basement apartment at Sawyer Mill. He and Catherine keep their long-distance relationship going, with him making regular trips to Pennsylvania. Seth told Catherine he'd lost his virginity only a few months before they'd met (perhaps with Barbara), but he had an advanced view of what made for pleasing sex. Much of it had to do with sadomasochism.

As Catherine later told *48 Hours*, Seth made special plans for her eighteenth birthday in March of 2002. He took her out for a night on the town, and then took her back to his hotel room. As they had sex, Seth's hand went from caressing Catherine's face to wrapping around her thin neck. Unsure of what was happening, Catherine told him to stop. Instead, he squeezed her throat harder. She grabbed his shoulders and threw him off of her.

"What the hell are you doing?"

Seth released his grip, then rolled off of her and onto his back. Catherine tried to catch her breath, placing her fingers where she was sure bruises would soon appear.

The choking hadn't been enough to knock her out, but it had startled her.

Seth whined about her reluctance to try something new. The mood was ruined, but he continued to badger her to at least finish the sex. Catherine surrendered.

Despite his distaste for crowds, Seth offered to escort Catherine to her senior prom. She bought an aquamarine dress with a beaded bust line and an empire waist over an A-line skirt and streaked her hair in blue to match her dress—an edgy contrast to her jeweled choker necklace and pearl-beaded handbag.

Seth dressed in all black, wearing a jacket but no necktie. His two top shirt buttons were left open, exposing a gold chain. He had grown his whiskers out and his hair was long, covering his neck. He looked in part like a dress-up Dracula, in part like an actor auditioning for *Jesus Christ Superstar.*

Seth picked Catherine up at the door and presented her with a wrist corsage, then posed for photos in her backyard. In recounting the night during interviews, Catherine said that, after the prom, Seth took her back to his hotel room, where they had a repeat of her birthday experience. During sex, Seth attempted to choke her by pinching her windpipe between this forefinger and thumb.

"What the fuck are you doing? Stop that!"

Seth's gaze was fixed on her throat. Catherine pushed against Seth's face, his shoulders, his chest, trying to shove him off. She was able to wiggle out from beneath him, coughing as she tried to catch her breath, then she leaped from the bed and started gathering her clothes.

"Fuck this. I'm out of here."

Before she could make her escape, Seth locked himself in the bathroom.

"If you go, I'm going to kill myself," he said through the bathroom door.

It was a childish ploy, but Catherine had grown up in an environment where drama was a comfort, threats a part of everyday life. She stayed that night, if only to convince herself she had saved him.

Catherine said she wanted someone to save, someone who needed her. Seth knew that, and he knew that's why she would find it hard to leave him.

For the entirety of their relationship, Seth was insistent that high school student Catherine leave Pennsylvania and move in with him in New Hampshire. The chance to leave home was too tempting to pass up. Catherine left town as soon as her last high school class was dismissed, even skipping graduation. Since her senior year had been so tumultuous, she hadn't made plans to attend college.

Seth began taking night classes at the University of New Hampshire. He heard about a small group of UNH students who had formed an unconventional club: a pagan circle. They would gather to talk about spirits and legends and magic and other otherworldly things. After Seth joined, Catherine told him she wanted to attend as well. She wasn't radically mystical, but she'd always felt like there was a male spirit who was watching over her.

"Who is this protector spirit?" Seth asked.

"His name is Cyrus," she said. It was a name that Seth would later say was among the several personas watching him from beyond the Veil of Separation.

At first Seth didn't want her to come to the pagan circle, but he eventually changed his mind. The circle was coed but predominantly female. One of the women, Gloria,[2] was an attractive redhead who was comfortable talking about sprites and pixies and Wiccan power. Gloria told the group she had a powerful essence in the spiritual world, a fairy named Anay.

In recounting the incident a decade later, Catherine said Seth proposed bringing Gloria into their bed. Although she had been in a same-sex relationship previously, Catherine wasn't interested in being part of some sort of polyamorous arrangement. But she wasn't going to leave Seth either. If he wanted to pursue Gloria, she told him, it would have to be something he did on his own.

Seth proceeded to hit on Gloria as well as most of the other women in the pagan circle. He let Catherine think that he slept with at least one of them, but whether he had or not, it wasn't with Gloria. She'd politely deflected his come-ons until she'd had to flat-out refuse him. The turmoil that followed among the club's members was enough to break up the circle for good.

After failing to sleep with Gloria, Seth left the circle believing Gloria's Anay was a spirit he had been chasing from one life to another—she inhabited the bodies of

---

2 Denotes pseudonym.

women for the purpose of tantalizing him. As women walked out of his real life, Seth kept their alter egos among his list of personas. He could not control those women, but he could control the spiritual versions of them.

————

Living in a basement apartment at Sawyer Mill was lonely for Catherine Fish. She didn't know anybody in New Hampshire. She landed a part-time job, but Seth made her quit because he didn't want her to work at night. He made all the decisions in their life, from what she could wear to what they would buy at the grocery store. He even insisted on doing all the cooking and would then decide what size portion Catherine was allowed to eat.

The young woman was conflicted. As she told *Foster's Daily Democrat*, she didn't consider Seth an abuser; he didn't strike her during an argument. But there were aspects of the relationship Catherine knew weren't right, like how rough Seth was with her in bed. But she was inexperienced, so she went along with it, first getting spanked, then slapped, then tied up as he had his way with her.

There were nights when Catherine was just too tired or not in the mood, but Seth never took no for an answer. Seth would cajole her by rubbing his hands on her or giving her unsolicited kisses on her body. She rebuffed his requests to do breath play (choking), knife play (running and scraping the dull edge of a blade on her skin), or blood play (drinking any blood these cuts might draw), but he would always have a different act to try, something different he wanted to insert in her. If she still said no, Seth would become enraged. He'd throw a tantrum like a child. He'd start flinging things around the apartment, yelling and berating her. If that didn't work, he'd say he'd kill himself if she didn't do what he wanted. Catherine would often give in just to calm Seth down, just to make the shouting and damage stop.

The intercourse was always brutal. Catherine was constantly getting urinary tract infections, and was treated for them so often she became drug-resistant to three of the most commonly prescribed medicines. In order to increase her protection against accidental pregnancies, Seth had a regimen he said was medically sound. Tearfully recalling the practice for interviewers, Catherine said Seth would turn on the water in the kitchen sink and wait until it got to its hottest point. Then he would fill a plastic watering can and pour the scalding water into Catherine's vaginal canal. She claims this procedure, combined with the vaginal tearing and persistent UTIs she suffered during the course of their relationship, caused permanent gynecological damage. Catherine would later say she didn't understand why no physician saw the string of infections for what she believed they were: symptoms of sexual abuse.

She told interviewers that Seth was deathly afraid of STDs and obsessive about preventing Catherine from getting pregnant. On more than one occasion, he said he would kill her before he'd pay child support. Catherine didn't think he was joking. Seth would remind Catherine of his karate training, and told her he could hurt his opponents effortlessly.

"Don't try to run," he said. "I would come and find you." Despite her outward denial about the state of her relationship, Catherine had been researching abuse and abusers. She knew that the second most common time for a man to kill his wife or girlfriend is when she becomes pregnant. The most common time, statistically speaking, is when she tries to leave.

————

Toward the end of their relationship, Seth was openly talking about his personas, which he said lived beyond the Veil. He told Catherine one of his alter egos was a dragon called "Akimeru."

"If I ever got into a car accident," he said, "I would become an enraged dragon larger than a building!"

The declaration was so ridiculous, even Catherine rolled her eyes.

One day, Seth sneaked up on Catherine, embracing her from behind. She told *Foster's Daily Democrat* she was wearing a short necklace, very much like the one she wore to the prom.

"You should avoid wearing necklaces around me," Seth said in her ear. "The urge for me to choke you is very strong."

Catherine slowly began to extract herself from Seth, but the relationship was so similar to her upbringing, it was hard for her to quit. Things started to change when she enrolled in an inexpensive business school in Dover.

She made friends on campus and had the chance to crash in the dorms if she needed time away from Sawyer Mill.

These mini-escapes did not sit well with Seth, and for a time he was able to manipulate Catherine to keep coming back. Ironically, his hold over her finally broke over something mundane, not something violent.

"Stop nagging me," he said to her one day over something inconsequential. "You're always nagging me."

The criticism broke the spell he held over Catherine like the sudden pop of a balloon. She knew what she had to say was valid, and calling it "nagging" was an insult.

What Seth Mazzaglia had finally given Catherine Fish was a rational reason to leave him. She could tell people he thought she nagged too much. That was the kind of break-up story people would understand. How could she tell people she ran from him because he was obsessed with choking her and violated her with a watering can?

The farther she got away from Seth, the more Catherine came to realize that during their time together he had been abusive physically, emotionally, and sexually. What he did in bed wasn't BDSM. It was sexual violence, pure and simple.

Through campus resources, she sought out help from the sexual harassment and rape prevention service at the University of New Hampshire and became an advocate for victims, eventually sharing her story at a Take Back the Night event. She moved to the West Coast, about as far away from Seth as she could get. In the years that followed, she would suffer from crippling bouts of post-traumatic stress disorder.

One of the most disturbing things Catherine recalled about Seth Mazzaglia was his preoccupation with murder and his bragging about how he would get away with it. All you had to do was drive the victim's car and wipe off the fingerprints, he told her.

"Just bring the body to the woods. The scavengers will do the rest."

Catherine told *48 Hours* that she suspected that Seth was destined to murder someone, that he would not be sexually satisfied until he had. She thought he would likely strangle someone to death in a moment of perverse ecstasy.

If anyone knew what Kat McDonough was getting herself into, it would have been Catherine Fish.

When Seth told Kat his version of his year-and-a-half relationship with Catherine, she had not been the great love of his life like the fabled Natasha had been. She had not been someone who had been inhabited by Anay or Akasia or some other ethereal spirit. She had just been a girl who hadn't understood him.

Catherine broke his heart, Seth said, and she'd made it even more difficult for him to feel secure in any relationship. He told Kat that's why he needed to keep her close. He was afraid this Kat would abandon him, just like the other Cat had.

Like every story Seth spun for her, Kat believed every word.

Kat had enjoyed the nonsexual role-playing with her new boyfriend. They seemed so perfect for each other in this life that it seemed natural to her that they had been together in past lives too. Her love, like the love of every teenaged girl, felt enormous and everlasting and all consuming. Despite this, Seth said they were not tethered in the Veil of Separation. Skarlet had not yet "paired" with Darkheart.

Seth said he could smell that Skarlet was a "dragon rider." He reported from his dream journal that Skarlet had been circling Darkheart, whose essence was that of a dragon. She was searching for Darkheart with the intention of capturing and taming him.

Once a dragon rider pairs with a dragon, "they are paired for eternity," he told Kat.

Each night while instant messaging, Seth reported on how tantalizingly close Skarlet had been to catching Darkheart. He said Skarlet's last test was to defeat a shadow dragon who was fortified behind a wall of fire. This dragon was named Akimeru, the same name he used with Catherine Fish.

It was a compelling story. It was also a powerful way for Seth to manipulate an impressionable girl. Over the course of a handful of days, Seth eventually told Kat he'd seen Skarlet defeat Akimeru and become Darkheart's dragon rider. Kat realized it meant that the two of them were now paired for eternity. Now she was tied to Darkheart and whatever he wanted.

If she recognized Seth's telling of Skarlet's journey as being nearly identical to the plot of the movie *Avatar*, she never said so.

———

Now that Seth had married Skarlet and Darkheart, he used this spiritual connection as a way of further manipulating Kat. He said the Hollow One was now trying to rip Skarlet and Darkheart apart. Seth said the Hollow One's power was so strong that it might hurt them in the real world too. Judging by her text messages, Kat seemed to believe wholeheartedly that the threat to them and their personas was real.

Seth said there was one way to keep the Hollow One away: destroy the spirit known as Violet and allow Darkheart—in the body of Seth—to sexually ravage Kitty in any way he wanted.

If Kat recognized the symbolism, she didn't say as much. Seth wanted her mother figure, Violet, out of the way. Since Kitty was actually Kat in real life, Seth was asking her to surrender unquestionably to him in real life.

To save the spiritual connection with her one true love, Kat agreed to play the part and give up control of her body to Seth. The bargain was set for November 5, four days after her eighteenth birthday.

———

As the sacrifice approached, Seth told Kat over Facebook that he had been seeing Skarlet everywhere—turning a corner, sneaking up on him, ducking from his peripheral vision. Seth said he'd had to keep Darkheart "in check" for several days.

"I know he's been itching for a chance to play."

Seth said Darkheart had been standing over Kat's bed watching her sleep. Hearing this, Kat agreed she had felt the dragon's presence in her room.

On Friday night, November 4, 2011, Kat could not get off the laptop despite her total physical exhaustion. Kat was taking her SATs in the morning and was desperate to get some sleep. For weeks she had been up past midnight Instant messaging with Seth.

"Dream not of madness and doubt," he said as she tried disconnecting, "but rather of a future with castles and wonder and fantasy and love."

She ended up clocking just four hours before it was time to wake up and get ready to take the five-hour test. After the exam, Kat was supposed to go to Seth's apartment, which he was now referring to as "the Lair," and surrender her body to Darkheart.

They had blocked off six or seven hours for this date. Seth insisted they needed that much time for their first experimentation with BDSM. Kat had told her mother she'd be spending the entire day with her friend Darla[3] and would be home after dinner. By now, lying to her parents about when she was with Seth had become an easy thing.

When Kat woke up on Saturday morning, Seth was

---

3 Denotes pseudonym.

already hailing her on Facebook, insisting that she text him the minute the test was over.

"Psychic craziness aside," he asked her in a message, "what were you thinking of going to college for before everything got all karmically nuts?"

Kat wrote back that she wanted to study graphic design and acting, and possibly aim for a minor in fashion or costuming. Though she knew she and Skarlet were now part of the Plan, she said she still wanted a high SAT score so she could get a college degree.

"I keep getting psychic sonar blips of you every time I think 'EMT.' Is that random?" said Seth. "Has Emergency Medical Technician crossed your mind as a thing to do?"

Kat said her grandfather had been a firefighter and conceded that a backup plan wouldn't be such a bad idea. To Seth, the idea of Kat joining him as an EMT would become something he couldn't let go.

———

After her SATs, Kat entered Seth's third-floor apartment at Sawyer Mill as if it were the first time. In a way, it was. She was there—not unwillingly—to make good on her promise to the Hollow One to give over her body completely to Seth.

Seth had explained that, in every relationship like theirs, each lover had a part to play. One was the Dominant, or, "Dom." The other was the Submissive, the "Sub." The Sub gave herself up to whatever the Dom wanted. That was okay, Seth said, because the Dom's role was to take care of the Sub. The Dom would ensure the Sub's pleasure in exchange for the Sub's obedience. The Dom would coordinate every move of the erotic dance, could demand his own pleasure come first, could demand in what manner it came. The Dom could do whatever he wanted to his Sub because she was a willing, consensual partner.

Seth asked Kat if she was willing. She said she was.

In his rundown of typical BDSM protocol, Seth left one crucial thing out. He never provided Kat with a safe word.

Seth pulled a length of white rope from under the futon's mattress. He ran it like a snake over Kat's bare skin. It was soft, made of cotton, nothing like the rough hemp ropes she had to climb in gym class.

Seth apologized for not knowing the Japanese art of Shibari, an advanced form of rope bondage that locked participants in "optimal positions." If done correctly, he explained, the knots were self-tightening—moving an arm tightened the loop on the leg, and so on. Kat had never heard of Shibari, but Seth promised he knew enough about BDSM rope play that she would enjoy it.

He started by making her interlock her fingers, then knotted the rope around her wrists. He crisscrossed the cord over her torso, made a loop around her neck, then continued to immobilize her with the line.

Kat's pulse was racing from excitement and fear. The braiding of her body didn't hurt. She felt like she was being swaddled, comforted. Kat liked the careful attention Seth gave her while tying her up. She couldn't move. She'd later say the bondage aroused her, physically stimulated her in every way.

Seth then produced a cold, flat object. It was the decorative short sword hanging on his wall. He used its dull edge to scrape and flick at her skin, the extreme form of BDSM known as knife play. It went by another name: "the kiss of steel."

Kat had given Kitty over to Darkheart to save Skarlet from the Hollow One. Or was it to save Violet? It didn't matter. They were bound together on Earth and in the Veil in a way no two other people would ever be. He was her dragon; she, the dragon rider.

———

Later that night, Seth texted Kat at home to see how she was and to relive all of their erotic activities. Kat was baking in the kitchen. She told him she had a bit of a headache but was otherwise blissful. She said she had found a cut on one of her fingers from the blade.

"Not sure how we didn't notice that," she wrote. "It's a pretty deep cut but it's not bleeding."

Seth said he had lots of cutlery that left hairline slices that were only detectable when pressure was put on that very spot.

"Hehehe," Seth typed. "Maybe next time Card'll come out to play and use something smaller than a short sword. Easier to handle."

He told his new sexual protégé that she'd worn him out.

"Woo hoo! I win," she wrote back.

They exchanged some more affectionate texts. Seth told her he wanted all of her free time up to Thanksgiving, then he signed off.

Kat, the high school senior who had just had her first experience with hard-core knife play, went back to baking her cupcakes.

PART TWO

PAIN

The only way to get rid of a
temptation is to yield to it.

—OSCAR WILDE,
THE PICTURE OF DORIAN GRAY

CHAPTER SIX

Mother Dragon

Seth Mazzaglia and Kat McDonough continued to have intense sexual encounters in which he indoctrinated her into his personal brand of BDSM. Seth said he wanted to punish her, to demonstrate his dominance over her, but that kind of "play" would leave bruises that would take days to fade. Fear of their relationship being discovered by Kat's parents kept those sadomasochistic games off the table for the time being.

"I feel like my powers were used for complete and total evil," he said, "and that makes me feel very warm and fuzzy inside."

The couple had also been talking about Kat moving into Seth's apartment. She didn't want to stay under her father's roof any longer than she had to. Kat was finding it harder and harder to contain her contempt for Peter

McDonough, which didn't improve his attitude toward her either. Kat began bringing small boxes of her things to the apartment, telling Denise that she was packing up old clothes to throw away. Graduation was just months away. The plan was for Kat to move out that summer.

Seth told Kat he'd be even happier if she moved in right away. Kat explained that things would be easier if they waited until school was over. Seth countered that he didn't like Kat living with her father, whom he now regularly referred to disparagingly as "Princess." He reminded her again and again that he was prepared to swoop in and rescue her from her family home at a moment's notice.

"Dream of the fortress that holds the dungeon where we torture everyone so exquisitely. Dream, my arms around you, of those screams lulling you to sleep."

Seth also began to refer to Denise as "Mother Dragon." At first it wasn't derisive, like calling her father "Princess." Seth recognized Kat's tight bond with her mom and hoped to use Denise's influence to his advantage. Despite her having initially discouraged Kat from dating him, Seth still believed that if Kat casually mentioned running into this wonderful guy again and again, Denise would come to see him as good for her daughter.

As time passed, however, Seth grew annoyed with Denise's insistence that her daughter come home after work or attend family functions on weekends. He felt the Mother Dragon's demands were cutting into his time with Kat.

While once he had been satisfied waiting in the Target

parking lot for Kat's fifteen-minute break, Seth now needed longer stretches of time to bring her from Portsmouth to his Dover lair, ravage her body, then get her home in time to start their nightly instant-message marathon. Mother Dragon was becoming a problem.

Seth began to sow seeds of discontent. He told Kat that he took her mother's rejection of him personally.

"She is stepping on my rock garden when I need my Zen," he said.

Kat always wanted to please her Mom, and the key to having it both ways was to keep Seth a secret. For her own part, Denise McDonough knew little of what was happening with her Kat. The daughter who had been attached to her hip for so many years was pushing away, vague about her activities, and often grumpy (due to being constantly tired), but that too Denise chalked up to Kat's being a teenager, at least at first.

She wasn't completely oblivious to the idea that Kat had a boyfriend. But the only person Kat had expressed any interest in was "Lex," and Denise had made her feelings clear. Denise's intuition told her something was up and it was likely with the older man, but she hoped the mismatched relationship would run its course, and she knew pressing the case was unlikely to do anything but push her daughter away.

Kat was beginning to make her own decisions, Denise knew, and that meant sometimes her daughter's heart would get broken. But she was not the kind of girl who would openly rebel—start smoking, go Goth, and scream,

"Fuck you, I'm seeing him anyway!" Despite her hunch, Denise refused to believe whatever Kat was doing behind her back was unhealthy or unsafe.

Kat could start to read the clues when Seth was upset. There was a blackness that would come over him, subtle changes in his body language.

At first he would pretend nothing was wrong, but his anger would soon emerge in petulant tantrums. If the problem was something she could solve, like faking a work shift so they could be together, she would. If it was something that was out of her hands, she'd tiptoe around it. She still longed for a chance to try out for Walt Disney World, but Seth had instead been insisting she sign up for an EMT-B course he was also going to take.

Kat wasn't opposed to the idea. There were EMT-B classes that began in the spring and in the summer. Kat told him she'd likely sign up after graduation, but Seth was insistent she take the class in the spring.

Seth's patience for Denise had worn thin. Mother Dragon's demands on Kat's time were too much for him to handle. He had asked Kat to spend several days of her Christmas vacation with him at the Lair. His girlfriend's answers were wishy-washy, because Kat wasn't sure if she could pull off such a prolonged absence from her family over the holidays.

Before Christmas, Seth gave Kat a promise ring. He meant it to be a symbol of his commitment to her in this life and in the others. For the girl waiting for Prince Charming, it was the most romantic gesture anyone had ever done for her.

"Every time I look at it or feel it there, I think of your love for me," she said.

"You should think of that every time you look at the ring we gave you."

Seth said "we," since he'd told her that the ring was a gift from both him and Darkheart.

———————

Seth was preparing the best he could for a flurry of police entrance exams in a half dozen New Hampshire communities. He had gotten disciplined about jogging, which kept his weight in check. His frame was more toned too, which he told Kat was the result of all of the sex they'd been having.

Seth soaked up everything he saw at the Citizens Police Academy. One of his classmates was a much older man Seth knew from the theater scene. This man fascinated Seth because, decades earlier, he'd done several years in prison for a nonviolent larceny. Seth always had questions for him about criminals and jail, and would use the man's stories as inspiration for his fiction writing.

He asked the ex-con if he'd act as a technical advisor of sorts, giving him a screenplay he'd written about the president's daughter getting kidnapped by thugs after she stopped to use an ATM. The old man gave the pages back at Seth, pointing out the president's daughter wouldn't *use* an ATM, and if she did, the kidnappers would never be able to guess which one or when. The guy was left with the impression that Seth had no sense of how the real world worked.

One evening at the academy in Portsmouth, an officer was explaining to the group how a Taser worked. He playfully asked if anyone wanted to volunteer to get zapped. Without hesitation, Seth raised his hand and walked to the front of the conference room.

The cop ran through several questions, variations on *Are you sure you really want to do this?* Seth didn't back down. With two of his classmates ready to catch him, the officer rested the nose of the pistol-shaped device against Seth's arm.

There was a loud crack as the quick burst of fifty thousand volts raced through his body. If Seth thought he could resist—that Wild Card or Darkheart or his martial arts training could keep him on his feet—he was wrong. He dropped straight to the floor, the electricity ordering his nervous system to contract every muscle in his body.

But in the time it took to help him up, Seth already appeared clearheaded. The officer led a round of appreciative applause.

The old ex-con noticed Seth's swagger as he went back to his seat. He'd seen it in prison before—that peacock walk when someone thinks he's proven he's a tough guy. In later interviews, the man said he questioned Seth's enthusiasm in volunteering to get Tasered. It was like Seth had something to prove.

Seth signed up at several local police departments holding entrance exams in December and January. The evening before each of the tests, he told Kat he wanted to log off Facebook early to get a full night's rest—a courtesy he hadn't afforded her before she took her SATs.

Seth thought he'd make an ideal candidate because, as he said in an IM, he was "clean, strong, healthy, educated, bold, intelligent."

He was convinced that every department would want him.

On the police exams, the essay questions were his biggest challenge. He was asked to detail his community involvement and to write about the qualities he possessed that would make him a good cop. Seth wrote about being hardworking, self-reliant, and a team player. He talked about his work as a karate instructor mentoring young students. He wrote that he'd seen people suffer and he wanted to help.

He said he was a "strong, unique, and passionate person who is devoted to the people around him." On the cover letter to one resume he wrote, "Yes, I am the Taser Guy from the recent Portsmouth Citizens Police Academy."

———

As Christmas approached, Seth amused himself by browsing online for lingerie. He trolled fetish-clothing websites and picked outfits he thought matched each of Kat's personas.

Kat told Seth that she had sliced her fingers on a cardboard box at work. Lasciviously he responded that he wanted to suck the blood from her cuts. After confessing to having "evil thoughts" about her, Seth said he had been eyeballing some chains at the local hardware store. He wanted to purchase more knives and some belts to use as restraints.

The couple made plans for Kat to raid Denise's supply of costume fabric. Seth instructed her to find fabric measuring one to three yards long and six to twelve inches wide, which would be ideal for crafting restraints. Shorter lengths would work for blindfolds. He wanted things in white, black, red, and blue.

Whatever time they could get together was filled with sex games at the Lair. Seth said each of their personas had different personalities in bed, different preferences. Kat got off on being restrained by ropes, but Seth no longer had the patience for tying knots. Instead he'd quickly belt her hands together or to the legs of the futon.

One time Kat complained about the bite marks and scratches he'd left on her stomach. Seth replied, "I wasn't exactly going easy on you."

A safe word was never invoked during any of these encounters.

Seth's temper was also getting shorter. Once, right before leaving to pick Kat up from the bowling alley, he got a Facebook message from Kat saying that Denise needed her to cover at the pottery studio.

Seth had had his heart set on a long afternoon with Kat in his bed. He threatened to come over and pick a fight, have Kat pack her bags and pull her right from her home.

"Mother Dragon is the enemy," he said. "Remove her. Remove the problem."

Seth never saw any of Denise McDonough's requests for help at work as coincidence, nor did he see Kat's required presence at family gatherings as anything other than an obstruction. He now saw Denise as an aggressive competitor for Kat's time and attention.

"She's deliberately psychically fucking with me!"

As soon as he stopped getting his way in the real world, Seth began telling Kat there was trouble brewing in the Veil. The Darkness was billowing. Darkheart must have his way. If Kat could not make the time to be with him, then Darkheart must find a minion—a sexual partner to ravage and throw away.

He took a keen interest in Kat's high school friends. They talked online about who might make a good partner in bed, discussions directed by Seth. There was Felicia,[1] who Kat described as a nice girl but a bit flighty. Seth, despite having never met this girl, said Felicia was likely his dark-haired woman from a previous life.

He also had his eye on Jill,[2] Kat's best friend since the first grade. Kat arranged for Seth to "bump into" her and Jill at the mall, and Jill had been friendly—even flirty— with him. Seth thought Jill was sexy, and the positive feedback he got from her electrified him. Seth told Kat that if she left him for Florida, the Darkness would drive him to take Jill as a lover—a minion—and that Kat would have to accept that fact. As with Felicia, he claimed Jill had already been a part of their sexual circle in their past lives, and that the persona Anay had inhabited Jill's body before fleeing again to the Veil, just out of his reach. He

---

1 Denotes pseudonym.

2 Denotes pseudonym.

wrote to Kat, "To be frank, I'd have to kiss her, and ultimately fuck her, to know for certain."

Seth also said there was an old girlfriend of his, someone named Bridget,[3] who'd recently tried to friend him on Facebook. He let Kat know she would be a good minion to use. Seth said he could regain control of the Darkness before it consumed him, but only if Kat gave him his sexual release first.

To accommodate his requests for time, Kat fabricated another story for her mother in order to get out of working at the studio. When she returned to her laptop, she messaged that her mom had agreed to push things back by three hours, but that Kat needed to be at the shop at the newly appointed time. Seth still wasn't satisfied.

"I'm still putting a black mark down against her for this one," he said, but he told Kat to prepare herself for "rough, wild, violent, Discovery Channel sex."

———

One night after work, Kat told Seth that while she was putting clothes on hangers in Target her four personas began arguing in her head. She told him Violet (who supposedly was destroyed in her sex sacrifice to Darkheart) was scolding Skarlet for the way she was treating their host's body. Bad food, too much sex, not enough sleep. Then Kitty complained about the way Skarlet had

---

3 Denotes pseudonym.

sex with Darkheart. Charlotte/Anay jumped in, reading all the others the riot act.

Seth was piqued. He asked for more details and expressed approval Kat was engaging her alter egos without his prompting.

It's impossible to know whether, while standing in the middle of Target's clothing section surrounded by shoppers and coworkers, Kat actually experienced this internal dialogue or whether she made up the story to entertain her restless boyfriend. It's impossible to know whether Seth believed her psychic encounter or was simply gratified Kat had become so invested in the spiritual narrative he'd drawn for her. Was Kat trying to find a way to tell Seth in his own language that their relationship was consuming her?

Either way, it was clear that Kat was working hard to emotionally sort out the real-world conflicts in her life: the struggle to maintain a relationship with her mother (Violet), her increasingly exotic sex life (Skarlet), her secret future with her boyfriend (Anay), and her own yearning to learn who Kat McDonough truly was (Kitty).

One evening after Seth dropped her off, Kat found her mother waiting up for her in the kitchen. Denise was no longer fooled by Kat's claims of attending extra play rehearsals.

"Whose car was that?"

Kat blurted out the name of a male cast member.

"It was Seth, wasn't it?"

Kat reached for something new to say, but Denise stopped her.

"I don't ever want to be lied to," she said.

Kat's silence was all the affirmation needed.

"I know how old he is," Denise said. "It's not normal for a guy his age to date an eighteen-year-old. A guy his age should be dating ladies in their twenties."

"But I like being with him. We really get along."

"You shouldn't be pursuing him either." Denise sighed then. "I'm only okay with you two being friends."

Kat said nothing more. She sat with her arms folded, throwing shade like an American teenager.

Denise tried to reason with her. She asked Kat to think about all the different men she'd meet when she got to college. She told her she'd find the right one after she'd had these experiences.

"Wait for the raspberry chocolate with sprinkles. Don't settle for plain vanilla," she told her daughter.

Hearing about it later, Seth Mazzaglia—the vessel of the Nameless One and Doomsday, the connoisseur of bondage and sexual sadism—bristled at Denise's characterization of him as "vanilla." He wouldn't say it at the time, but Seth told Kat later that the ice cream comment hurt his feelings far more than it angered him. He said Darkheart was also insulted.

Seth reported back that there were visions from the Hollow One foretelling Kat would move out after New Years in order to avoid an epic battle to slay Mother Dragon.

Seth warned that the stress of Mother Dragon's interference was making it hard to hold the Darkness back. He said he'd have to seek out a minion to control the urges roiling inside of him. Seth talked about calling up his ex-girlfriend Bridget for a hookup or "seizing the first young woman I see and doing something horrible."

Kat promised to make it all up to him after Christmas, when she had a week's vacation.

———

Kat texted Seth on Christmas morning.

"I fucking love you. I'm in a sex mood."

They would not see each other on the holiday, but the day after would be free once Kat got off from work. Before leaving, she messaged Seth to pick her up at four from Target. Moments later, she IMed again saying she couldn't make it.

"Did Mother Dragon just put her foot down? What happened?"

Kat explained the house needed to be picked up and her room needed to be cleaned because relatives were coming in from Florida and Denise needed an extra hand getting things done.

Seth was apoplectic. They had planned a two-hour visit, two hours that were set aside to relieve the Darkness, he said. Mother Dragon was once again getting in the way.

"Fine," he wrote. "She gets you today—but she is going to let me see you for at least four hours every day for the rest of the week."

Kat wasn't sure how to answer. "It doesn't work like that."

"Then how does it work?"

"I'm not just some little toy you two are trading off."

Seth continued his tantrum. He'd been through so much leading up to Christmas, he said. He'd struggled to push down the Darkness and resisted the urge find some minion to satisfy his needs. How could Denise do this to him?

Unable to deal with him any longer, Kat switched off her computer and went to work.

Seth waited to hear from Kat after her shift ended at four o'clock, but she didn't return his calls or respond to his instant messages. With nothing but time on his hands, Seth composed a series of long letters appealing to Kat and Skarlet. He wrote to each of them as if they were separate people and begged them for forgiveness and proclaimed his love. He spent the entire night writing, explaining, pleading.

"You are my lady. The mighty, chaotic, bloodthirsty and powerful Skarlet Tempest. And I am your ferocious, loyal, cunning, and primal Darkheart."

The next morning, when she finally received the message, Kat responded, "You are my dragon . . . I found you, pulled you from your other dragons, and will never give you up."

Seth said that Denise's reaction had been "truly unexpected" by the Hollow One and the Nameless One; it had not been foretold in the tarot cards. He said that Mother Dragon was threatening everything and Kat needed to leave home. She agreed to make it happen.

In the struggle over who would pull the toy away from the other, Seth believed he had won.

Seth then made a strange promise to Kat.

"If my Darkness is ever going to drive me to do something horrific to another person," he said, "I will first check with you."

CHAPTER SEVEN

Akasia

Seth was planning a New Year's Eve get-together, a quick dinner with guests at his mother's house, before returning to the Lair. He was going to invite Kat along with his gaming friends, Andy and Peggy. There'd be no liquor or loud music. He wanted to ring in 2012 eating snacks and playing video games well into the morning. It would be a sort of "coming out" party for Kat, still only known to his friends as the "mysterious disappearing dragon."

Seth recognized that getting Kat out of the house for New Year's would take some advance planning, so he'd been advising Kat to start early, sowing the seeds with her parents that friends from school were going to be having a party. He brought up the importance of her coming over for New Year's almost daily, and in order to please him, Kat concocted a series of false parties and invitations from friends in the days leading up to New Year's.

Seth's motivation for wanting Kat with him for concurrent days was about more than her uninterrupted company. He told her that, for the kind of sex he had in mind, she would need a couple of days to heal. Seth planned to teach Kat about impact play. She told him she was turned on just thinking about it.

"Mmmm cut me please," she typed as they messaged about his plan.

"You apparently need to be cut," Seth said, promising her more knife play. "I need to feed. Blood feeding might actually help with the Darkness."

As his Submissive, Kat had been allowed to draw the knife across Seth's chest and suck the ribbon of blood that flowered from the narrow cut. It was a rare and violent sex act that, as Dom, Seth permitted her to perform on him.

He wrote, "The thought of my blood in your body makes me . . . hard."

She responded, "The thought of you cutting my skin makes me wet."

Seth confessed that violence hadn't always excited him. "Natasha drew it out of me," he said, "and now bloodshed is a downright turn-on for me."

Seth told Kat she might enjoy hot wax play. He claimed he once had a submissive who liked to have her nipples encased in wax, then have Seth rip it off once it cooled. He'd then use clamps on her burnt nipples, then drip more wax from the candle.

"I was very sadistic with her," he said, boasting that he'd made her orgasm each time with this foreplay alone.

Seth said their night of passion would begin with impact play. He told her he was going to bind her to a chair with leather straps—ankles and wrists secured. He would then strike her with a belt across her thighs and torso. He'd whip her along the triceps, careful not to leave visible marks on her forearms, but Kat said that as long as she covered the bruises with her clothes she'd be fine.

Seth told her that if she got a long-sleeved shirt in the required shade of red for her job at Target, it would open up "more possibilities." Given the extra time they planned together for her recovery, Seth said, "We can have much rougher fun than usual."

When the evening arrived, they did all of these things and more. Seth fully dominated Kat's body, restrained, cut, and flogged her. Not once during her extended stay at his apartment did he ever suggest they use a safe word.

———

After attending the party at his mother's house that he'd so adamantly cajoled Kat to attend, the group went back to the Lair and played video games all night. There was no beer; there was no pot. There wasn't even a champagne toast at midnight. There was just friends slaying Thundering Boulderkins, Cloud Serpents, and thistleshrubs in *World of Warcraft*.

The group also played Dungeons & Dragons, using Seth's personas as characters in the game. Doomsday was a barbarian fighter. Darkheart was a paladin. Cyrus was a bard and an assassin. They used the game's dice to guide these characters for hours through a fantasy world of pillaging and plundering.

When Kat finally returned home, her brother informed her that while she was away he had used a computer program to track her cell phone. He said the phone had pinged off a tower in Dover, not near the party in Portsmouth Kat had claimed to be attending on New Year's Eve. He'd told their mother that Kat was lying about her whereabouts, and that she was probably with Seth. But he said their mom had just shrugged him off, saying that Kat could have been with any of her friends in Dover and he should let it go.

Kat was enraged at her brother's treachery, though both she and Seth were relieved to hear their cover story had worked to fool Mother Dragon. It wouldn't do for Kat to be caught in another lie. But the more they thought about it, the more uncertain they became. Was it some sort of test? Had Denise been so nonchalant because she already knew that Kat was in Dover with Seth?

―――――

The New Year's party had gone so well that Kat wanted to meet more of Seth's friends. In particular, she wanted to meet the one she only knew as "the psychic lady."

Kat knew this was someone Seth had confided in about his personas and that her views seemed very valuable to him. But Kat also had worries about her. She told Seth she wasn't jealous of the woman, romantically or otherwise. At least that's what she said.

Kat said people with psychic powers had always bothered her, making some kind of unspoken distinction between the powers she and Seth claimed to have and those that might belong to others. She said she worried psychics could hurt her in the spiritual world. Seth promised to arrange a meeting.

Seth's friend's name was Roberta Gerkin. She billed herself as a professional psychic, available for readings in New Hampshire and southern Maine. Seth and Roberta met the year before he met Kat, at a Halloween haunted house where Roberta had been hired to read tarot cards. Seth had introduced himself to Roberta as Lex and showed a keen interest in her interpretation of the cards.

Roberta was in her early forties and had been doing tarot card readings for many years. She had carrot-colored hair that hung in twisting curls that brushed her shoulders. Roberta didn't wear much makeup and carried herself like a sage of the New Age. She didn't fit Seth's preferred waifish mold, not that it mattered much. Roberta was going through a divorce, and romance wasn't on her mind when they met.

But the two hit it off right away, and they had a long discussion about all things spiritual. Roberta was impressed with the intellectual way Seth spoke about otherworldly things. She was used to people asking silly questions about the tarot, but he took her work seriously.

The night they met, nearly a year before he met Kat and began sharing his many personas, Seth told Roberta about Darkheart, Cyrus, and the Nameless One. Roberta would later testify she sensed his true belief in these spirits' presence beyond the Veil and she did tarot readings for several of his personas. Seth told Roberta that Darkheart was in control most of the time. He also told her about Doomsday, but she would later say she considered Doomsday less of a persona and more of an "event."

Seth and Roberta's friendship ran in streaks. Seth would contact her and they would see each other frequently to talk or read tarot cards, then they wouldn't see each other for several weeks until Seth reached out again. Seth asked Roberta for guidance from the tarot cards about how to handle the Darkness. He asked Roberta to predict his future, to read what the cards said about his prospects of becoming a police officer. Her interpretations were frequently favorable.

One time when they met up to read cards, Roberta later said that Seth was twitchy, charged up like a spark plug. This was still months before he dated Kat, and he told his psychic friend he needed a release, otherwise the Darkness would overcome him. Seth asked Roberta to give him a blow job to help him control the Darkness. Roberta would later tell a jury she thought the request was "odd," but she felt he needed it to keep from "overloading his circuits." Roberta went down on him and gave him the release he wanted.

Seth called Roberta "the Valkyrie" after the flying female guardians of Viking myth. The Valkyrie were angels of the battlefield who selected which warriors lived and died, taking the slain to the Norse heaven, Valhalla. Seth saw Roberta as a kind of spiritual protector, a magical figure who could guide him, even protect him.

After Seth began dating Kat, he gave Roberta a version of her backstory. The tarot card reader said she was told his girlfriend was a high school student and a performer who came from a bad home where her father abused her and her mother refused to stop it because she didn't want the neighbors to gossip about the family. Seth told Roberta he and Kat had plans to move in together imminently.

Seth eventually introduced Roberta and Kat at a party Roberta threw before moving into a new apartment with her boyfriend, Paul Hickok. Neither woman made a significant impression on the other, but Kat seemed satisfied that Seth and Roberta weren't having an affair. Although if he were, Kat reassured herself, it would only be because Seth was going to make Roberta his minion.

———

During their midnight chats, Seth would not stop pressuring Kat to set aside her college plans and instead take the EMT-B course with him. Kat was now resigned to the fact that, if she wanted to stay in her relationship with Seth, she couldn't leave the area for college and she should give the EMT-B training a try.

Seth's obsession with the EMT-B course seeped into everything. Kat said she wanted to buy a new pair of shoes and a skirt. Seth told her not to. He said money spent on shoes was money not spent on EMT-B training.

"Shoes aren't a thing I see futures about."

With Kat still on the fence, Seth tried to elicit a decision by warning her that there would be serious consequences on both sides of the Veil if she didn't take the course at the same time as he did. Seth said taking the spring class would be "a woman in red." She was Akasia, he said, an enemy spirit sent from the Veil to turn Seth into Doomsday. He said if he were to take the class alone—without Kat—Akasia would slip into a nearby body and seduce him. As if the consequences in "this world" weren't enough, Seth threatened Akasia could "sever the connection" between Skarlet and Darkheart for all eternity.

"How could she possibly do that?" Kat sounded frightened. "How could she possibly dispose of me?"

Seth said there were thousands of ways Akasia could do it. "I only need to slip up once . . . you taking the EMT-B this spring, ahead of schedule, is the only way I know to prevent it."

Kat was now terrified that her spiritual presence was in danger, and that Seth could be taken from her if she didn't comply with his vision. Her mind was made up. Seth had used her belief in this magical dimension to manipulate her . . . again.

Kat decided to empty her bank account to cover the seven-hundred-dollar tuition, but it was a joint account with her father, and he wasn't keen on her blowing her savings. Kat overheard her father say he was afraid she'd fail the course and waste all of her money.

"He is a stupid fucking prick who I will kill . . . I hate him so much," she wrote to Seth.

In response, he told Kat she should never be disrespected, then added, "The only 'disrespect' you should ever have to endure is purely for sexual kink and fetish reasons."

Kat told Seth how he provided the love she had never felt from her father. Seth's power over her was growing from submission to dependency.

"I have always been hurt in this life, and I feared that I would never escape it, that it would always find me. But no, I'm actually going to be safe with you. You're not going to attack me over petty things like he does. You're not going to insult me constantly. I'm actually safe from that. You don't know how much that means."

Kat and Denise eventually convinced Peter to let his daughter get her money. She took the cash and, with Seth picking her up at a secret location, drove directly to the campus on the last day of registration.

It was declared that Akasia would *not* be stealing Seth from her. At no time did Seth ever offer to give or to loan Kat the money he pressured her to spend. He did receive quite a dividend from the incident: Kat was even more disgruntled with family life, she was going to accompany him to the class, and she demonstrated again that she was willing to do whatever it took in this world to ensure unity in the other.

———

Even with Kat's continued compliance with helping him "control the Darkness," Seth's hunt for a minion to join the couple in bed continued. Though it wasn't one of her fantasies, bi-curious Kat thought the idea of a threesome was sexy. Seth, whose sexual appetite never seemed completely sated, talked constantly about sharing another woman. He didn't speak of these potential partners in a loving or erotic manner; he spoke of them in terms that indicated disdain; in his view they were dispensable, disposable, and dehumanized.

"You could always drag some hapless pretty little thing along and watch the carnage," Seth said, "but I'm not sure we have any viable victims in our immediate orbit."

He said he wasn't making progress with seducing his ex-girlfriend Bridget, and Kat wasn't certain any of her school friends would be up for a threesome. Seth was still infatuated with Jill but conceded she was likely not ready for what he wanted from her.

"Do we subject poor Jill to untold horror before she even realizes she's a part of this?" he messaged, "or do I discharge enough of the rage so we can have a slightly easier afternoon and evening?"

Kat chose to let him take out the rage on her instead.

As she fell asleep, he wrote to her, "Dream of lots and lots of fucking and orgasms and the redonkulous soreness of your hips and between your legs that you are going to feel for the rest of your life from the moment you move into your true home, the Lair."

One evening, Kat could hear her parents fighting. Her father said it was time for Kat to start paying her own way. He wanted her to pay for her cell phone, for her medical bills, and for her auto insurance once she got her license. Denise was arguing against it. Kat was still in high school, she said, paying her own way wasn't appropriate. Kat also heard them talking about charging her rent.

"If they try to make me pay rent," she complained, "that's the instant [I] move out."

When he heard that, Seth told Kat trouble was brewing in the spiritual world. Both Cyrus and the Nameless One were shifting into combat modes.

"Something big is about to go down," he wrote, egging her on.

———

On Valentine's Day 2012, Denise returned from work to a suspiciously quiet house. She went into her bedroom to change clothes. That's when she saw a note propped up on her pillow.

Denise snatched up the paper and quickly scanned the paragraphs of Kat's handwriting. As she began reading it a second time, she walked back into the kitchen to grab her car keys, her eyes never leaving the paper.

"I love you, but I can't stay here anymore," the letter said. "I need to leave. I need to be free."

Denise would later say that reading the note felt surreal, like finding herself in a bad TV show. She knew Kat was working at Target, so she drove directly to the store. She didn't wait for her daughter's shift to end. When she saw her mother looking around the store for her, Kat asked her manager if she could go on break and followed Denise to the parking lot.

"What is this?" her mother said, waving the note under Kat's chin.

"Mom, you don't understand," she said softly. "I love you but I need a break."

Denise tried to reason with her daughter. She said they could work things out with her father, with her brothers. Whatever it took.

"I'm staying at a friend's house," Kat said. "I'll contact you when I'm ready."

As she watched her daughter hurry back into the store, Denise wondered how she could have been so naïve. She knew the "friend" was Seth Mazzaglia. She'd really believed the relationship would have fizzled out by now. Denise was especially troubled because, with Kat gone, she'd lose the ability to guide her, to comfort her, to mentor her. She'd no longer be able to be a mother to her.

Kat had moved out only hours earlier and Denise felt like she had already lost the war. Maybe that was the point.

Denise was pained by one thing in particular: As an actress, she'd learned to study dialogue through playing different characters. Real or fictional, each person has a way of talking that is completely unique to him or her. It occurred to Denise that, in the note and during their confrontation, none of what her daughter had said sounded like Kat's dialogue. She knew her daughter better than anyone else, and the words she'd used hadn't sounded like Kat's.

It was like someone else was putting those words in Kat's mouth.

CHAPTER EIGHT

The Lair

"I don't want to get too addicted to the drug of you," Seth told Kat in instant messages just before she moved in to the Sawyer Mill apartment.

"My side effects are bite and scratch marks," she playfully replied.

Instead of sleeping in, Seth now had to wake up early each morning and drive Kat to Portsmouth High School, and then pick her up again in the afternoon, unless she could get a friend to drive her to Dover.

Kat's relationships with her friends remained mostly unchanged, but she was cold to her family. Both of her brothers also attended Portsmouth High, and when they would pass in the hallways, Kat walked by without looking at them. If either tried to say hello, she acted as though she didn't hear.

Despite Kat's estrangement, Denise wanted to stay in touch with her daughter. But Kat wouldn't respond to her mother's texts or her instant messages on Facebook.

Because Denise had been so active in the local theater scene, she had been longtime Facebook friends with Seth. Despite his oversized ego, Seth kept a pretty small public digital footprint, and his posts revealed very little about what he was up to. Denise tried to reach out to Seth through Facebook, asking him if he would like to come over for dinner with Kat or if he could pass on a message to have her daughter get in touch.

Her messages went ignored, and soon after she sent them, Seth unfriended Denise and blocked her from viewing his account. He made Kat do the same.

The Lair, still resplendent with fantasy battle and video game paraphernalia, was now Kat's place too. But neighbors in Sawyer Mill found the couple strangely mismatched. One neighbor, an assistant football coach from UNH who lived on the same floor, was of the impression that Kat was a very quiet, shy girl while Seth was a braggart who loved to engage him in conversation and boast about his karate skills. Used to the braggadocio of young men, the coach thought Seth perceived him as another "alpha male."

Seth had long lived like a slob and knew the apartment was a disaster. The bathroom had never seen a thorough cleaning, and evidence of at least two previous meals could always be found on the counter or in the cluttered kitchen sink. Before Kat would visit, he'd make a quick run through, wiping and picking up only the most egregious offenses. He'd make the futon bed and made sure there were walking paths through any books or CDs left on the floor.

In preparation for Kat moving in, Seth made room for her clothes and belongings by packing away some of his own things and making space in the apartment's small closet. He also purchased all sorts of cleaning supplies and vowed to stay on top of the housework. He had a large box of blue latex gloves he took from an ambulance company he'd worked for and wore them to scrub the apartment's grimy surfaces with chemical cleaners.

Kat found the relative peace of Seth's apartment relaxing. She set up a chair next to one of the two industrial windows preserved from the original mill. The sun would warm her face, and she had a nice view of the river running past. Sometimes Seth's cat, Raven, would jump on her lap while she daydreamed. He reminded her of the cat named Merlin she'd left behind in Portsmouth.

Their financial situation was tight. Seth never asked Kat to pay rent—he couldn't, not after he had used her father's rent demand to put pressure on her to move in—and they instead agreed that Kat would contribute a predetermined amount of money for groceries and gas. The sum was a hefty chunk of her take-home pay, so it was hard for her to save any money.

There were parallels between Seth's lifestyle with Kat and with Catherine Fish. If Kat did splurge on something like lunch or new clothes, Seth would become upset.

"You already have a lot of clothes," he'd scold.

When Seth felt a wave of anger or depression coming on—the condition he referred to as "the Darkness"—he would get antsy and want to leave the apartment. He'd hint that Darkheart was making him leave, possibly to hurt someone. Catherine would chase him, passing his test to see if he was wanted. Likewise, Kat's reaction would be to grab his arm and convince him to stay.

"You keep me calm," he'd say with a smile, which made Kat feel like she was taking care of him. It pushed every button in her; she was a person born to please others.

When Kat moved out, Denise had stopped paying for her daughter's cell phone, but although he and Kat no longer had to rely on Facebook for communication, Seth wanted to be able to reach Kat during the day and decided to open a joint account despite the expense. They each bought cell phones with slide-out keyboards for easy texting. Kat had Seth listed in the contacts on her phone as "Darkheart."

Seth hadn't heard back from the police departments where he'd applied, but he couldn't put off getting a steady job in order to supplement his piecemeal income. He took a position at Best Buy working in the video game section. The store was located close to the Target where Kat worked, and the extra money he earned at Best Buy was just enough to cover their meager lifestyle. The couple didn't eat out, and a big night out might mean going to see an action movie or a local theater production. Most of the couple's free time was spent playing video games, watching DVDs, or having sex, which they did with the frequency of newlyweds.

The sex didn't get more conventional now that Seth and Kat were sharing a bed. If anything, the novelty of being together without interference took them even further from what most people would consider normal. Seth's preferred style of intercourse didn't change—it was still intense and almost always aggressive. He suggested that the rough sex was a measure of their intense desire for each other, proof that their passion was all-consuming. Kat agreed.

Once Kat was inside the Lair full-time, Seth demanded sex multiple times a day every day, once demanding that she have sex with him nine times. Kat gave him whatever he wanted, checking off every letter in BDSM and several that weren't part of the practice.

He'd bind her with brown leather buckles. He'd make her crawl around. He'd called her horrible and humiliating names. He'd spank and hit and whip and cut and cause Kat whatever pain he desired to inflict. When he felt like slowing down, Seth would insist on other kinds of sex play. A box under the futon held all of the couple's accessories: ropes, blindfolds, a leather bra, multiple collars and leather belts, knives, packages of condoms. Kat had created the box herself. Did it indicate she was an enthusiastic participant or someone trying to pacify an erratic lover?

Kat still enjoyed being tied up by Seth, especially all the gentle attention the process required. She was a fan of being confined by corsets too; the complicated laces squeezing her together felt almost comforting, like being swaddled. Bored and impatient with the effort required to lace her corsets or tie complicated knots, however, Seth started using the ropes for their bondage play less frequently. Instead he would reach for leather straps and belts with which he could quickly immobilize her. Kat was disappointed by this, missing the careful attention Seth paid her while tying complicated knots. The ropes did not disappear completely, however. A cord of the soft cotton line remained fastened to each of the futon's four legs for easy access.

Seth told Kat he wanted to practice more erotic asphyxiation, or "breath control," the act of cutting off a lover's airway during sex. It was something Darkheart wanted to do with Skarlet, he claimed. Seth would most often use his hands, reaching around Kat's neck and squeezing her windpipe. He also used a belt threaded through the buckle like a noose. Asphyxiation was one among the most physically dangerous of the "edgeplay" sex acts any couple could engage in.

But not even when doing this did Seth and Kat ever employ a safe word or other signal of distress.

Until now, they had played the role of Dominant and Submissive. As Dom, Seth had guided their sexual play. As Sub, Kat had followed his lead. But now Kat felt she had some control over the direction of their encounters. There were times Seth wanted to perform a certain act and Kat suggested something else instead. If she turned him down, however, he would usually become angry, and

Kat would acquiesce and let him do what he wanted to her. Despite this pattern of submission, Kat no longer considered herself strictly a Sub. She instead saw herself as a "Switch," someone who could play either Dom or Sub.

During one encounter, Seth allowed Kat to tie him up to let her play the role of Dominant. But he didn't exactly submit as a Sub would, instead granting her permission to use the ropes rather than giving himself over to her desires. She used the knife, carved an X in his back. It was the only time he actually allowed Kat to "Switch," and even then, her taking the lead was largely an illusion.

After she moved in, Seth gave Kat new lessons in his version of BDSM. There were more than just Dom and Subs, he told her. There were also Masters and Slaves.

Unlike a Sub, a slave had no say in the acts the Master could choose to perform. While a Dom takes a Sub's pleasure into consideration, a Master does not do so with a Slave's. A Sub is a lady, Seth said. A Slave is a slut, and must be treated like one. A Slave must obey her Master without question, without hesitation.

Seth said that he would be in control always, but that sometimes Kat would be his Sub and sometimes she would be his Slave. When they had sex as Slave and Master, Kat had to address Seth as "Lord" or "Sire." Seth would call her "whore" or "slut," forcing her to get on the floor and beg for his forgiveness or affection. But the Slave never got affection. She only received more punishment.

Kat, by all accounts, seemed to embrace the hedonism, to enjoy it. She even penned a BDSM love poem to

Seth, saying, "I want you to attack me/I need to be dominated . . . I want to be hit and thrown down/I really want to be tied up. Tight." and referring to herself as "The Willing."

Seth responded with a note of his own. He said to his "Willing" that he would dominate her "brutally, without mercy." He wrote: "Others will watch as I command your submission."

He ended his letter with this sentiment: "I am your Lord. You, my Lady, are my toy."

They had been through so much, they would say to each other. This world and the next had tried to come between them. She was his Skarlet, his dragon rider. He was her Darkheart, his dragon. Of course she was his "Willing."

———

If Kat thought moving into his apartment would quell Seth's desire to find a second girl to join them in bed, she was sadly mistaken. She had done what was asked of her to keep the Darkness in check, so it followed logic that the Darkness would not force him to take another woman as a minion, but Seth never stopped talking about a ménage à trois. If anything, his interest in it increased. He told Kat that only finding another girl to fuck would keep the Darkness under control.

Seth's weekly video game get-togethers with his friend Andy didn't stop when Kat moved in either. Now that Kat was in the apartment, the futon was never folded into the couch position. It was always pulled out like a bed, the sheets and comforter tucked under the thin mattress.

Andy would sit on the floor, his back up against the edge of the mattress. Seth would join Andy on the floor while they tapped and clicked on their wireless game controllers. Kat sometimes played too, but she mostly watched. Or she did her homework. She still had to get up early to attend high school, but there was no going to bed in the studio apartment when it was time to play video games.

Andy would later recall to officials that one evening while he sat on the floor blasting his way through a one-player game, Kat took a seat behind him on the futon. Seth turned his attention away from Andy's score and climbed up to join her. It got quiet as everyone became preoccupied with their own endeavors. Andy could hear the couple making out, gasping for air between their tongues. He went on playing the video game.

Seth called out to his friend in a matter-of-fact tone.

"Would you mind if I had sex with my girlfriend?"

Andy wasn't sure what to say. He liked to think of himself as open-minded and accepting of his friend. He told them to do what they wanted.

As Andy tried to focus solely on the small TV screen, the noises from behind him changed. He heard a rustle of blankets, the tink of a belt buckle prong bouncing off its frame. The smacking of lips and tongues was replaced by guttural breathing in rhythm with the groans of the futon's frame. No one spoke.

Andy was uncomfortable, but he never turned around to watch. After what felt like an excruciating eternity, Andy heard Kat let out a squeak of pleasure. The bouncing on the futon stopped. Andy saw Kat walk past him to the bathroom in his peripheral vision. She was naked from the waist down. Seth got up to dispose of a condom, then rejoined his friend's campaign through the virtual battlefield.

After Andy left, Seth and Kat discussed how the evening went. Seth declared the evening was fine, the sex was hot, and Andy seemed none the worse for having been there. "I knew he could deal with somewhat vanilla behavior," Seth said of his friend. "The more violent and festishy stuff might weird him out."

Seth never shared his personas with his longtime friend Andy. They never delved into each other's sex lives (never even discussing *that night*), so Andy was unaware of Seth's penchant for rough sex. All Andy knew was what Seth did tell him: that he and Kat were looking for a willing partner to join them for a threesome.

That spring, Andy got a job in central New Hampshire, about an hour away from Dover, and never resumed their gaming get-togethers.

Other than her own embarrassment that Andy had seen her nude, Kat admitted to having liked it too. The "vanilla behavior" was a satisfying change of pace. She'd felt like neither Sub nor Slave, just a young and impulsive lover.

But Seth also had a different takeaway from the encounter. Here was a way to entice a girl into a three-way. He and Kat could get the action going on the futon and then ask their guest to join. All they needed to do was convince a potential lover to visit the apartment long enough for them to get it on.

Seth's focus on bringing another woman into their bed meant that he and Kat were now juggling several potential relationships. Four of Kat's friends from school and theater groups had been targeted by Seth for their potential to become his minions. He also suggested that Bridget, his old girlfriend, might be a good choice. She'd had sex with him in the past, so he believed she might do so again. It was unclear to Kat how their relationship had ended, but Seth licked his lips at the thought of bringing Bridget back into his orbit.

At this point, Kat was actually interested. In the weeks she'd lived in the Lair with Seth, she'd crossed so many sexual boundaries that having a threesome no longer seemed foreign. When it came to their sexual pecking order, Seth declared he was the "alpha" and Kat was the "beta," but that if there were another woman in their bed, Seth said Kat would be the "alpha" over her.

———

In late spring, Kat finally began attending the EMT-B class in Durham with Seth. After finishing up her final semester in high school by day, she accompanied Seth to the EMT-B class at night.

The material was old hat for Seth as he worked toward his recertification. One classmate would later comment that it looked more like Kat was following Seth around like a puppy, not attending class to achieve some vocational goal of her own.

The curriculum included learning lifesaving techniques, like how to stop bleeding and how to help someone who was struggling to breathe. Kat realized acquiring these skills would look good on a future resumé. It was nearly summer, and she would finally be a full-fledged counselor at Camp CenterStage; adding "EMT certification" to her credentials would likely heighten her standing with the staff. But Kat had not yet reminded Seth of her commitment to work at theater camp that August. She had no idea how her Master would respond when she finally did.

———

Kat was still trying to fulfill Seth's desire to bring another woman to bed, and so she asked Wendy,[1] another good high school friend, over. As before, the plan was to watch a movie and see what happened afterward. When Kat extended the invitation, Wendy wanted to know if she could bring her boyfriend. Kat ran the idea past Seth, who nixed it.

"Just say I'm skittish and only willing to meeting one new person at a time."

Wendy wanted to know more about "Lex." Kat again asked Seth how she should respond. He wanted her to play up to Wendy how dark he was, how he'd "seen things" in life. Kat asked if she could tell Wendy that someone had died in Seth's arms, thinking it might seal the deal. Seth approved.

---

1 Denotes pseudonym.

Kat told investigators that when Wendy arrived at Sawyer Mill, "Lex" offered everyone apple cider and movie snacks. The three of them then sat on the floor rather than on the unfolded futon and watched a film.

As the movie went on, Seth and Kat climbed back on the futon and began to make out. Wendy turned to investigate the noise and giggled to see that Seth had pulled off Kat's shirt. Seth turned to stare soulfully at Wendy.

"I want to fuck my girlfriend," he said, producing a condom from thin air. "Is that okay with you?"

Wendy stared back and nodded. Her head swiveled back and forth from the TV screen to the show happening behind her. The couple was naked, Seth taking Kat from behind as she braced herself on her hands and knees. As they had sex, they both stared at Wendy, wordlessly imploring her to join them.

Wendy turned around, took Kat's face in her hands, and began to make out with her. They kissed each other's necks and ears before returning to each other's lips. Behind Kat, Seth announced his orgasm with a guttural grunt. The girls' kisses tapered off and the encounter ended with awkward glances and stifled laughs.

It seemed all had gone according to plan. But on the scorecard, Kat had only gotten to first base with Wendy. Worse, there had been no sexual contact between Wendy and Seth. Although he was encouraged by their progress toward drawing in a minion, Seth told Kat he was disappointed that it had not been more of a "three-way."

———

Seth had a female video gaming friend from his old pagan circle, Zoey,[2] who visited the Lair once in a while. Together, Seth and Zoey slashed their way through digital fantasy worlds as they sat on the floor sipping soft drinks and munching on snacks.

One night, Seth asked Zoey if she wanted to continue in one-player mode while he took a break. She pressed onward, thumbing the joystick and pressing the controller's buttons. As they had with Wendy, Seth and Kat slid back onto the futon and began making out loudly. When they had captured Zoey's attention, Seth asked whether she'd object to him having sex with his girlfriend in front of her.

Zoey turned away from the game and watched the couple as their clothes came off. With Seth lying on his back, Kat mounted him and began grinding. After spying them for a while, Zoey approached Kat from behind and ran her hands over Kat's breasts. Kat moaned encouragement, pleading for Zoey to continue. There were also invitations for Zoey to do more, to give some attention to Seth, but she only massaged Kat's breasts until Kat reached her climax. Afterward, Zoey offered shy apologies and polite regrets as she excused herself from the apartment.

Kat told Seth the sex was hot and thought the night was a victory. Seth was once again less than satisfied. Twice they'd drawn women into their bed, he complained,

---

2 Denotes pseudonym.

and both times all of their attention had been focused on Kat.

———

Seth decided not to limit his search to the few female friends the couple had. He opened accounts on dating sites both mainstream and obscure.

His profile on OKCupid bore the name "DarkKaiser," but it wasn't so different from the thousands of others on the site. It featured several color photographs of him and described him as a twenty-nine-year-old straight single male living in Dover. He described himself as "In a word, enigmatic," and posted that he didn't drink or do drugs, and his hobbies were "gaming" and "watching movies." There was no indication he was into anything other than a conventional relationship.

Seth also posted a profile on an alternative matchmaking site called bondage.com, dedicated to connecting people with certain fetishes, like BDSM. Seth used the profile name "DarkKaiser" there as well, describing himself as a "master seeking slave," interested in a "lifetime relationship, a play partner, princess by day, slut by night, a Sub."

Kat was also active online, doing research to learn more about the BDSM lifestyle Seth had introduced her to. She later said that when she had questions, she'd write them down on Post-it notes and leave them on her computer so she wouldn't forget what to look up.

Seth and Kat both created profiles on a site called fetlife.com, whose members self-identified as straight, bi, pansexual, heteroflexible, evolving—whatever term best fit their orientation. Categories of interest included "experimentalist," "exhibitionist," "brat," and "degradation receiver." Kinks listed on the site included everything under the sun: foot fetishes, leather and latex, cross-dressing, body shaving, forced womanhood, cosplay, nipple torture, flogging, and erotic cuddling.

Seth signed up on fetlife.com as "enigmaticshadows," while Kat chose the handle "roguetemptress." Their hope was to use the website to find women interested in getting together with couples. Their desire was to find someone willing to move in with them for sex, to be their maid, and to submit to being their minion.

The couple posted a personal ad on the fetish website hoping to find the perfect Slave for them. The ad was signed by Kat, but it's unclear whether she was the sole author or—based on the unrealistic demands in the post—whether she was taking dictation.

Kat wrote that her "Lord" was the Dom and described herself as a "nymphomaniac switch." She laid out their wish list: a Slave who would cook, clean, do the dishes, and "be available for some form of sex at any given time." They would have a one-month "trial period," after which the Slave could be terminated.

Despite the honest solicitation, there seemed to be no interest among fetlife users for such an arrangement.

———

Denise McDonough waited outside Portsmouth High School and scanned for her daughter among the stream of students exiting the doorways. She spied Kat, who looked both surprised and embarrassed to see her. Her mother still couldn't wrap her head around why Kat had moved out and cut all ties with her family.

"Kathryn, come home," she begged her daughter.

Denise offered to give Kat her own basement bedroom—secluded from the rest of the family—if she moved back in. There was something in Kat's body language that revealed to Denise she was struggling with the decision.

"Okay," Kat agreed. "Pick me up after work on Saturday. I'm closing. I'll come home with you."

Denise was thrilled and hugged her daughter.

That Saturday night, Denise sat in the Target parking lot and watched the last of the customers leave the building. She waited as employees in red shirts and tan pants exited the darkened store, but Kat was not among them. She flagged down one of the workers and asked if Kat was coming out soon.

"She didn't come into work today. She called in sick."

Denise couldn't dial Kat's number fast enough.

"Where are you? Why aren't you here at work like you said?"

Kat's voice wavered as she answered. She said she had cramps and hadn't felt like working that day. Denise thought she could hear someone coaching her.

Kat suddenly blurted, "Stop stalking me!" and hung up on her mother.

Denise later told interviewers that she stared at her phone, gripping it until her fingers turned white.

"Oh, you want to see some stalking? Fine, I'll show you some stalking."

Denise called her sister and her father and asked if they'd go with her to Sawyer Mill to get Kat. She didn't know what to expect from Seth, and she was willing to drag Kat out by her curly hair if necessary.

A friend of Denise's who also lived in the complex let them into the building. When the elevator opened to the third floor, she marched straight down the hall, her father and sister struggling to keep up. Before rapping on the door, she could hear Kat and Seth inside talking and watching TV. When she knocked, their voices hushed, and Denise realized they were likely waiting for her to simply go away.

"I can hear you in there! Open the door!"

Denise knocked again, harder this time. After a few moments of murmuring from inside the apartment, Seth emerged in the doorway, blocking the threshold. Denise observed him puff out his chest in an effort to look more intimidating. Seth pulled the knob and closed the door behind him, leaving it open only a crack.

"I need to talk to Kathryn," Denise said without any pretense of courtesy.

"No," was all Seth said in reply.

Something inside Denise McDonough snapped. Her face turned red and the voice she had used for years to project from the stage was suddenly turned all the way up, booming down the building's industrial hallway.

"I need to see her!"

"You can't."

Denise started jabbing a finger in the air at Seth.

"You're a fucking pedophile!" she exploded. "You're a fucking loser! You can't get a girl your own age!"

That was enough to get other doors on the floor to swing open. Heads shot out. Eyes summed up the situation. Neighbors ducked back into their apartments to call the cops.

"You need to leave," Seth said to Denise, his arms folded across his chest.

"Not until I talk to Kathryn!"

Seth remained unmoved.

"Hey," said Denise's father from over her shoulder. "Why are you being such an asshole?"

Hearing that, Kat pounced through the cracked door.

"Don't you call my boyfriend an asshole!" she yelled at her grandfather.

Denise reached out and grabbed Kat's hand.

"Kathryn. Just talk to me."

Seth whined, "You're going to steal her from me."

"Kathryn, I just need to know why you're doing this."

Kat choked back a sob. "You don't understand. I don't want to live at home."

Denise understood. *She* didn't want to live at home either—but it was hardly an abusive or dangerous situation. And it was the far more appropriate place for her eighteen-year-old daughter.

"Fine, but this isn't the right way. You can still date him. Go to school. Graduate. Find some girls your own age to move in with. But he"—she motioned to Seth—"needs to talk to your parents and be respectful."

Kat shook her head in disagreement, but her body language betrayed her wavering commitment as she seemed to lean a bit toward her mother.

"Come on," Denise said. "You want to sit on the floor and talk? Let's just sit and talk."

Denise moved slightly down the hall and slid down the wall to the floor. Kat followed and sat down across from her. The others gave them their space but watched protectively.

"What is going on? This isn't you."

Kat shrugged her shoulders. She couldn't articulate why she felt the way she did. Mother and daughter sat weeping on the hallway floor.

"I can't live at home. Dad is an immature bully."

Denise rolled her eyes. "You've got to be kidding me." She conceded that her husband's behavior was often child-like, and she suppressed the desire to remind Kat that she was just as responsible for the constant bickering as her father was. Then, as if remembering the mission that brought her to Sawyer Mill, she told Kat something she thought would have an impact on her daughter, the girl who had always imagined a time in which her name would be displayed in lights.

"You have a bigger future than this, Kathryn. Don't throw it away."

The elevator doors opened then, and two Dover police officers walked down the hall, their utility belts jangling with equipment.

"What's the problem here?"

Denise tried to plead her case as succinctly as she could to the officers, explaining how her teenage daughter had run away from home to live with Seth, a twenty-nine-year-old man.

"Guys, she's still in high school."

An officer asked Kat how old she was.

"Mama," the cop said kindly when he heard Kat's response, "she's eighteen."

Denise knew that was the end of the conversation, that in the eyes of the law, Kat was an adult. Denise was contrite though oblivious to the fact that she could have been arrested on a number of misdemeanor charges. She opened her arms, and mother and daughter hugged and kissed good-bye.

"I'm always your mommy," Denise said. "I love you."

The cops escorted her and her father and sister away as Kat and Seth disappeared behind the door, locking it behind them.

The officers stayed behind as the family got on the elevator. Denise apologized again and again to the policemen for the way she'd reacted.

"That's okay, Mama," said one of the cops. "I would have done the same thing." As the elevator doors began to close, he added, "I would have done worse."

CHAPTER NINE

Camp

Despite the discouraging confrontation at Sawyer Mill, Denise McDonough wasn't finished trying to reestablish ties with her daughter. She'd try to flag Kat down at school when picking up the boys or stand in her way on the sidewalk. But her daughter would ignore her, walk around, or reverse direction.

One afternoon, their paths crossed at the mall. Kat was alone, so Denise hoped they could speak freely. Kat wouldn't look her mother in the eye and brushed Denise off, saying something about needing to be by the phone in case Seth called.

Denise would go to Target with the hope of catching Kat at work. When she did find her daughter, she noted a marked change in her personality. When Denise would talk to her, Kat would appear preoccupied, looking furtively around the store. She told Denise it wouldn't be good if Seth saw them talking. Denise inferred this meant Kat's boyfriend would yell at her mother for interfering with her daughter's relationship. It didn't occur to her that it could be bad for Kat.

On Portsmouth High School's graduation day, Seth was scheduled to work and told Kat he couldn't get out of his shift. He knew Kat's parents would be there, and he didn't want them trying to take her away from him, so he asked Roberta Gerkin if she would accompany Kat to and from graduation. Kat wasn't entirely comfortable with this arrangement. She still wasn't convinced that the psychic wasn't a threat.

Denise and Peter McDonough were able to get two tickets to the graduation ceremony through their sons. After the diplomas were passed out and families began to gather for photos, Denise and Peter tried to maneuver their way through the crowd. They saw Kat, still in her gown, being pulled away by Roberta.

Soon after, Denise's friend who lived at Sawyer Mill asked Denise if she could babysit for a couple of hours. Denise resisted the temptation to stop by Seth's apartment and went directly to her friend's place, but when she spotted Kat hauling a bag of trash to the Dumpster outside the building, Denise opened the window and yelled out a friendly hello. Kat froze and refused to come any closer.

"Why won't you come over here and just talk to me?" Denise asked.

"Because if I saw you, I'd have to lie to him," Kat said. "And I don't want to lie to him."

———

Kat got a new laptop to replace the one she'd used at her parents' house, but she was somewhat limited in her on-line activities. There was no Wi-Fi in the apartment, so she had to tether the portable computer to the Internet through a gray Ethernet cable. It stretched only as far as the futon, so she kept the computer on the floor next to where the couple slept.

While there was no need to continue her midnight chats with Seth, Kat still liked to communicate with her friends via Facebook. Seth, however, did not approve of these chats. He said that any time spent IMing with other people was time spent away from him—even if the two of them were in the same room.

The new computer was state of the art. Instead of a login password, it had a biometric security feature, a fingerprint reader that allowed Kat to simply swipe her finger across a tiny scanner in order to boot up the machine.

Seth didn't like the feature because it meant he couldn't use Kat's computer at will. He made Kat give him the backup password so he could also log on. When he used the laptop, he would usually sign in under Kat's profile, despite her having set one up for his use. This gave him access to all of Kat's e-mails, chat logs, and social media accounts and allowed him to post content and interact with other users as if he were Kat. Seth had a similar rule for Kat's cellphone. He made her share her four-digit PIN number to unlock the phone and would regularly read her call log and text messages.

Seth didn't reciprocate with his own passwords, so Kat had no access to his computer or cell phone or any of his online accounts.

———

Seth didn't respond well to the news that Kat would be leaving in late August for Camp CenterStage. Her being gone for two weeks was unacceptable, he told her, *completely* unacceptable.

Kat argued back, telling Seth the camp job wasn't a surprise. He'd known since he met her that she'd finished her training the previous summer in order to return as a camp counselor. Seth grumbled and pouted petulantly. The following day, he told Kat he'd laid down tarot cards in order to consider the option of her going to camp. He told Kat he'd make her a deal, one he expressed in a way that sounded less like a compromise and more like a mandate. Kat could go to camp for two weeks, he said, but only if she found a sexual surrogate to serve him in her place.

Kat immediately offered to skip camp instead, but now Seth was insistent. She could go, he told her, but she had to find a minion for him to play with. It was the only way to keep the Darkness in check.

Kat knew this was a tall order. It had been hard enough to get anyone to agree to watch her and Seth have sex, much less participate even in a limited way. Now Seth was demanding that someone be her sexual replacement for a full two weeks. She knew she couldn't ask any of her friends, and he didn't have any other women to call upon. The only chance Kat had to hold up her end of the bargain was to find someone online. Agreeing to try, she joined Seth in starting the search on BDSM websites.

Together, Seth and Kat scrolled through the dozens—hundreds—of profiles of people on the Seacoast who claimed to enjoy an alternative lifestyle. Their focus was on finding a woman that fit Seth's preferred type—young, slender, and blond. If she were a lesbian or bisexual, that was considered a plus.

He wanted someone he could be a Dom with, someone who would then either be a Dom or a Sub to Kat when she returned from camp. Seth selected a few of his favorites from the profiles as if ordering off a wine list. He said it was better for Kat to make first contact with them, that it would be less intimidating if the invitation came from his willing girlfriend and not from him. They composed the message together.

Writing as "Skar," she told the woman about her upcoming two-week absence. "We just want someone to keep him company, and for some sexual activities."

They got no responses from any of the women they messaged. It shouldn't have come as a surprise. What Seth and Kat were looking for was "a unicorn"—something known in alternative sex circles as a beautiful, sexy, unattached woman willing to join a couple in bed, attend to their individual pleasures, without any strings or drama.

The name, of course, refers to a creature that doesn't exist.

The impossible quest didn't stop them from trying obsessively, however. Even during sex with Kat, Seth would set up the laptop so he could simultaneously scroll through digital profiles, as if shopping for his surrogate Slave. As the camp date approached, more and more posts attributed to Kat popped up on the websites, each sounding slightly more desperate than the last. Kat knew that going to camp depended on this.

Right before she was to leave, Kat told Seth she'd found someone. A blonde in her thirties, someone who agreed to be a sexual surrogate and do some light housework. Kat had arranged all the details. The woman was going to meet him at the apartment the night after she left.

The Master was thrilled with his Slave. That night, Seth let Kat get on top of him during sex, her reward for a job well done.

————————

Seth got up early and made Kat breakfast in bed. Her suitcase was packed for camp, and he was going to drive her to the drop-off point. They'd had sex the previous night, and it had been uncharacteristically tender. Seth was being clingy. He was already missing her.

"You are my Skarlet."

"And you are my Darkheart."

Kat explained there was a no-phone policy in place at the camp, even for the counselors. Seth instructed her to disregard the policy, and to call him every night after lights-out. Kat said she would try to call and possibly text, but it wouldn't be easy. She didn't even know if she could get a signal there.

Seth ignored her and repeated that Kat needed to call every night.

In the parking lot at the drop-off, he grabbed his girlfriend one last time. "Until the tides bring you back to me."

Kat got on the bus with the rest of the theater brats and waved good-bye through the window.

When they finally arrived in Maine, Kat fell back into a familiar and comforting rhythm. Old friends. Ice breakers. Cabin assignments. Songs at dinnertime, the meal served family style. All the campers finally settled into their cabins and slid into sleeping bags with hardly any complaints of homesickness.

A safe amount of time after lights out, Kat snuck into an empty counselors' lounge and powered up her cell phone. When the device finally connected to a remote network, a series of text messages sent earlier in the day began to fill the inbox. The phone buzzed again and again. There were also many notices of missed calls, Kat saw. They were all from "Darkheart."

Seth texted that the surrogate had bailed on him. She hadn't shown up. He wanted to know if there was some mistake about the day? Were they supposed to meet somewhere other than the Lair? Was she able to get her contact information for this mystery woman? Did she even exist?

When they first dated, Kat lied to her parents over and

over to get out of the house, making up parties and work obligations and play practices for cover. She lied so she could do the thing she really wanted—to go to Seth's. Was it such a stretch to think Kat would have done the same thing to get what she really wanted now—to go to camp? Seth was never able to track down his promised surrogate, but Kat later said under oath the woman and the arrangement were real.

It wasn't just Kat's past behaviors on display. Seth was in full-on temper mode. His behavior mimicked how he'd reacted at Christmas, the unbearable thought of not having his woman behind closed doors for uninterrupted hours. His inability to confront Kat about the situation only made it worse.

Kat didn't check her phone again until two nights later. Hiding in the counselors' lounge, the cell came to life with another flurry of unanswered phone calls and text messages. The surrogate was a no-show for the third straight night, Seth wrote. Darkheart was demanding Kat respond. Why had she not replied to his text messages the night before?

Kat wrote back that there was a lot going on at night and it wasn't a good time to slink away. Darkheart didn't want to hear how she had been socializing with friends when she was supposed to be calling at the appointed time, Seth wrote. Kat said it was much too quiet at camp for her to make a phone call, but that she'd try to text.

Darkheart then said that Kat had been a bad Slave to her Master. He said she would pay when she got home.

Back in Dover, Seth was crawling up the walls. He'd been so looking forward to having a new plaything—and now he had nothing. As the two weeks wore on, his mood continued to blacken.

He went to see Roberta Gerkin and asked for a tarot reading. He said the situation with Kat had made the Darkness more intense, more difficult to control. Seth said he felt like Doomsday was coming and that he couldn't control him. He told Roberta that if Kat didn't start checking in with him at the appointed time, someone "would be dead."

On August 25, toward the end of the second week, Seth composed an epic text message, detailing the elaborate, humiliating punishments he had planned for her failure in securing a sexual replacement for him while she was at camp.

When Kat read what Seth wrote, she was appalled. She had never seen anything like this from him before. Even when doing it as "the Nameless One" or "the Hollow One," the roughest of the sex personas, he had never threatened his Slave with such violence. It horrified her. Just as he had disproportionately demanded four nights of dates because he lost one night to Mother Dragon, his response to her not obtaining a temporary sex Slave was also disproportionate. It was disturbing and extreme.

Kat deleted all of the other text messages from her phone, but couldn't bring herself to get rid of this one.

Like a hideous screenplay, Seth even dictated the dialogue for them both. " 'You've been a naughty slut.' 'Yes, sire. I'm sorry,' you will reply," he wrote. "I stop halfway and listen to your whimpers and yelp. 'Beg for the rest of it,' I say."

He told her she was then supposed to ask him to do more. The text went on and on, with Seth gleefully describing how he would continue to strike her all over her body. She was to constantly say, "Thank you," to apologize for leaving him alone, and to submit to a laundry list of sex acts that would denigrate her body.

"I will twist, slap, whip with a chain, pull hair, and punish you as you ride me."

Seth even threatened to do something he had never done in bed with Kat, the one thing that truly terrified her. He was going to sodomize her.

And yet, the long list of what he had just described would only be Kat's *first* punishment. The text continued.

"The second price of this—you choose a friend," he wrote. "I may do *anything* I wish with her while you watch and assist."

The text message ended on a sinister note.

"I think it would be fitting if the first thing you saw me do when you got back is pleasure one of your friends until they died of orgasms. And only then turn my brutal attention back to you."

———

Months later, while on the witness stand, Kat said a friend dropped her off at the apartment when the bus returned from Maine. When she opened the door, she found Seth waiting in the Lair with all of the contents of their special box laid out on the bed. She rolled her suitcase into the cluttered apartment and left it by the closet.

Darkheart ordered Kat to take off her clothes. She began to beg Seth not to sodomize to her. She begged as hard as she could. It wasn't the kind of play begging that Subs did for their Doms, where they pretend not to want the thing they know comes next. It wasn't even the kind of begging Seth had made her do as his *Slave*. Seth ignored the pleas, seemingly determined to hurt her.

Tears were rolling down Kat's cheeks. She offered to do anything else Seth wanted, any kind of impact play he could dream of. She said she would be his Slave for however long he wanted. She appealed and sobbed and bargained and pleaded.

Darkheart's will was strong, Seth reminded her as he unbuckled his belt. He'd told her there would be two punishments and this was just the first.

He pulled Kat over to the futon and made good on his promise.

CHAPTER TEN

The Punishment

The sexual punishment Kat McDonough endured continued for days. Even as their lives returned to normal routines—going to work, making dinner, picking out a movie to watch—the brutality of the sex continued as a cycle of cruel thrusts, hard pinching, hitting, and throat grabbing.

The couple's earlier conspiracies to find a minion to use and abuse were no longer wishful fantasies. Seth now told Kat that she *must* fulfill the terms of her second punishment, and he was unrelenting about it. She had no choice, he told her. She had to find a woman to offer up to him.

Kat continued to solicit—and to throw herself at—women on fetish websites, but no one was tempted by what she was selling. She'd already gone through her high school friends, most of them having been summarily banished from the Lair for escaping the erotic trap they had laid. Neither Wendy nor Zoey were coming back, their encounters with Seth and Kat having made them feel awkward and uncomfortable in the apartment. Even Jill, Kat's best friend since first grade, didn't want to come over.

The number of women in Kat's real-life orbit was limited as well—she was no longer in school, just working part-time and doing plays. There were only a few women her age on staff at Target. The more Kat thought about it, there was really only one candidate who kept coming to mind. And she might be Kat's only hope.

———

Lizzi Marriott—the twenty-year-old former prom queen with the huge blue eyes and sandy-blond hair—had started working at the Greenland Target about a month earlier.

Kat and Lizzi both worked the night shift a couple of times a week. They spent hours together organizing store shelves and moving clothes from boxes to hangers. Lizzi was quick to help her coworkers with whatever needed to get done. She was silly and made Kat laugh. Lizzi was effervescent even when slogging cardboard boxes through the department store. She was always friendly, even if she'd come straight from the University of New Hampshire ocean lab to her shift, wearing salt and exhaustion like a second skin. It seemed impossible to wipe the smile from Lizzi's face, and because of that, she was impossible to ignore.

Lizzi's curiosity had no bounds; she was driven to make friends with her coworkers and wanted to learn everything about them, and she was open with the details of her own life as well. During the night shift at Target, there was plenty of time for small talk. Kat knew that Lizzi was a transfer student to UNH and was studying marine biology. She knew Lizzi grew up in Massachusetts but was living with her aunt and uncle about twenty-five miles from campus. She also knew that Lizzi was bisexual and that she had a girlfriend who sounded pretty cool.

When she shared the details of her life, Kat was surprised by how much they seemed to have in common. Lizzi also enjoyed performing and had a great singing voice. They were both interested in nerd culture, things like science fiction and superheroes and role-playing games. Kat had just learned to play Dungeons & Dragons, and Lizzi was dying to learn too. Kat, whose mom sewed costumes, was blown away upon hearing that Lizzi had made her own prom dress.

Both young women lived with cats, although Lizzi admitted she was allergic and that her aunt and uncle's cat wouldn't leave her alone. Lizzi squealed when Kat shared her obsession with Harry Potter and how she'd dressed as the character Tonks for a movie premiere. Lizzi told Kat that the Harry Potter books were her favorite too. They'd been the first books she'd learned to read on her own.

Kat saw Lizzi the way everyone did: undeniably charismatic and keenly intelligent, but a little bit ditzy. It was testament to both her likability and her absentmindedness that one day, when Lizzi managed to lock her keys in her Mazda while it was running, the store's employees fell over themselves to help her out. When with some luck and ingenuity they were finally able to open her car, what struck Kat most was Lizzi's unflappable attitude about the incident. If Kat had locked her keys in the car, she would probably have walked into work swearing up a storm or holding back sobs. Lizzi had just shrugged and laughed at her own silliness—as if understanding just how unimportant such a mistake was in the scheme of things.

One night in the break room, as a group of workers gathered to chat, one woman said she'd been stocking the book section and couldn't believe a mainstream retailer like Target was selling *Fifty Shades of Grey*. There was tittering among the group, as some explained the BDSM-themed novel's plot and others admitted they either knew too much or not enough about what people did behind closed doors.

Kat had never shared her own alternative lifestyle with her coworkers, but when someone asked if Kat had read the book, she said no.

"That's my life every day."

That silenced the group, and everyone avoided eye contact with Kat when they grasped her meaning. But Kat noticed Lizzi looked at her and made some kind of funny face. Later, testifying under oath, Kat said she wondered if that was a signal that Lizzi was intrigued. She didn't wonder whether Lizzi was just trying to be kind.

After days of brutal treatment at Seth's hands, Kat told him she might have thought of a candidate who could fulfill the second part of her punishment. Seth still thought there were other fish on the line. He was holding out hope they could still land a unicorn, a real "ten," through the BDSM personal ads.

Seth also had his eye on Kat's friend Darla. She had a new boyfriend who was interested in bondage, and she'd told Kat they had been experimenting but neither of them really knew what they were doing. Kat hinted that "Lex" could likely be convinced to teach them a few things.

"We've even messed with blood/knife play," Kat told her via text message. "He has plenty of experience in it and I've found it psychotically fun."

"I'm looking at electricity stuff," Darla responded.

Kat said that, although that seemed fun, she was into rougher stuff.

"I like chains, whips, leather, rope, and knives."

The complication was Darla's boyfriend, Eli.[1] Seth wanted a three-way not a four-way. They were hoping to get Darla to come to the Lair alone the way Wendy had, but they agreed that they would allow her to bring Eli if that were a deal breaker.

Seth agreed to vet Lizzi as well, and the next night Kat and Lizzi were scheduled to work together, he dropped by the store to casually bump into them both. Kat intro-

---

1 Denotes pseudonym.

duced him to Lizzi, who proceeded to go on and on to Seth about what a great girlfriend he had.

Seth found Lizzi to be everything Kat said she would be. He liked her looks and loved her personality. The fact that she was bisexual gave him hope she wouldn't be opposed to having sex with both of them. He took out the tarot cards and did a reading on Lizzi when they got home.

"She was flirting with you," Seth later told Kat.

Her smile, her laugh . . . that was just the way Lizzi always was, Kat thought. But as Seth insisted there was more to it than Lizzi just being friendly, Kat found herself wondering why it was that she was always so oblivious.

———

Midway through September 2012, Kat quit her job at the Target in Greenland and started working at the Michaels arts and crafts store in Newington, across the street from the Best Buy where Seth now worked. Kat and Lizzi exchanged phone numbers on Kat's final day but didn't make any specific plans to get together.

The punishment was now routine. At any moment Seth might turn to Kat and order her to have sex. Kat would later tell her mother that she feared for her physical safety, aware that Seth was a third-degree black belt who vastly outweighed her. Kat claimed Seth threatened to track her down if she left—the same thing he told Catherine Fish.

The rough treatment Kat described was not noted by anyone else around them. At this same time, Seth and Kat were regularly visiting his mother, Heather, and by all accounts these trips were polite and drama-free. Heather was planning some home improvements, and it was agreed that Seth and Kat would come over to do some painting. They said they'd pick up all the items needed for the job, including a new painting tarp.

Despite the disastrous experience she'd had around the summer-camp surrogate, Kat did not abandon the hope she could attract a Sub for Seth through an online BDSM personal ad. Kat thought she had a pretty appealing profile. She was a thin and pretty eighteen-year-old girl—how could she not be receiving messages or responses to her e-mails?

Most of the members on the website seemed to be in their forties or fifties, their profile pictures showing balding men with paunches or wrinkled women with fat bottoms. Everyone knew those with photos featuring only close-ups of eyes or sexy shoes or genitalia belonged to people who were obese or ugly or pretending to be someone else. But Kat's alter ego "roguetemptress" was the real deal.

The string of virtual rejections on top of the punishing sex she'd endured for a month was wearing Kat down. On September 25, 2012, at two o'clock in the morning, Kat switched on her computer and started writing a letter to herself.

"I feel like such a fucking loner," she began. Seth had been telling her she was this sexy woman, but her failures at attracting any partner undermined that feeling. It played into all of her other insecurities and feelings of rejection.

"I can handle being called a slut or a Slave to a Master. It's better than no attention at all."

Kat said "Skarlet" had been a powerful, desirable woman in her past lives and behind the Veil. If that were so, she wondered, why can't she have the same power in this world? Cracks were finally showing in Kat's state of mind when it came to the hard-core BDSM she was being subjected to. Seth still claimed it was Darkheart or Wild Card having his way with Skarlet or Anay, but Kat seemed to have doubts about whether the sexual experience she wanted was the same as what Seth was telling her was taking place.

She wondered how she could be so blind as not to know—as Seth had tried to convince her—that Lizzi was flirting with her.

"God somedays I just want to give up on all of it and just submit myself completely to Darkheart, but I know that I don't really want that completely [in] this life." She was vacillating between the life she was living and the life she was promised. Kat was having a crisis of conscience.

Kat closed her laptop and sat in the dark. Only she could say what other thoughts were running through her head that night. But she didn't say much more, not in her journal anyway. She'd finished the entry with a resolution.

"I've gotta figure out what to do about this."

―――――

Kat and Lizzi hadn't really stayed in touch in the few weeks since Kat had left Target, and they'd never actually seen each other outside of the store when she did work there. But they'd become Facebook friends, and Kat could keep tabs on her there. And she did keep tabs, because Seth had decided that Lizzi was the one.

Kat dialed Lizzi's number and asked if she wanted to come over to watch *The Avengers*, which had come out on DVD the previous week. She asked Lizzi if she remembered when they'd found the Avengers underwear in the boys clothing section and how they'd joked they would wear them if they came in bigger sizes. Lizzi laughed and agreed to come over, saying it would be fun to hang out.

Lizzi was still new to UNH and new to the area. She was looking to make friends and also felt she and Kat had a lot in common. It would have to be Tuesday night, she told Kat, because of her evening class schedule. They set a time of around ten P.M., and Lizzi asked for Kat's address so she could plug it into her TomTom GPS.

Kat waited outside the entrance to the Sawyer Mill Apartments looking for Lizzi's Mazda on the night of October 2, 2012. When she finally pulled up, Kat jumped in the front seat. The parking lots were hidden along a confusing tangle of streets and behind the mill, so Kat needed to show her where to go.

They had the apartment to themselves because Seth was at play practice, Kat said. Seth had a role in local productions of *A Midsummer Night's Dream* (Kat was in it too, but her smaller role didn't require so many rehearsals). She apologized for the level of clutter.

In addition to the ubiquitous piles of laundry and video game paraphernalia, in the corner there were some painting supplies, which they'd bought to complete the work at Heather Mazzaglia's place. As the movie started and they settled in to watch it on the futon, Lizzi and Kat dug into the individual bowls of microwave popcorn they'd each perched on their laps. Seth came home from play practice a few minutes before the end of the movie, said hi, and then waited until the film was over to make small talk. He told Lizzi it was great to have her visit and that she should come back again. They could watch another movie or play video games or Dungeons & Dragons, he said. Because it was nearly an hour's ride from UNH to her aunt and uncle's house in Chester, Seth also offered the apartment as a place to crash if Lizzi ever felt like it.

Lizzi said she was grateful and would absolutely come back to hang out. The conversation lasted about ten minutes before she said good-bye.

"She had definite potential," Seth said after Lizzi left. "We have to get her back."

He then told Kat that Lizzi was almost certainly someone they had met in a past life—perhaps someone Skarlet met the night she burned down Portsmouth.

Kat thought Seth would be pleased with her for bringing Lizzi to the Lair, but instead he only offered a rebuke.

"You were too friendly."

"What do you mean?" Kat asked him.

"You should have been more flirty. Less friendly, more flirty."

Seth told Kat she should have sat closer to Lizzi. Instead of each of them eating popcorn from separate bowls, he said, Kat should have put both microwaved bags into one large bowl. Seth said that would have been more sexual, their buttery fingers touching again and again as they reached into the bowl.

Seth also said that, if Lizzi were to come over again, Kat should suggest they all play a game of strip poker.

———

The following week, Seth and Kat got an unexpected nibble from Darla, when she said she was ready to experiment with bondage. Not the common "tie my wrists to the headboard" stuff, she told Kat. She wanted to learn more about rope play and how to tie complicated harnesses. She wasn't 100 percent sure that her boyfriend, Eli, would be on board, however. He'd hinted at trying some kinky stuff, but Darla was afraid to freak him out.

Darla asked Kat if she and Eli could come to the Lair and have "Lex" show them a few things. *Could Lex teach Eli how to be a Dom? Could he show him some ways to tie her up?* Seth was all for it when he heard about the plan. He would demonstrate a few things on Kat, like a teacher imparting his wisdom on eager students.

Seth saw this as a great opportunity. If they played it smart, a sensual Dom at work on a nude Sub could get their observers aroused. When the moment was right, Seth could invite Darla to get up close to the vulnerable Kat. Or he could help Eli as he practiced on his girlfriend, but Seth would have to insist Darla be nude so that Eli could learn the proper amount of pressure to apply to the skin.

Darla set a date for Monday, October 8, but she texted Kat at the last minute asking to put the date off until the following night, Tuesday evening, October 9.

As she had promised Seth, Kat also followed up on her invitation to Lizzi, who said she'd love to come back and hang out again. Kat tried to book her for Wednesday the tenth, but Lizzi said her work and class schedule was very tight. The only night she could get together was on Tuesday the ninth. Her chemistry lab started at 6:10, but she could come over when it was done.

The irony was rich and wasn't lost on the couple. After months of no takers, suddenly they were double booked.

Their solution was simple. Lizzi wouldn't arrive until around nine P.M. Kat told Darla and Eli they had late play rehearsal and that the couple should come over at ten thirty. Kat told Lizzi she and Seth needed to leave just after ten o'clock to pick up a friend of Seth's at the airport.

If things got romantic with Lizzi, they'd cancel their BDSM demonstration with Darla and Eli and pretend as if the airport pickup got cancelled. Otherwise, they'd usher Lizzi out just after ten o'clock and wait for the second shift to clock in.

———

Seth clocked in at Best Buy on Tuesday, October 9, at 10:59 A.M., looking forward to the kind of evening he'd been waiting for since before Kat left for camp. He told Kat that their personas for the evening would be Skarlet and Darkheart—two particularly sexual alter egos.

In the meantime, Kat was playing air traffic control via text message with all the principal players. In the early afternoon, she pinged Lizzi to confirm that she'd be coming over after class.

"Okeydokey." Lizzi punctuated it with the smiley face emoticon :) "Can't wait, darling!"

The "darling" comment made Kat wonder again if Seth was right and Lizzi had been flirting with her all this time.

After confirming with Darla, Kat messaged Seth to say that both plans were in place.

"Perfect," he texted back, and Kat congratulated herself with the return text, "Win for Skar!"

Shortly after six P.M., Seth texted the director of *A Midsummer Night's Dream* and told her he had a work conflict and couldn't come to rehearsal that night. He said Kat was unavailable too. (Though she had her own phone, Seth was the contact person for all theater communication with Kat. It was yet another way of him exerting control and reducing Kat's autonomy.)

He then sent a message to Roberta Gerkin, claiming that psychic activity had been "shorting out my radar" and asking her to just "let me know you're alive."

At 7:20, although she knew Lizzi was likely still in class, Kat sent her a text saying she was hopping in the shower, just in case she showed up early.

Lizzi didn't respond until an hour later. "Okeydokey, just got outta class!"

At that moment, Seth got home and realized he had time to take a shower himself. While he scrubbed the day from his skin, his cellphone buzzed once. Roberta had finally returned his previous text, reporting she was okay. Her second text was more ominous.

"Keep yourself guarded for a while. Someone is looking for you and I can't tell if they're friend or foe."

———

Earlier that evening, Lizzi Marriott had relaxed at the UNH student center, the Memorial Union Building in the heart of the enormous Durham campus. She grabbed a bite in the MUB's massive dining hall and texted with her girlfriend, Brittany Atwood.

Lizzi headed to her chemistry lab, and while she was there, she received several affectionate messages from Brittany. She sent a text back, saying she was wearing the gift Brittany had given her two days earlier, a black hoodie sweatshirt bearing the logo for *Avenue Q*. The musical was one of Lizzi's favorites, a *Sesame Street* parody featuring Muppet knockoffs singing subversive songs like, "It Sucks to Be Me" and "The Internet Is for Porn."

When class ended and she climbed into her Mazda Tribute, Lizzi and Brittany traded more text messages. Lizzi knew she shouldn't text while driving—the way deer and wild turkeys suddenly appeared on New Hampshire roads, she was taking her life in her hands—but she didn't want to put Brittany on pause.

Lizzi's TomTom GPS reminded her of the way from Durham to Dover, and she found the Sawyer Mill visitors' parking lot without trouble. As she walked to the complex's back door, she kept typing texts to Brittany on her iPhone.

"U should do more poetry baby," Brittany responded to something she wrote. "Ur really good with words."

"I can be eloquent when I want to be."

As she so often did, Lizzi ended the message with :P, a sticking-tongue-out smiley face. Once she hit send, she switched over to text Kat.

"I'm at the outer door :D"

Lizzi and Brittany exchanged texts with <3, the combination that looks like a heart—shorthand for "I love you."

As Kat opened the locked door for Lizzi, she sent one final text message to Brittany. "You're so cute!"

It was 8:55 P.M.

PART THREE

SUBMISSION

One has always had too much when
one has had enough.

—MARQUIS DE SADE

CHAPTER ELEVEN

Missing

When Becky Hanna woke up on Wednesday, October 10, 2012, she headed downstairs to the kitchen and immediately noticed that her niece, Lizzi Marriott, wasn't home. Lizzi was very responsible, and although there was no need for her to check in with her aunt and uncle, she almost always did so as a courtesy. She was an adult, though, and didn't have a curfew. But Becky hadn't heard her niece come in late or head out early.

She saw that Lizzi's SUV wasn't in the driveway and, checking the attic bedroom, noted that Lizzi's bed hadn't been slept in. She later told *48 Hours* she was concerned but not particularly panicked. Becky respected her niece's privacy and imagined she might have gone to a party or slept over at a friend's dorm room. When push came to shove, Lizzi wasn't her daughter, and it was a delicate balance to both adore the girl and to give her the space a college sophomore was entitled to.

The last sign of Lizzi's presence in the house had been left on Monday night. Lizzi had said her class was taking a field trip to a tidal pool to study the aquatic life, and she told her aunt she needed some boots because the terrain would be rocky. At Becky's urging, Lizzi borrowed her cousin's pair and dashed off to UNH.

At the estuary, every slimy thing captivated Lizzi, just as it had at the New England Aquarium. Her lab partner didn't find it nearly as interesting, though, and wandered away from the group—only to fall into a deep tidal pool. Lizzi turned when she heard the splash and went over to fish her partner out, but instead she found herself yanked in up to her thighs by the struggling student. The water was cold but not nearly as frigid as the chill from the wind blowing through her wet jeans when she climbed out. She shared this calamity with friends on social media, not in words that cut down her clumsy classmate, but rather with that self-deprecating tone that celebrated another of her harmless misadventures.

The tale had been her final post to her Facebook page.

When Lizzi returned home to the Hannas, she'd left a note of apology on the soaking boots by the door. The note was still there.

Her confidence in her niece aside, Becky still felt something wasn't right about her absence on this Wednesday morning. Becky consulted the family calendar where Lizzi often wrote her schedule. For Tuesday night, Lizzi had noted that she had an evening chemistry class, then plans with a friend. "School til 9, might to a friend's after, back at 12 at latest."

Becky's husband, Anthony Hanna, also tried to tamp down his concern. If Lizzi had stayed out all night, he rationalized, she'd come home eventually to change her clothes and freshen up, if not before class, then before her shift at Target later that night.

But Tony was anxious for another reason. He loved Lizzi's spirit and friendly personality, but he'd sometimes worried she could be *too* friendly, too trusting.

Back in Massachusetts, Lizzi's girlfriend, Brittany Atwood, was also uneasy. She had sent three more texts to Lizzi the previous night around nine P.M., but when there had been no response after "You're so cute!", she figured Lizzi had arrived at her destination and their conversation was over.

Brittany knew the friend Lizzi was visiting that night was Kat McDonough. They'd never met, but she felt a pang of jealousy whenever Lizzi would talk about Kat. Lizzi had introduced Kat through a text that listed all of the things they were both into.

"And she is bi!!!" Lizzi wrote, which rattled Brittany. Distance, new circles of friends, and time spent apart were always a dangerous combination for relationships. In October 2012, Brittany was living in a tiny apartment with her sister— an arrangement that wasn't working out—and her girlfriend was in another state. Brittany would later admit that it was much easier for her when Lizzi was ten minutes away at her parents' house in central Massachusetts. They'd had a great summer together, and she was still getting used to only seeing her girlfriend on the weekends.

She also was uneasy about her girlfriend's affection for a guy she'd met who also worked at Target. Nate McNeal was one of the few people who were friends with both Lizzi and Kat. Like the two of them, he also considered himself a nerd—he was into video games and fantasy novels like *A Game of Thrones*.

Nate told journalists he had known Kat for much longer—his sister had been her friend in kindergarten—but he was much closer to Lizzi. The two of them texted jokes about killer octopuses leveling cities and destroying modern civilization.

"Can you speak fluent octopus yet?" Nate had texted Lizzi on the afternoon of Tuesday, October 9.

"Pfft, was I ever unable?" she wisecracked.

Nate laughed and typed back on the cracked screen of his iPhone. "Now we shall raise an army . . ."

Lizzi texted back that theirs would be an army of huggably betentacled cephalopods. Nate asked his aspiring marine biologist friend how terrifying it would be if someone gave steroids to an octopus.

"OCTOPUZILLAAA," she texted back in mock terror.

They made a date to have lunch on Wednesday, but when he texted Lizzi to confirm the plans at 11:33 P.M. on Tuesday, she didn't respond. At noon on Wednesday, he went to the restaurant anyway and waited for her for more than an hour. Lizzi had told him that Brittany was jealous of their friendship, and as he sat there waiting, he wondered whether the couple had quarreled about the lunch date being out of bounds, or whether Lizzi had simply forgotten their plans.

"Ay!" he texted Lizzi at 1:15, hoping pinging her would be enough to jog her memory about their tête-à-tête. Lizzi didn't respond.

He tried again later. "L-sizzle? :D"

As the hours passed, Nate's worry grew.

"Friend? Art thou okay?!" he texted, followed by the D: emoticon, an expression of great concern.

That evening, Lizzi didn't turn up for her five-to-ten P.M. shift at Target. Calls to her iPhone went straight to voicemail.

On Thursday morning, when it was clear Lizzi hadn't come home for a second straight night, Tony and Becky Hanna could no longer deny something was seriously wrong. As they struggled to think straight about what their next move should be, the wall phone in the kitchen rang.

Tony snatched up the receiver and Becky moved close, hoping to hear Lizzi's apology ringing through the earpiece. Instead, she heard Lizzi's father's voice.

"Hi, Tony. It's Bob. Have you heard from Lizzi?"

"No," Tony replied to his brother-in-law. "We were just about to call you."

———

Bob Marriott and his wife, Melissa, hadn't known there was a problem until Brittany called them the morning of Thursday, October 11. She told them that Lizzi had not responded to any of her calls or texts for more than twenty-four hours, which was very unlike her, and that there hadn't been any activity on her usually lively Facebook account.

The Marriotts knew Lizzi and Brittany were in constant contact with each other. They had hoped Tony and Becky knew what was going on, but now panic passed through the telephone like a contagion.

Lizzi's father hung up the phone in utter disbelief. Bob was an engineer, but he found it hard to think analytically about the situation. Should they call the cops? Should they call the FBI? How long did Lizzi have to be missing before authorities could start looking for her? He could only guess at what those answers might be.

Later, recounting the day for CBS, the parents told how they each picked up a phone and began calling everyone they could think of.

No, she hasn't shown up for work. No, she didn't make it to her class. No, I haven't seen but I'll try to reach her for you.

After two hours of dialing with no results, Bob and Melissa Marriott could no longer just sit around their kitchen table. They got in their car and made the ninety-minute drive from Westborough to Chester, Bob driving while Melissa continued making calls.

When they arrived at Becky and Tony Hanna's house in Chester, the foursome put their heads together about what they should do next. Tony pointed to the note Lizzi had written on the calendar for Tuesday.

"Going to a friend's?" he said. "What friend?"

Brittany had told Bob Marriott all she knew about Lizzi's Tuesday night plans, how after chemistry lab, Lizzi had said she was meeting up with her former Target co worker, Kat. Brittany wasn't sure, but she thought Kat's last name was McDonough and that she lived with her boyfriend somewhere near Portsmouth.

Around two P.M., Bob and Melissa talked to Nicholas McLellan, a patrolman from the tiny Chester Police Department. Officer McLellan contacted the county dispatch center to put a BOLO ("be on the lookout") for Lizzi's Mazda. He also had Dispatch trace the last GPS coordinates for Lizzi's cell phone, which placed the device in Dover on Tuesday night.

After spending much of his day searching local databases and reaching out to the same people whom the Marriotts had already called, Officer McLellan was able to connect the dots between Kat McDonough and her boyfriend, and he retrieved the phone number for an apartment listed under *S Mazzaglia* in Dover.

Seth answered the officer's call, but denied that Lizzi had come to his apartment on Tuesday night. Seth claimed to have been home until around nine P.M., then left to go on a two-mile run. His legs began to hurt, he said, and he'd had to slow down and walk. He didn't get home until ten.

Seth told McLellan there wasn't anyone in the apartment when he got back. He said that his girlfriend, Kat, didn't arrive home until midnight.

There was something about the conversation that McLellan didn't like. He thought Seth sounded very nervous and had gone out of his way to put distance between himself and his apartment. Before McLellan hung up, he asked Seth to have Kat call him as soon as she could.

About twenty minutes later the officer received a call from Kat. She told him that, yes, Lizzi was supposed to have come over on Tuesday, but she'd never made it. She'd said her chemistry lab could go as late as ten P.M., Kat explained, so there had been no set time for her arrival. When ten o'clock rolled around, Kat said, she went outside the building to wait for her. They had plans to walk to a nearby cemetery.

"Why were you going to a cemetery?" McLellan asked Kat.

"We were going to take some pictures at night," she responded. "I wanted to prove to her that ghosts are real."

Kat said that she waited and waited but ultimately decided to go to the cemetery alone. She got back at midnight and went to bed.

McLellan wrote up everything he could and told his supervisors that there was something more going on with this missing persons case. The decision was made to get other agencies involved in the search for Lizzi Marriott.

An hour later, James Yerardi of the Dover Police Department knocked on the door of Seth's apartment at Sawyer Mill. Both Seth and Kat were home. The officer explained that he was looking for Lizzi Marriott and was there to collect some information.

The couple sprang to life with niceties and invited the officer inside. Seth listened as Kat explained to Yerardi

Lizzi Marriott was a bright, silly, lovable nineteen-year-old studying marine biology at the University of New Hampshire. Loved ones say her only fault was that she was "too trusting." *AP Photo/Jim Cole*

MISSING
$10,000 Reward

Cell phone last used in DOVER
10:11pm on 10/9

ELIZABETH "LIZZI" MARRIOTT, Age 19

- She is 5' 5", about 130 lbs.
  blond hair and blue eyes.
- She was driving
  2001 tan Mazda Tribute
  NH plates 304-5397

Any Info – Contact Chester Police Chief William Burke
603-887-2000
Reward for the safe return of Elizabeth

On October 9, 2012, Lizzi went missing. Family only knew that she planned on visiting a friend after class. *Chester Police Department/ New Hampshire Department of Justice*

All photographs courtesy of the authors, unless otherwise noted.

From an early age, "Kat" McDonough dreamed of being an actress. Her mother encouraged her to explore her artistic side.   *Photo used with permission*

When she became a teenager, Kat felt unwanted at home. She was ready for someone to sweep her off her feet.   *Photo used with permission*

Seth was a regular in the local theater scene, where castmates often found his personality off-putting. Given his dark looks, he was often cast as a villian. Few knew the truly dark side of his personality.

Photo used with permission

Seth took Catherine Fish to her senior prom in 2001. She later moved in with him and had a year-and-a-half relationship she said was filled with sexual and emotional abuse.

Photo used with permission

Seth pressured Kat to move into the Sawyer Mill apartments on the Bellamy River. He called his apartment "the Lair," which was where they were free to pursue all sorts of wicked intentions.

Seth's studio apartment was filled with tokens of his interests: video games, fantasy tales, and violent sex. *New Hampshire Department of Justice*

Lizzi's disappearance set in motion a huge manhunt for her safe return. Her Mazda Tribute was later found abandoned in a parking lot at UNH, its GPS missing. *New Hampshire Department of Justice*

This scenic overlook on Peirce Island provides a grand view of the Piscataqua River, where its swift-moving currents bank east and empty into the Atlantic Ocean.

Authorities from New Hampshire Marine Patrol examined the jagged shoreline of the Piscataqua for evidence in Lizzi's disappearance, a search that would continue on land as well as in the air and water for weeks. *AP Photo/Jim Cole*

 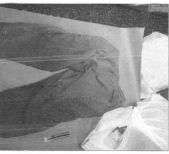

[LEFT] Prosecutors say these were the gloves the suspect wore when Lizzi was killed. [RIGHT] The hunt for evidence turned up clothes from the night Lizzi disappeared. DNA recovered was critical to the case. *New Hampshire Department of Justice*

Seth walks out of a Strafford County Superior courtroom, as the world is ready to hear what happened the night Lizzi Marriott died.

Escorted by guards, Kat is hurried past reporters as she prepares for another long day of cross-examination.

The job of securing a conviction fell to Assistant Attorney General Peter Hinckley, who often looked like the weight of the world was on his shoulders.

Public defender Joachim Barth presented a rigorous defense, boiling the trial down to a case of "Who do you believe?"

Kat McDonough spent ten grueling days on the stand, during which public opinion about her truthfulness constantly swayed back and forth.

After the verdict, Bob Marriott addressed the media about the profound impact the loss of Lizzi had had on their family.

Photo used with permission

that she had been expecting Lizzi that night but that her friend had never shown up. Kat also said Lizzi had sent a text around nine P.M. saying her class was over, but that was the last time she'd heard from her. Yerardi made a note of the text message, a detail that wasn't part of the story Kat told the Chester police officer.

Yerardi asked Seth and Kat to call the police station if they heard from Lizzi.

Then he asked, "Do you mind if I take a quick look around? Just to see that Lizzi isn't hiding here?"

Seth and Kat said they didn't mind and that he should take as much time as he needed. There wasn't much to go through in the small apartment, but Yerardi scanned it efficiently, briefly inspecting the small kitchen and the living room/bedroom studio combo. With his foot, he poked around piles of dirty clothes and video game cases on the floor. He checked the bathroom and pulled back the shower curtain, revealing more of Seth and Kat's poor housekeeping.

The visit lasted only a few minutes. There was no sign of Lizzi in the apartment, and no sign of foul play. Officer Yerardi thanked Seth and Kat and left.

Lizzi's family and friends began to mobilize. They gathered the most recent pictures of Lizzi they could find. She was smiling in every one of them. Full-color Missing posters were printed. The flyers were straightforward, the text framing Lizzi's face, her blue eyes jumping out from the portraits they chose:

Lizzi Marriott: five foot five, blond hair and blue eyes,
130 pounds. Last seen driving a Mazda SUV with New
Hampshire license plates. A $10,000 reward for infor-
mation leading to her safe return.

Within hours, the posters were distributed to police
and were plastered all over Chester, Portsmouth, and the
sprawling UNH campus in Durham. Posters were even
hung throughout the Sawyer Mill complex.

The local media took note of the pretty girl being
sought on the posters and followed up with the police,
suspecting there might be a story worth following.

The initial reports of Lizzi's disappearance were rele-
gated to the inside sections of New Hampshire's Seacoast
papers and the newspaper in Lizzi's home town of Westborough, Massachusetts.

"I hope she's with someone where she wants to be and
that she'll come home," her father told a reporter.

The University of New Hampshire Police Department
tracked down both Lizzi's chemistry teacher and her lab
partner. Both confirmed that she'd been in class on Tuesday, October 9. The investigators considered the possibility that she had never made it to her car or that something
had happened after class that prevented her from arriving
in Dover, and an officer spent the day canvassing UNH
campus parking lots for Lizzi's Mazda Tribute.

Nate McNeal was also contacting everyone he could
in the search for Lizzi.

He texted Kat, "Hey have you heard from Lizzi lately?
Or did she come over Tuesday night?"

"No. She was supposed to but never showed up," Kat replied. "I'm worried as well."

"Have you told the police that?"

"Yea they called and told me she was missing, i told them everything i knew."

Nate frowned at the broken iPhone screen in his hands. He texted back a symbol meant to mimic the look he wore on his face:

[:

———

By Friday, October 12, as wider news coverage of the missing coed began to break, officials were beginning to doubt that Lizzi Marriott would turn up safe and sound. The investigation was in the command of the Chester police, but it was already crossing jurisdictional lines. With only five full-time officers and a handful of part-timers, the small-town department didn't have the manpower for such an operation. It was time for the New Hampshire State Police to take control of the search.

New Hampshire's state police are relied upon for more than patrolling highways for drunk drivers and speeders. Because of its great number of small towns and villages, close to two hundred communities rely on the NHSP to back up their local police forces. Even in cities with large departments, like Manchester or Portsmouth, the NHSP provides resources for large-scale investigations.

The NHSP can deploy crisis negotiators, bomb disposal units, and forensic analysts, but for the most part these towns lean on the state police for the everyday public safety services they can't fully supply, from responding to car accidents or burglaries to domestic disturbances. Many municipalities without officers on nighttime duty route emergency calls to troopers, even though in some of the northernmost points of the state, those troopers could be an hour away.

The elite squad at the New Hampshire State Police is the Major Crime Unit, composed of seasoned veteran detectives and a forensic support staff ready for deployment anywhere they are called upon in the Granite State. Major Crime is most often in the news as the team that leads homicide investigations, and they work with local and federal authorities on cases like kidnappings, bank robberies, or police standoffs.

While assaults and robberies can be prosecuted by county attorneys, in New Hampshire, homicide cases can only be prosecuted by the state's Attorney General's office. Given concerns about Lizzi's disappearance, the NHSP brought in the AG from the start. The level of coordination between the NHSP and the AG is critical to closing murder cases, with AGs involved even in the very early stages of an investigation, whether it be working with police at a crime scene, or responding to late-night calls to deliver emergency press conferences.

When the NHSP became involved in Lizzi's disappearance, their first step was to acquire her cell phone records. Investigators quickly confirmed the text messages between

Lizzi and Kat and between Lizzi and Brittany. The last message she sent to Kat was at 8:51 P.M.:"I'm at the outer door :)."

She sent one more text to Brittany at 8:55 P.M.— "You're so cute!"—and that was the final message on the record.

Around 9:30 P.M., Lizzi's iPhone had pinged a tower in Dover, indicating that, even if it wasn't in use, it was powered on and within range of that tower. It certainly appeared from the records that she'd gotten as far as the door to the Sawyer Mill apartments.

Armed with what they knew, the Attorney General's office called a press conference on Friday, October 12, at the Chester police station. The Marriott family joined officials from the state police and the FBI and Associate Attorney General Jane Young in seeking the public's help in finding Lizzi.

Young took the lead. She said there was no evidence that anything "nefarious" had happened to Lizzi, but that all possibilities were open. Wet, falling leaves and darkened, unfamiliar roads could have caused her car to veer into the woods, Young said. She added that helicopters were searching all of the routes Lizzi might have taken and that a nationwide BOLO for Lizzi's car had been issued.

Bob Marriott also spoke at the press conference and said that they planned to canvass popular college hangouts like Hampton Beach and off-campus bars with the hope of finding someone who knew something. He admitted the week's events had left him in a fragile state but that family and friends in both states had given him shoulders to cry on when necessary.

Acknowledging his greatest hope—that Lizzi had taken off on a whim and was now afraid to return because of the fuss she'd caused—Bob Marriott just said, "Lizzi, come home."

CHAPTER TWELVE

Good Cop

At the same time officials were holding their press conference in Chester, four plainclothes troopers from Major Crime—three men and one woman, all of them sergeants—were heading to Dover to follow up on their strongest lead. There they met up with a Dover Police Department detective with the plan of visiting Kat McDonough and Seth Mazzaglia at their apartment and talking with them some more.

Detective Jeff Ladieu called Kat's cell and asked if he could come over to ask more questions about Lizzi Marriott's disappearance. Kat told Ladieu neither she nor Seth was home because they were both at work in Newington. She said she would be meeting up with her boyfriend when he went on his break, and would be willing to meet with the detectives at Best Buy, where he worked. It was clear to the investigators that Kat didn't want to talk to them unless Seth was with her.

The five officers took a pair of unmarked cruisers from Dover to the Newington Best Buy. Ladieu went into the store by himself and asked a worker where he could find Seth Mazzaglia. He was directed to the video game section of the store.

Ladieu introduced himself to Seth as a state police detective and asked if he could borrow some of Seth's time to get more details about Lizzi Marriott's whereabouts on the evening she was last heard from. Ladieu then asked Seth if he'd be willing to accompany him to the Newington police station to answer questions.

"How long do you think it will take?" Seth asked.

"I don't know," Ladieu said.

Ladieu noted that Seth remained calm and friendly, asking his store supervisor if he could leave early from work. Kat, whose job at Michaels was across the street, arrived at Best Buy as Ladieu and Seth were preparing to leave. They all walked out the front door together.

The investigators phoned ahead to the Newington Police Department and obtained clearance to use two of the department's interview rooms for as long as they needed them.

Kat got into the car with Ladieu and Sergeant Sara Hennessey, the two officers who it had been decided beforehand would question Kat, while Seth got into the other car with Sergeants Joe Ebert and Brian Strong, who had been assigned to conduct his interrogation.

Seth said he recognized the third man in the car, Dover Detective Scott Pettingill.

"We met before," he said to Pettingill, "I remember you from when I applied for a job at the Dover Police Department."

———

Seth sat at a large table in a second-floor conference room at the Newington PD. When the two-car caravan arrived at the department at around four P.M., he'd been escorted to the room along with NHSP Sergeants Ebert and Strong and Detective Pettingill. He had no opportunity to speak with Kat, as she'd been led to a separate room on the first floor of the department along with the other two state cops, Ladieu and Hennessey.

Seth's back was to the room's door, and as he looked across the table at the three investigators, he realized he'd been in this room before under very different circumstances. The conference room had served as a classroom for some of the Citizens Police Academy classes he'd attended a year earlier.

Ebert spoke first, asking Seth if he had any objection to his recording their conversation. Seth said he was fine with it, and Ebert activated two small recorders he'd placed on the table between the investigators and Seth. Ebert asked Seth to repeat for the recording that he assented to the interview being taped. Seth confirmed that he did.

Ebert then asked Seth whether he understood that,

although he'd been driven to the department in a state police car, he was there voluntarily and that the door to the room was closed only for privacy. Seth said he understood the situation, and the officers then began asking him questions about October 9, the night Lizzi Marriott disappeared.

One of Joseph Ebert's areas of expertise was in crisis negotiations. He had to read people quickly and figure out which buttons would work best when pressed. Seth wanted to be a police officer, and there was an awkward earnestness to him. Ebert would use that. He wasn't going to treat him as if he were stupid or pound his fist on the table. Seth was acting like he wanted to help, so Ebert would let him help. He'd take the "good cop" approach.

For about an hour, Seth told the three men the same basic outline—that he'd arrived home from work around nine P.M., gone out for a jog, and returned at ten P.M.

Kat, he said, wasn't home at either point, and when she finally arrived at the apartment at midnight, she told him she'd been walking at a local cemetery because she thought Lizzi Marriott might be there.

Sergeant Ebert asked Seth if he'd received any phone calls that evening, and Seth said he had. Ebert then asked Seth if he minded if Sergeant Strong looked at his phone while they continued to talk.

"Yeah, sure," Seth said, pulling out his phone and punching the password on the keys, then handing the phone to Strong.

Ebert asked Seth if he believed something had happened to Lizzi Marriott.

"I don't know," Seth said. "I really don't."

If Seth was surprised by the directness of the question, he didn't show it. But what he said next got everyone's attention.

"I'm concerned that something might have, though, and that Kat is covering it up."

When Ebert asked what kind of cover-up he was concerned about, Seth's answer was even stranger. He suggested that Kat and Lizzi might have encountered an "aggressive prowler" while out walking in the cemetery.

Something bothered Ebert about Seth, and it went beyond the bizarre response he'd given to the question about Lizzi. It was something in the way he addressed the three officers, at once open and helpful but also glib and more than a little shady.

Seth's affect was off. He had a swagger that didn't match up with reality. He was a twenty-nine-year-old man working a part-time job at Best Buy. He'd tried to make small talk with cops by bringing up his failed police academy application. His girlfriend looked like a little kid and acted like Seth was the boss, yet Seth was talking about her as if *she* were someone who kept secrets from *him*.

Following what he would later say was a pure hunch, Ebert asked Seth to talk more about his girlfriend, Kat, in particular their sexual relationship. Without hesitation or embarrassment, Seth told the officers that he and Kat enjoyed rough sex, even going into detail describing the leather belts he liked to use to restrain her. He launched into a casual lecture on BDSM, explaining that he and Kat frequently took part in bondage, domination, and other kinky sex acts.

Ebert asked whether Seth and Kat had ever involved a third person in their bedroom activities. Seth responded that they had done so on several occasions.

"Did you have an interest in involving Lizzi Marriott in intercourse with Kat?"

Seth shrugged. "Down the road, maybe."

Seth's cell phone was now on the conference table in front of Sergeant Ebert. Ebert asked Seth if he understood the mechanics of how cell phones search for signals, how they "bounce off towers" when seeking to connect to the network. Seth replied that he didn't know much, but he'd heard it was possible to track a person's location using their cell phone.

Ebert then swung the conversation back to Lizzi, asking what Seth thought might have happened to her.

"I don't know," Seth said, "I could theorize and speculate all day, but I wasn't there."

"Seth," Ebert asked thoughtfully, "if something did happen to Lizzi, what do you think should happen to the person who committed that crime?"

"It would depend on what they did," Seth replied. "You know, the more extreme the crime, the more extreme the punishment."

"How about if it wasn't extreme at all?" Ebert asked. "How about if it was accidental?"

Ebert then told Seth that Lizzi's cell phone records put her in the vicinity of the Sawyer Mill apartments on the night she disappeared. Given what they'd just discussed about Seth and Kat's personal life, he said, he was worried that perhaps Lizzi had been harmed at some kind of "party gone wrong" at the apartment.

"Let me ask you this, Seth—understanding the type of sexual gratification that both you and Kat enjoy, do you think it's possible that's what happened that night?"

"My memory is good," Seth replied. "It's not a hundred percent. But how something like that could happen without me knowing or seeing or without someone saying, 'Hey, guess what happened in your apartment while you were running,' you know? Like, I . . . That's the kind of thing I might need a little air to think about."

"Yeah," was all Ebert said.

"That's—I—because if something like that happened in my apartment, I . . . that's . . ."

"Accidental, though," Ebert interjected, "I want you to consider that."

"And I mean what . . . okay," Seth stammered. "If it were an accident, what would happen to the person?"

The detective told Seth a story about a previous investigation he'd worked in which a man lied about having contact with a missing woman, when in actuality, that woman had died during sex with the man and another woman. Because the man lied at the outset, Ebert said, he faced serious consequences. No one believed him when he tried to explain later that the woman's death had been an accident.

Ebert's story was a fabrication, but he'd quickly formed a theory and hoped Seth would rise to the bait.

Seth nibbled, asking what happened to the people in the story.

"There were consequences for them," Ebert said, "for lying to us and not being truthful with us, in the front, but there weren't consequences for them in terms of what had taken place."

He paused to let that sink in.

"And it depends very much on how something takes place."

Ebert reminded Seth of the importance of being able to tell the Marriotts what had happened to their daughter, and he admitted that if something had happened to Lizzi, he would have to hold *someone* accountable for it. Seth said he did have suspicions, but was afraid of what might happen if he talked about it.

"Seth, here's the thing," Ebert said. "Before we go even one second further, I want you to . . ."

"I feel like maybe I should be asking for a lawyer," Seth suddenly blurted. "I don't want to be accused of something I didn't do . . ."

"Oh, hey, look—" Ebert tried to interrupt.

". . . that happened in my apartment," Seth said. "I mean that's literally what's going on in my head right now."

"Let me say this to you," Ebert was looking directly

at Seth. "If you told me, 'Hey, I want an attorney,' I would never tell you not to get one. If you told me, 'I want to leave,' I told you that you're here voluntarily."

Seth told Ebert that he wanted to be cooperative, but he was scared he was being accused of something. The cop reassured Seth he wasn't targeting him, he just wanted to know the truth about what happened that night.

Seth waited a few moments, seeming to weigh Ebert's words. His head was bowed. His leg bounced nervously on the floor.

Finally, he spoke.

"She's gone."

———

"She's gone, she's gone," Ebert repeated. "Now I'm not pointing anything at you. I'm just saying if she was here and there was some type of—something of *play* that ended with an accidental death . . ."

"Yeah," Seth muttered.

". . . if you had a suspicion of that, hey, now is the time to be honest with me and tell me that. And if you are telling me, 'I'm not going to tell you without an attorney,' I'm never going to—I'm not going to beat it out of you."

"Yeah," Seth repeated.

Seth then said it was possible that some of his friends might have been inside his apartment at Sawyer Mill without his knowledge, explaining he hadn't mentioned it previously because he was trying to protect them. He said he had exchanged text messages with those friends, but said he was not at the apartment when something may have happened to Lizzi. Seth then said he was concerned Kat might have been involved.

"If what I do know leads to Kat being locked away for a lifetime?" Seth said. "It would shatter me."

Seth told Ebert that there were things he knew but that he was scared of getting his friends in trouble, in particular, two friends who had come over to his apartment later that night. As he talked, Seth's earlier swagger seemed to melt, and he became increasingly agitated.

"I'm sorry," he said to Ebert. "I'm getting worked up. And I could probably use some air, but I really . . . I really . . . I really want to help."

Ebert said, "I know you do."

Detective Pettingill excused himself from the conference room and made sure he was out of earshot before pulling out his cell phone to call his own department headquarters in Dover. He told the shift supervisor to send a squad car over to Sawyer Mill to secure the entrance to Seth's apartment. The unit, he said, was a potential crime scene.

———

"Is there any way I can speak off the record, like, no record just for a few minutes? Is that possible?" Seth had been answering Sergeant Ebert's questions for two hours.

Ebert convinced Seth to leave the recorders running, and then Seth told him something new. He claimed that he sometimes suffered blackouts, which made him worry that he might have information that he couldn't access.

He then changed another detail of his story, telling Ebert that the night Lizzi went missing, he'd come home from work and put on his running clothes, but then blacked out. He said it wasn't just him and Kat in the apartment that night; another couple did come over, but much later.

"I think something did—something bad happened that night," Seth said, but he continued to claim that, since he'd blacked out, he couldn't get at the memory.

For another twenty minutes, Seth repeated his assertion that something bad might have happened at his apartment, but he couldn't remember anything else. He also told the officers his parents would be worried about his absence and perhaps he should leave.

Ebert posed a scenario to Seth. If Kat and this other couple were able to tell the police what had happened, he suggested, wouldn't it be in Seth's interest to do so now himself, rather than let others speak for him?

"And here's the other thing that should be of concern," Ebert added. "As I sit here, you're talking to a couple of guys from the state police and the Dover Police Department. When I left the debriefing this morning, there were a hundred law enforcement officers from across the country. The FBI is here . . . there is no stone that will be left unturned."

Seth posed a scenario of his own: If something had happened as the result of a "horrible BDSM-related accident," he asked, "what are the consequences? What happens to the people in it?"

Ebert told Seth that *if* he were able to help the police find Lizzi, he would have to answer for what took place, but that his cooperation would be taken into consideration.

"I don't want to walk out on the interview like I—I—but—I do—I do need air." Seth's agitation was ticking up a notch. "It's like there's this voice just screaming inside of me."

Ebert didn't want to lose him.

"Look at me, brother," he said, looking Seth in the eye. "You and I can take a walk outside, catch some air. We'll get a glass of water."

As they walked toward the door, Seth asked Ebert if Kat was okay. The detective assured him they were treating her in the same manner in which they were treating Seth.

———

NHSP Sergeants Jeff Ladieu and Sara Hennessey had been questioning Kat McDonough in a room on the ground floor of the Newington PD. They'd figured Kat might open up to another woman, so Hennessey had asked most of the questions. Kat didn't say much of substance and largely stuck to her original story.

While it was true that she'd had plans to meet Lizzi at the Sawyer Mill apartment, Kat told the officers, Lizzi never showed up.

Kat claimed that she'd looked for Lizzi outside the building for a while, and then headed on foot to a nearby cemetery. Her cell phone had died while she was in the graveyard, she said, which was why she didn't know that

Lizzi had texted her from the back door of the apartment building.

Kat said she spent several hours taking photos in an attempt to capture ghosts before returning to Sawyer Mill at midnight. Seth was home when she got there, Kat said, and they went to sleep like any other night.

Ladieu and Hennessey asked Kat to sign forms giving consent to a search of her cell phone and her apartment. Hennessey scrolled through the phone, past some texts from Darla, and pulled up a text in the Sent folder, dated October 9.

"Did you send this text to Lizzi the night she went missing?"

The message read, "Hey dahling i expected you a 10? i passed out and lost track of time. you still coming?"

Kat said she did send the text, and that she now remembered wondering why Lizzi never showed up.

"But the text was sent at 11:04 P.M.," Hennessey pointed out. "You said your phone died when you were in the cemetery and you didn't recharge it until you got home."

Kat stared blankly at Hennessey, then said she must have gotten the time wrong.

Ladieu excused himself and walked upstairs to the room where Seth was being questioned. In the hallway, he traded notes with Sergeant Strong about what each team was learning. Strong gave Ladieu the names of the other couple Seth claimed had come over to the apartment. They were working the angle in the other room that something sexual might have happened among them all, and he suggested the detectives ask Kat about it too.

Ladieu returned to the downstairs conference room around the same time Ebert took Seth outside for a breath of fresh air. He passed the couple's names to Hennessey, who then asked Kat if these friends had anything to do with what happened to Lizzi.

Kat began to shake visibly and the color drained from her face. When she spoke, it sounded as if her tongue had swelled, slurring her speech.

"I don't want to answer any more questions without talking to a lawyer," she said.

And just like that, Kat's interrogation was over.

———

Seth and Ebert stood in the cold, leaning against the building like smokers taking a break. Newington's police department occupies a modern building, set back from the road in a grove of trees. Seth gestured to an open area on the grass.

"That's where I saw the K-9 demonstration for the Citizens Police Academy," he said.

Ebert knew Seth was still trying to make some sort of connection to the investigator. His "good cop" technique was still working.

They walked back into the building and Ebert asked Seth to keep his voice down as they passed the area where Kat was being interviewed. When they returned to the upstairs conference room, Ebert picked up the thread of the question Seth had asked him earlier. He told Seth that the extent to which he would be held criminally responsible for what happened to Lizzi would be based on whatever information he provided.

"The only person who asked me that question . . ." Ebert began.

"Is someone who's done something," Seth finished.

"Exactly," Ebert said.

"I know."

Ebert asked Seth if he'd meant to hurt Lizzi Marriott on the night she disappeared.

"Well, no more than in the BDSM kind of stuff," he started, then added quickly, "If that's what happened . . . the intention . . . I certainly would not have meant to kill her."

Pushing a pen and paper in front of Seth, Ebert told him that, if he wanted to, he could draw a map to where Lizzi was located. Seth asked whether he would be taken to jail immediately if he told the investigators where she was, and Ebert told him not to make that assumption.

"Step one is 'Where she at? Where she at?' Let's get over the hill together," Ebert said. "Let's get over that, then let's work on 'What happens to me?' We'll get to that."

"Would I get to see my parents and Kat before going to jail?" Seth asked, suddenly sounding like a little boy.

"When you tell me where she's at and what happened, I will ensure that you get to see your parents tonight."

Seth picked up the pen and began drawing.

CHAPTER THIRTEEN

Peirce Island

Sergeant Joseph Ebert looked at Seth Mazzaglia's crude drawing of a map, which he understood depicted a location in Portsmouth, although Seth hadn't wanted to say it.

"Where did she go?"

Seth tapped a spot on the map three times.

"She went in the water there? Okay. How did she get there?"

Seth stared at the paper and said nothing.

"Seth, you just told me that a young girl is in the water right here."

"I know," Seth said softly.

"What's done is done," Ebert said. "There's no more stress now."

Seth didn't reply.

"Look at me, Seth," Ebert said. "You've come so far. You're telling me you put her in the Piscataqua River. There should be no more barriers. No more barriers . . . I'll tell you what, I'll trade you for exactly where."

Ebert pointed at the map. "Do you know where the salt piles are?"

He was referring to a prominent commercial landmark along the river—a mineral holding yard where mountains of rock salt is stockpiled for use on New England's winter roads.

"So you know what's on my mind," Seth said.

"Absolutely."

"My holding back is that part of me that does look out for my friends is still fighting," Seth said cryptically. "I do plead the Fifth on saying who or what . . . but I can't let her family go without the chance of finding her."

Seth then admitted that Lizzi Marriott's body was in the Piscataqua River. Ebert asked him point-blank how she got there, and Seth hesitated.

"Okay, how about this?" Ebert offered. "Where did her car go? I mean, you told me the hard part, man . . ."

"Yeah," Seth said.

"Don't hold me back on the car . . . There is absolutely no reason—there is no detriment to you from this car. The detriment to you could be that you told me where her body is."

Mazzaglia then told Ebert that Lizzi's car was parked in one of UNH's more obscure lots, the one tucked behind the agricultural program's greenhouses and horse stables at the far end of campus. Detective Scott Pettingill left the room once again, this time to call the university police.

Ebert walked Seth backward from the car, asking him again what happened to Lizzi before her body was put into the Piscataqua.

"When I pull her body out of that water—and I will—what am I going to see?"

Seth paused before answering. "Whatever happened in that time block, I can't remember."

"How about this? When you put her in the water, was she bleeding?" If she had been, Ebert knew, it would indicate her heart was still beating when she went in.

"No, not that I remember," Seth said.

"So I can assume that she died through asphyxia, strangulation?"

"I guess," Seth said. "I—I don't—I don't remember."

Ebert let a beat pass.

"Are you hungry, Seth?"

"Yeah, a little," Seth said. "I'm having dinner with my parents."

"I don't know if I can assure you of dinner with your parents, but I can assure you dinner. How's that?"

"I've lost a lot of people in my life," Seth said suddenly, raising his voice. "That's why I want you to be able to at least tell the family that we're searching for the body . . . I want you to be able to tell them that, because I know the pain."

Ebert pointed at the crudely drawn map.

"Do you know one hundred percent for certain that that's where her body went in the water?"

"Initially," Seth said. "Tides could have come in and out since then."

Ebert left the room to let the others know they were going on a field trip. It was 7:20 P.M.

————

Twenty minutes later, Sergeants Ebert and Strong, along with Dover PD Detective Pettingill, were getting ready to leave the Newington police station so that Seth could show them the places he'd drawn on his map. Seth requested his cell phone back, but when Ebert asked if he could hang on to it for a while longer, Seth agreed that he could.

Ebert asked if Seth needed to use the bathroom before getting in the car, and Seth said he did. Ebert asked him for a favor before he walked into the restroom.

"You need to look at what's in my pockets?" Seth asked.

"You got it, brother."

When Seth emerged from the bathroom, the four men climbed into the same unmarked car they'd driven from Best Buy to the police station, Seth up front in the passenger seat.

Ebert picked up the receiver on his car radio and signaled the dispatcher: "Ten-eight, one noncustodial." He hoped Seth would understand the code. They were transporting a subject, someone who was not in police custody.

They drove at a regular speed with no lights or sirens. Ebert told Seth he should "relax" during the drive. He made some casual conversation and then asked Seth who had gone with him that night to the location he'd drawn on the map. Seth refused to answer the question, adding he was "taking the Fifth."

The foursome's first stop was Sawyer Mill. The men saw a few police cars parked outside the building but no other sign of law enforcement activity. After a brief stop, Ebert asked Seth to direct him to the Portsmouth location he'd drawn. Before they pulled out of the complex parking lot, Seth pointed to an area in the back of the building, saying he had a flash of memory in which his friends were standing together before entering the building on the night Lizzi disappeared.

Ebert said he found it hard to believe Seth couldn't remember what happened in the apartment. As a road trooper, he said, he'd once seen someone die in a car accident.

"Seeing somebody die, unless you're a sociopath, you remember those details."

Seth didn't respond. The detective let it sink in for a moment.

"What do you suppose your mom would think," Ebert asked, "if I told her you'd tell me where [Lizzi's] body was, but you wouldn't tell me what the last moments of her life were like?"

In the passenger seat, Seth began to cry softly as Ebert pointed the car toward Portsmouth and pushed down on the accelerator.

———

In Durham, an officer from the UNH campus police picked up his radio. Lizzi Marriott's Mazda Tribute had been found in the parking lot behind the university's horse barn, exactly where Seth had said it would be.

———

Detective Timothy Burt of the Dover Police Department arrived at Sawyer Mill with investigators from the crime-scene unit around 8:20, the same time Seth was directing Ebert to Peirce Island. Having heard that Officer James Yerardi's cursory scan of the inside of the apartment the day before hadn't yielded any evidence, Burt circled the exterior of the building.

He saw several Dumpsters in the complex parking lot, including one in the rear of Sawyer Mill that looked like it hadn't been emptied in a few days. After contacting the building's owner, he secured the container, instructing his team that no one was to approach it or disturb its contents.

———

By the time they reached the access road to Peirce Island at about eight thirty, several Portsmouth patrol cars had blocked off the entrance. As the cops let them pass, Ebert said, "Seth, you see the law enforcement down here? You get the idea there's no changing things up now."

After they parked, Ebert asked Seth to show him what he'd done with Lizzi's body. Seth began to lose his composure again.

"I can't. I just want to see Skar."

Ebert let him cool off for a few minutes, and then Seth agreed to take the officers on a walk.

It was dark on Peirce Island. The temperature had

fallen, and Ebert lent Seth a jacket from the trunk of the car, a forest green state trooper's jacket with a badge on the breast. If Seth wanted to fit in with the police, to show him he was their equal in the investigation, he now looked the part. The question was, would he play the part?

Seth showed the detectives where he'd parked that night, saying he'd driven Lizzi's car from Dover to Portsmouth, but again refusing to talk about who had been with him. He led them down the path to the island's overlook, where he said Lizzi's body went into the water.

After a few minutes of searching the area, the investigators weren't seeing any obvious evidence of foul play.

At around nine P.M., Ebert and Pettingill walked Seth back to the car, where they continued to interview him. Seth wavered between claims of memory loss, hallucinations, and something he called "theoretical reconstructions" of the events of October 9. Finally, he landed on a new version of events.

Although he didn't know what actually happened that night, Seth now said, he did remember being inside his apartment and realizing that something was "not right."

He said he remembered seeing Lizzi, and that it looked to him like she'd been choked.

———

Ebert started the car and drove out of the Peirce Island parking area.

"I'd like to take a ride and go to the local police department so we can sit down, have a bite to eat, and continue our conversation," the sergeant said.

"I want to see my parents and Kat," Seth replied.

Ebert assured Seth he would make arrangements to call his parents when they arrived at the Portsmouth Police Department, and he asked Seth what he wanted them to know. Seth said he didn't want them to hear anything about rough sex or Lizzi's dying as the result of something bad, just that he was trying to do the right thing by helping the police.

Seth asked again about seeing Kat. "Even with you watching," he said. "I just want to see her, hear her voice . . . I want to see if the love is still there . . . I just . . . I risk my life for her . . ."

"I can work on that," Ebert told him before turning the conversation back to Lizzi.

"The last thing in the world I want to do is put words in your mouth," Ebert said, "but I think from what you said to me and feel comfortable saying is that's how she died. That she died from strangulation."

Seth replied, "Your guess is as good as mine."

When they arrived at the Portsmouth police station, Seth was led to a small interrogation room equipped with both audio and video recorders. Seth sat in the middle of the room with Sergeant Ebert sitting on one side of him and Strong and Pettingill on the other side, between Seth and the door.

"We're at a difficult point," Ebert confided. "And what you've told me is that Lizzi died in your apartment and that you disposed of the body. I don't know that there's much difference between being the one who physically caused her death or being just part of the act because those are the parts you're leaving out."

"Even if I say it was an accident," Seth said, "whoever out of that group who might have done that, you're not going to help them out that much."

Ebert responded sharply, telling him he believed Seth was lying.

Seth then claimed to have another recollection, telling Ebert that "the five of them" had all been in the apartment together, and that "everyone was excited before everything went wrong."

Ebert reminded Seth that investigators would be searching his apartment for evidence. Seth replied that his only concern was the cops letting his cat out.

"We didn't do anything," Seth insisted. "We panicked."

"You know what the sense I get from that is?" Ebert asked. "More and more I believe that—unfortunately—it was *you* who took this girl's life."

"We were all having fun and then an accident happened!" Seth cried. "I'm just trying to protect my friends."

———

During a break, the investigators escorted Seth to the bathroom, but this time they accompanied him inside. After asking what he wanted to eat, an officer went to get him a meal from McDonald's while the rest of the investigators ordered pizza.

When his interview at the Portsmouth Police Department resumed at around eleven P.M., Seth was edgy. He asked to see Kat again. This time Ebert didn't respond to the request and continued to ask him questions about Lizzi.

"Can I have a few minutes to breathe?"

Ebert offered Seth some "air," but instead of taking him outside, the officers walked him around inside the station. Seth continued to evade Ebert's questions. He looked hard at the door leading to the lobby and said he thought he might like to leave so he could go and see Kat.

"Please, Seth," Ebert begged. "I'm meeting with [Lizzi's] parents in a few hours. I have to give them an answer. They know something's going on. There's fucking police every-where, on the news, on the Internet."

They were frozen in place. It was the make-or-break moment.

"Please, Seth," he said. "Don't force me to go to them and tell them I don't know what happened."

Seth slumped. He wanted to see Kat, he said again. Ebert promised Seth that if he told him everything, he'd bring him to Kat. The detective then asked what he would say when he saw her.

"That I love her."

"What else?"

"I love her and it's all going to be okay somehow."

"Then let's do it. Let's do it," Ebert said. "You keep your end of the bargain, and I'll keep mine."

———

The story took shape slowly, with continued claims of memory lapses and blackouts, and then began to evolve and shift into a series of contradictory admissions, new iterations being spun each time Ebert asked Seth to go over it again.

Seth finally arrived at a version of events in which he admitted having been in the apartment when Lizzi died. First, he told Ebert that it was the *other guy* who'd killed her. They were having consensual sex, Seth claimed, and the guy choked her.

At around one A.M., Seth broke again. Lizzi had come over to the apartment to hang out, he admitted, and Kat had suggested they play a game of strip poker.

"One thing led to another," he said, and BDSM came into the conversation.

It turned Lizzi on, Seth claimed, and then he had intercourse with her while using a soft rope meant for sex play. When he climaxed, Seth said, "I pulled a little tighter and she began to seize."

Then Lizzi stopped breathing. Once they realized their mistake, Seth said he and Kat took Lizzi's things and got rid of them in different Dumpsters after dumping her body in the river.

At 1:40 A.M., Sergeant Ebert advised Seth of his Miranda rights, nearly ten hours after picking him up at the Newington Best Buy.

Ebert walked Seth back to the unmarked car for one more ride around the Seacoast. Seth pointed out the Dumpsters in which he remembered disposing of evidence. Seth told the troopers he was sorry and wanted Lizzi's family to know he was sorry.

Ebert told Seth that he was going to drive him to the Dover Police Department.

"I'd like to speak to an attorney if you're going to question me further," Seth said.

It was 3:21 A.M.

————

As the sun came up, search warrants were secured for a number of locations. Dover investigators combed Seth's apartment and the Dumpster behind the complex. In some trash bags they recovered household garbage and men's and women's clothes and shoes. They also found a single used condom.

In the meantime, the NHSP Major Crime Unit began scouring Peirce Island. They did a cursory search of the water but would need boats to do more. They did find something above the waterline of the rushing Piscataqua: Tangled on the weather-beaten rocks were several strands of sandy-blond hair.

CHAPTER FOURTEEN

Current Events

On Saturday, October 13, 2012, the TV cameras knew precisely where to be, even if the Marine Patrol didn't. Their boats chugged slowly off the shore of Peirce Island, an officer leaning over the rail to scan the water, even though visibility was limited to just below the surface. It was a solemn scene that filled onlookers with dread. Everyone knew the patrol boats had something to do with the disappearance of Lizzi Marriott, but there was no explanation for why they were so focused on this tiny area of water.

The motley islands and inlets along the Piscataqua River create a chaotic maelstrom of currents and whirlpools, all powered by some of the fastest-running water on the continent. The danger zones can be so turbulent that even the industrial tankers that navigate the river get shoved off course if they hit a rough patch.

The riverbed would also be a problem for divers. The currents surge with the tides, racing upstream and then rushing in the opposite direction with a powerful undertow. The Piscataqua runs very deep, and its bed is littered with lobster traps, mooring balls, debris from wrecked vessels of wood or iron, and other remnants of centuries of shipbuilding and piloting blunders.

The river's shoreline offers no refuge either. Sudden waves could effortlessly slam a diver into the sharp surface of dangerous rock formations that could get in the way.

But on the morning of Saturday, October 13, the biggest obstacle to the Marine Patrol search was the murky state of the fast-moving water, a condition that could last for a couple of days.

As he'd told Seth Mazzaglia it would, it fell to Sergeant Joseph Ebert to break the news about Lizzi to Bob and Melissa Marriott. At the Chester command center, he asked the parents to step into a private room. Melissa later said she knew right then what he would say.

Ebert told the Marriotts their daughter Lizzi was dead, and that her body had been placed in the Piscataqua River. The likelihood of recovering her was slim, he said.

Their first question was one any parent would ask— they wanted to know how Lizzi had died.

Homicide detectives understand from the start that telling families their loved ones have been murdered is part of the job, and they are well trained in setting their own emotions aside for the families' benefit. It's a task that doesn't get easier with time, but there is a sort of emotional muscle experienced cops call on for the task.

But *how* Lizzi had died—there's no training, no amount of time that made it tolerable to deliver that news.

It was Kat McDonough's boyfriend, Ebert told them. He then told them what Seth said had happened and said that evidence was still being collected.

"What about Kat? Is she under arrest too?" the Marriotts asked. It was a natural question.

"No," Ebert told them. But the investigation was ongoing, he explained, and they couldn't rule out one or more people also being charged.

Sergeant Ebert got up to leave Bob and Melissa Marriott alone in the room. A homicide detective understands that this moment is important too, that once the officer shuts the door behind him, a family is no longer learning about their loved one's murder. It's the moment in which they begin learning to live *with* it, and it marks them forever.

———

Assistant Attorney General James Vara announced the arrest of Seth Mazzaglia at a press conference that afternoon.

New Hampshire homicide prosecutors are notoriously stingy with details on arrests or motives or the strength of their case, in part because of strict state ethical conduct rules designed to ensure fair treatment of the accused, and also because they are involved in the case from the beginning and are as aware of the many perils of ongoing investigations as the police are.

Although they had not yet recovered Lizzi's body, Vara

told reporters, police and the AG's office had "credible evidence" that she was dead.

Vara said there was little else he could share because of the ongoing nature of the investigation, but he did drop a few bread crumbs for journalists to follow.

He confirmed that the activity off Peirce Island was related to the case. Pens furiously scratched spiral-bound pads, noting that the specific location must mean authorities had solid information about where she was dumped.

Vara also told them that Seth Mazzaglia would be arraigned on Monday in Dover District Court, not in Portsmouth, a hint as to the location where investigators thought the crime had occurred. Sawyer Mill is a hulking landmark in Dover, and a quick drive-by would quickly uncover the scene of detectives and technicians coming into and out of the building.

Finally, Vara said, the charge would be second-degree murder. This implied the death wasn't premeditated, but veteran reporters knew not to read too much into the second-degree charge; sometimes it was merely used as an opening gambit, with the state later seeking a first-degree indictment from the grand jury after an investigation turns up new evidence.

Without much to go on, reporters working the weekend shift needed to come up with stories that would sustain their outlets through Monday morning. Like a coordinated and hungry pack, newspapers, TV stations, and radio outlets turned their focus away from the slow-moving boats and instead focused on Seth Mazzaglia. Who was he? How was he connected to Lizzi Marriott?

It didn't take much effort to find enough material to fill the news cycle. A cursory Internet search uncovered the online dating profile of the man from Dover: twenty-nine, an actor and stuntman, someone who was "enigmatic." He went by the name of "DarkKaiser." Cross-checking this profile with other websites—darker, more deviant websites—a portrait of the man was painted in newsprint. Daily headlines were infused with a bold new vocabulary.

"BONDAGE"
"DOMINATION"
"SEX SLAVES"

———

Lizzi's former coworker Nate McNeal was crushed upon hearing the news of her murder and Seth's arrest. He pulled out his iPhone and texted the one person who might know something.

"Kat, please tell me you were ignorant of all this. And if you weren't, at least tell me why."

Kat McDonough never responded to that text.

The remembrances for Lizzi began that Saturday night. At the UNH hockey game, the Wildcats held a moment of silence. The president of the university issued a statement: "Lizzi was a new member of the university community and will be missed in our classrooms. Our focus now will be on supporting our campus community during this difficult time."

There would be grief counselors available on campus that Monday, the statement said. The president also expressed "shock" that the accused killer was also an alumnus of the school's theater program.

In Lizzi's hometown of Westborough, Massachusetts, a candlelight vigil was held at a public park. The event was organized in part by a stranger to the Marriott family, the Reverend John Taylor. That morning, members of his First United Methodist church had planned to drive from Westborough to New Hampshire to help with the search, only to learn it was too late. The Marriotts were not religious, but Taylor asked if members of his congregation could surround them in a prayer circle to ask for the Lord's comfort before the vigil began.

Lizzi's aunt and uncle, Tony and Becky Hanna, and her girlfriend, Brittany Atwood, along with a few family friends, joined Bob and Melissa and Lizzi's brother on the park's gazebo. Hundreds of people streamed in slowly to show their support. Many only knew of Lizzi through the news coverage but wanted to pay their respects. The park flickered from the growing light of handheld candles. Pastor Taylor asked for a prayer, and those gathered sang "Amazing Grace."

Bob Marriott summoned the strength to step to the microphone.

"Together we made an angel," he said, choking back his emotions.

He mentioned all of the law enforcement officials who

had spent the week looking for Lizzi, and he said he hoped they would be able to find her and bring her home. He thanked all of the friends and family who knew Lizzi, who had watched her grow into "an amazing young woman."

"Lizzi is a great tribute to everyone here."

Then, no longer holding his tears at bay, he said, "She is now home in heaven."

At that, Bob broke down into sobs, unable to continue.

Reporters covering the event asked for quotes about Lizzi from loved ones. A picture of an optimistic, adventurous girl with a bright future began to take shape. Those insights into who Lizzi was were the beginning of a story that would emerge over time, but it was a narrative that would never waver, no matter how many sources the press talked to in the weeks and months that followed.

"She was just a good girl. That's probably what got her in trouble," one family friend told a newspaper. "She was too trusting and she was beautiful. Those two things will kill you."

On Sunday morning, the Marine Patrol assessed conditions on the water before resuming the search. Even in the tumultuous waters of the Piscataqua, it was still possible that Lizzi's body was very close to Peirce Island. They had seen such things happen countless times before.

Often, when a person drowns, their lungs fill up with water, creating a heaviness that sinks them straight to the bottom. Then, after some time passes, gasses build and a breakdown of tissue takes place, releasing that weight and causing the body to pop to the surface like a cork.

But the suspect's statements made it far more likely that Lizzi hadn't drowned, that she hadn't been breathing when she entered the water. That meant their best chance was if Lizzi had gotten tangled in one of the natural or man-made traps that made scuba diving in the search zone so treacherous. Otherwise, there was little that would have prevented her body from being pulled out into the Atlantic.

That morning, the Piscataqua River saw gusty winds, an extra strong current, and rough chop. The Marine Patrol deemed it too dangerous for their vessels and divers to resume the search, so it was called off for the day.

Back in Westborough, the mood was somber at First United Methodist. Pastor Taylor knew the community tragedy had to be addressed. He dismissed the congregation's children to leave the main service for Sunday school early so he could speak freely to the adults.

"This evil act will not define Lizzi. We will remember her smiling and laughing," quoted the *Worcester Telegram & Gazette*. "That evil that befell her could not deny her soul for shining forever so bright. I know when Lizzi died, God's light was present. She knew she was loved. She wasn't alone."

It was then that he spotted Bob Marriott in the back row of the church's pews. No one had noticed him slip in. He was alone, his wife and son choosing not to venture outside their home. He'd never been to this church, but at the vigil the night before, the pastor's words had comforted him in a way he hadn't realized he needed.

Pastor Taylor said that Lizzi would see her parents and brother again in heaven. But for now, he asked the congregation to pray for Mr. Marriott.

It was then that the congregation followed Taylor's gaze and saw Lizzi's father in the back of the church. Without speaking, people sitting on either side of Bob hugged him. Everyone in the church turned around and raised their hands toward him in prayer.

"Get him through the day," Taylor called out. "Bear him up."

The tears were flowing freely now. Everyone shared in Bob Marriott's grief. Everyone shared the shock that such a random act of evil could happen to a family who lived among them.

———

On Monday, October 15, search crews were back on the water. Marine Patrol and the U.S. Coast Guard rotated four vessels to keep the operation going nonstop. They were using side-scan sonar and an underwater camera, but visibility was still poor.

Peirce Island, which had been closed to the public for three days, was now searched with teams led by cadaver-sniffing dogs. A New Hampshire State Police helicopter swept over the area looking for anything that seemed out of place along the shoreline.

In nearby labs, experts used computer modeling to

map the tidal patterns back to October 9, trying to project where Lizzi's body might have been taken. New Hampshire officials asked authorities in Maine and Massachusetts to keep an eye out for a body washing up on shore.

The public wasn't giving up on Lizzi either. A pair of seventy-year-old twin brothers, who claimed to know the craggy inlets of Portsmouth better than anyone alive, turned their morning walking routine into their own search, looking for signs of anything unusual along the shoreline.

At a press conference, Associate Attorney General Jane Young said that there were no plans to call off the search. She said they planned to keep on looking for Lizzi Marriott until they found her.

———

At Dover District Court, Seth Mazzaglia appeared on a TV screen for his video arraignment. He wore a gray county jail uniform, his hair disheveled. The charge was read.

Felony charges can only be tried at the superior court level, so no plea of guilt or innocence was entered. Seth was ordered held without bail and a probable cause hearing was scheduled for a few weeks later. He stepped away from the camera, not to be seen again in public for many months.

———

The marine search teams struggled through another day of rough conditions on Tuesday, but the waters were calm and the skies clear on Wednesday, October 17. Crews noted these were ideal conditions in which to search, and that it was probably their last, best chance of finding Lizzi's body. Multiple boats worked the area around Peirce Island, and helicopters circled above them, covering as much shoreline as their fuel tanks would allow. The effort yielded nothing.

———

On Thursday, October 18, the University of New Hampshire held an outdoor service to honor Lizzi. Again, Bob Marriott was there to represent the family.

In the days since her disappearance, Scott Chesney, an official with UNH Academic Affairs, had been in constant touch with the Marriotts. Lizzi had only attended the school for a few weeks, and although her hope had been to move to the dorms in the spring, she wasn't a resident student. Scott said that made her no less a part of the campus community. His own daughter was also a UNH student, so he empathized deeply with the grieving father. He was among the first from the school to offer his condolences.

"I know it's raining and I know you're off-campus right now," Bob told Scott on the phone, "but I want you to drive into campus, go to your daughter's room, and hug her as hard as you've ever hugged her. Tell her why she's important to you."

After the call, Scott Chesney did exactly that. He got into his car, drove to the dorm, and squeezed his daughter as hard as he could.

Students gathered on the large grassy hill outside the campus administrative building. As with all of the public remembrances, the crowd was mixed, with some who knew Lizzi and many more who had simply been touched by her story. In the crowd was also grumbling about some of the lurid details emerging in the press and of the unfair insinuations made about Lizzi.

She isn't here to defend herself, the crowd whispered. *It isn't right.*

Friends from high school and her time at Manchester Community College spoke about her sparkle and her kindness. The crowd heard from a boy she'd helped through a math class as well as from a young singer who'd performed with Lizzi in a chorus.

"There was a light to her. I can't explain it," one speaker said. "Lizzi's spirit is connecting everyone together. Even though she is not with us, she is living inside us."

The university president called Lizzi's death "heartbreaking" and praised the community for coming together.

Bob Marriott finally got up to speak, the swelling under his eyes visible from the back of the crowd. He put on another brave face as he paid tribute to his daughter, maintaining his composure as he spun tales about her life, her love of the ocean, and how much it meant to her to finally be studying marine biology.

He told the students that because she was no longer able to make new friends, those assembled should make that effort.

"Make a connection and spread the light that was

Lizzi," he said. "Please reach out to your parents and tell them you love them and the next time you see them, give them a giant hug."

Bob's voice cracked as he thanked the UNH community for caring about his daughter. He took a seat in a folding chair as the service reached its final act. The event concluded with music playing on a loudspeaker, a recording of Lizzi singing "Into the West," the Oscar-winning ballad written for the *Lord of the Rings* movies. But as he heard his daughter sing the lyrics, "Why do you weep? What are these tears upon your face?" he collapsed in sobs, his shoulders heaving and a handkerchief covering his eyes.

It was as if Lizzi's haunting voice were singing directly to him.

"The ships have come to carry you home."

———

The active search for Lizzi Marriott's body continued on the Piscataqua for weeks. By Halloween, there were boats making daily trips past Peirce Island hoping to find something. When contacted by the student newspaper at UNH in December, officials said that boats on the river were still keeping an eye out.

The tremendous effort put into recovering Lizzi wasn't solely for the benefit of her family. The Attorney General's office had a murder case pending trial, and they were missing the most important piece of evidence of all: Lizzi's body.

It is possible to win a conviction without a body. Some

lawyer might attempt to argue that there was no *proof* Lizzi was dead, but the defense had already stipulated to that fact.

The AG's office had been able to proceed with these kinds of prosecutions in the past, often because there was some biological evidence a person had died, like the discovery of incinerated human remains or the recovery of brain matter after a shooting. Although there was a statement from Seth, Lizzi's missing body posed other vulnerabilities in the prosecution's case, and the AG's office knew the defense would exploit them.

Without Lizzi's body, the state wouldn't be able to medically prove what had caused her death, wouldn't be able to prove that the manner of her death pointed to homicide, wouldn't be able to prove it hadn't been an accident, and wouldn't be able to forensically prove who her killer was.

Without Lizzi's body, it was undeniable what was needed for a conviction at trial: The state desperately needed Kat McDonough to testify as their star witness against her boyfriend.

———

There were times, after the police reopened Peirce Island, that Bob Marriott would drive there and walk to the same overlook where Seth and Kat had once watched the tankers pushing upriver, walk past the same tree the couple had claimed was magic.

Bob made the trip alone, as Melissa couldn't bring herself to spend any time gazing out across the water while her daughter was still missing. The winds blew harder and colder at the outlook as the autumn wore on. The salt air filled his nose as he scanned the coastline.

Any father would feel ambivalent. Any father would feel the opposing pulls of hope and dread as the search for his dead child stretched from days into weeks.

Lizzi had always wanted to live in the ocean. Now, it seemed, the ocean would be her tomb.

CHAPTER FIFTEEN

"Take Care of This"

Kat McDonough was devastated by Seth Mazzaglia's arrest. She had said many times that he was all she had in the world, and she didn't want to let him go. She left the Newington Police Department thinking Seth would be outside waiting for her. She went numb when she learned he had been arrested for Lizzi's death.

With their apartment closed off by police, Kat needed a place to go. She could not afford an apartment on her own and felt there was no way she could go home. In moving out, she had rejected her mother and disowned her father. If she went back, she'd have to face all that, and they'd probably make her pay rent on top of it.

Kat took the only option she thought she had available: She moved in with Seth's mother, Heather Mazzaglia, in Portsmouth. She thought she would only be there until

Seth got out on bail, but when that didn't happen, Heather said Kat could stay as long as she needed.

Kat's decision not to move home was heartbreaking to her mother, Denise McDonough. How could she not want to be with her family? Denise wondered. How much power did Seth have over her even when he was in jail? When would Kat stop viewing her as "Mother Dragon" and start seeing her as her mother?

––––––––

Seth had to decide who would represent him in court. Based on his income, he qualified for a public defender, but his father, Joseph, had some money and offered to pay for a private criminal attorney, one who could presumably focus more closely on his case. Seth met with both teams and was uncertain which one to choose.

Less than a week after his arrival at the Strafford County jail where he would be detained until trial, Seth was granted telephone privileges, and he called Kat at his mother's house. He explained his quandary, telling her he was genuinely conflicted about whether to hire the private attorney or take the public defender.

Seth seemed unsure whether the smart move was to go with a lawyer with many years of experience who "does murder cases for fun or money" versus the team "looking to cut their teeth on a challenge."

He told Kat to find a deck of tarot cards and do a reading to help him decide who should defend him against the murder charges.

"You don't even have to know the meaning," he told

her. "Just tell me which card comes up and I will know the answer."

Kat drew three cards, announcing the name of each as she did so. Seth sighed deeply.

"I'm going to go with the public defenders," he announced. "They seem a little inexperienced, but they really have their crap together. It really does seem like they're going to put everything they have into it to prove themselves."

Seth's voice turned sweet. He urged Kat to go to his father and to tell him to use the money he would have spent on his son's defense to send her to UNH, to help her finish her paramedic training, or to spend it on whatever she wanted.

Kat told him she thought the decision was a good one. She'd met with the public defenders and their investigators the day before.

"I really like them," she said, adding that she'd told them all about what had happened that night.

On October 15, 2012, Kat had gone to the local office of the New Hampshire public defender, where she met with three attorneys and a defense investigator, who escorted Kat into a private room and began scribbling notes.

The team noted that Kat was calm, very fluid and reflective, and seemed eager to help. Kat told them the story she'd earlier told the police—that she had been in the cemetery taking pictures of ghosts when Lizzi didn't show up—was a lie.

The meeting lasted four hours, with Kat recounting everything she could about Lizzi's visit to the apartment.

When it was done, Kat asked the lawyers if they thought she had helped Seth's chances of an acquittal, and they told her she had.

When she left, the four looked incredulously at one another. Kat had done far more than help Seth's chances. She had just incriminated herself in Lizzi Marriott's death.

———

After creating a twenty-five-page report from her hand-written notes, investigator Lisa Greenwaldt asked Kat to come back to the public defender's office and review her statement. This time, Greenwaldt wanted to get Kat's admission on video. Even if Kat later recanted her statement, they wanted an ironclad record of what she'd told them.

Many times, a witness will say one thing in a private meeting and something completely different at trial. The public defender's investigators interview hundreds of people each year in preparation for their many cases, and while it's not feasible to videotape all of them—especially as the investigators are most often chasing down reluctant witnesses at home, at their jobs, or in jail—the defense felt they had to nail this case down. But Greenwaldt didn't even know where the office video camera was stored. When she finally found it, she realized there were no blank tapes, and she ran to the store to buy some.

On October 17, 2012, two days after making her initial statement, Kat sat in the conference room wearing a cable-knit cardigan over a red T-shirt (one she'd likely purchased to wear to work at Target). Her curly hair was pulled back and she wore her eyeglasses. She seemed comfortable and friendly, even smiling and laughing during the discussion. She spoke freely about her sex life and what turned her on.

"I knew I liked being overpowered or tied up," she said, describing her proclivities in terms of a damsel-in-distress fantasy. "There was a certain amount of pain I actually liked."

Kat told them she'd worried that she was crazy for being aroused by bondage, thinking she was the only person in the world who enjoyed the fetish, until Internet research had dispelled any notion she was alone.

Kat said she and Seth purchased a variety of harnesses, each used for a different sexual purpose.

Greenwaldt would occasionally stop Kat to point out a passage in the report, and the two would agree on a slight edit. Kat would then pick up the thread again.

She told the investigator that she and Seth had been seeking a third person for a consensual, polyamorous relationship. They thought Lizzi could be that person, so they'd invited her over to have some fun.

Kat said the night began with the threesome playing strip poker. She giggled as she described how badly she'd been losing, ending up naked after only a few hands, she said, but Seth and Lizzi quickly caught up to her.

Kat said that the sexual electricity in the air led to kissing between her and Lizzi while Seth watched. Then they'd all gotten naked and started a game of Truth or Dare, which led to group kissing. Kat and Lizzi gave Seth and each other lap dances. Kat then straddled Seth and began to ride him.

Kat told Greenwaldt that Seth then turned and offered her up to Lizzi as if presenting a gift.

" 'If you want, you can do this,' " she quoted him as saying.

"She seemed to understand that?"

Kat nodded yes, that Lizzi did understand what Seth meant.

Lizzi lay on the floor, Kat said, and they each took turns having sex with her. Then, Kat claimed, Lizzi asked about the ropes and harnesses she knew they liked using, so Seth and Kat pulled their box of BDSM supplies from under the futon and helped her into a complicated harness that restricted her arms and applied pressure to her chest if she moved a certain way. Kat told the investigator how the harness was also designed to prevent its wearer from lifting her head. Asking Greenwaldt for a pen, Kat sketched out on the report how the harness fit on Lizzi, drawing straps that crossed at the breasts and wrapped around the torso.

That's when Kat brought up Seth's confession, saying the statement he'd given to the police was also a lie. Lizzi didn't die when Seth accidentally strangled her with a rope during sex, Kat said. There was no rope involved at all, no manual choking. The threesome had had sex for about an hour, Kat said, and Lizzi did die accidentally, but it was during an act called "queening."

Greenwaldt asked Kat to explain. "What is that?"

Frustrated that she couldn't quite explain it, Kat said, "I could show you."

She got out of her chair and moved around the table,

lowering herself to the floor. Greenwaldt moved the video camera to frame Kat in the viewfinder.

Kat knelt on the floor, her legs spread. She explained that, as Lizzi lay on the floor, Kat covered the other girl's mouth and nose with her vagina, squeezing Lizzi's head between her thighs. Kat demonstrated how being on her knees gave her leverage to rock back and forth, grinding against Lizzi's mouth to get the sensation she wanted.

As she lay there immobilized, Seth performed oral sex on Lizzi and then penetrated her for a second time. They both felt her squirm beneath them, which they attributed to her pleasure.

Kat said that she straddled Lizzi's face for between ten and fifteen minutes, about the time it took for Seth to climax inside of her and wash up in the sink. Kat said it wasn't until Seth returned from the bathroom that they noticed Lizzi was having some kind of seizure.

Kat said she moved off Lizzi and they both saw her face had turned purple. Even with their EMT training, they knew there was nothing they could do to save Lizzi's life, she said. They panicked and almost immediately began concocting a plan to dispose of her body.

That was the start of a series of events, Kat said, which ended with her and Seth dumping Lizzi Marriott in the Piscataqua River.

Lisa Greenwaldt kept the camera rolling as she took more notes, the defense investigator still amazed not only by what Kat was saying but by how she was saying it.

At no point during the videotaped interview did Kat get emotional about the death of her former coworker and supposed friend, or express any contrition for the role she described having played in it. Instead, she projected an easy calm, a casual happiness. It was just what Seth's defense team had been hoping to capture.

————————

The Marriott family was only partially satisfied when Seth Mazzaglia was arrested. They knew it was Kat Mc-Donough who had lured Lizzi to the apartment. They knew Kat was complicit in her death or, at the very least, in covering it up. They knew she'd helped bring their dead daughter's body to Peirce Island and had dumped her into the water as if she were a piece of rubbish. They knew she'd taken measures to obstruct justice and protect Lizzi's murderer.

Why isn't Kat McDonough in jail? they asked New Hampshire investigators time and time again.

Detectives gave largely unsatisfactory answers. They urged patience. The investigation was still ongoing. *Give us time to pull all of the pieces together*, they said.

Even with the families of victims, police almost always keep their cards close to the chest. It's an essential tactic designed to keep them in control of all the information around a case.

If a cop tells a grieving widow her husband was shot with a .22, for instance, there's no telling with whom she might share that information. Keeping that detail secret could mean that only the killer knows the caliber of the pistol, making it valuable evidence. But a sharp defense attorney might get that evidence excluded if he could prove the widow had talked about it with her neighbors.

The New Hampshire State Police was being coy. The absence of Lizzi's body loomed large over the entire investigation, which meant they already had to rely on other avenues to get what they needed to secure a conviction. Hanging an entire prosecution on a confession is a dangerous proposition. Confessions are recanted or ruled inadmissible all the time.

Having Kat on the street was good for them, they knew. Seth was calling her frequently, and even though inmates know their calls are recorded, they often slip up.

It was of little consolation to the Marriotts, however. They wanted swift justice, but the NHSP knew time was on their side.

———

Seth and Kat carried on as if they were in a typical long-distance relationship. Kat was able to e-mail him at the jail, and though he couldn't e-mail back, he wrote her letters.

When they spoke, it wasn't in the voices of their BDSM personas. The tone was soft and shyly romantic. Sometimes Kat sounded dreamy. She told Seth that she couldn't imagine a world without him, and he told her the same. During one call, he started telling her how he was trying to fix things so Kat could have access to his bank account.

"Wow," she said in a teenaged voice, aglow with puppy love.

Seth said he'd been coming up against some logistical walls because the two of them weren't married.

"They keep on asking: 'What's your marital status? Single? Married? Divorced?' I keep wanting to say, 'Married, and this is my wife.'"

Kat then asked him why they couldn't be. They discussed it some more and talked themselves right into an engagement.

"We can figure it out, and I say let's do it," Seth exclaimed. "I'm all for that!"

Seth told Kat he'd been researching how to get married in jail, but that it would take him at least a week to get the information through the proper channels. She said she would start doing research too.

Seth also said he was glad Kat had brought up the idea, conveniently disregarding that he had been the one to do so.

"I have been trying to figure out how to approach you with it . . . We are on the same wavelength, I guess. It's nice."

At that, Kat giggled, her voice taking on the tone of a blushing schoolgirl.

Seth apologized that he couldn't give Kat a proper wedding, one with all the trappings. He was distraught he couldn't get down on one knee and give her a ring, he said. Kat reminded him she already had a ring, the ring that he and Darkheart had given her nearly a year earlier. He told her, his voice dripping with confidence, that it would all work out for the two of them in the end.

"We are a couple who can find a way. We are the aberration. We may have to set some records here, but we are the aberration."

When they hung up the phone twenty minutes later, Kat was no longer Seth's girlfriend. She was his fiancée.

And that was good for Seth.

———

Ryan Bachman was Seth's cellmate, his "bunkie." He was tall and gaunt, his appearance hinting at the heroin addiction that had landed him in the Strafford County jail.

Bachman played chess with Seth often; they were equally matched. But Bachman found his bunkie to be a bit of a curiosity and more than a little bit annoying. Seth's reading material was always about fantasy and mysticism. He spent a lot of time reading about magic spells and the afterlife in a copy of the Egyptian *Book of the Dead*, and he talked about his interests constantly.

Bachman was okay asking Seth for a game of chess, but he knew better than to tell the guy he shared a cell with for twenty-four hours a day that he thought Seth was crazy.

In stark contrast to Bachman's cadaverous appearance, Seth was slowly putting on weight. After many months of training for his dream job in law enforcement, now his face and body were rounding out. Seth blamed it on the anxiety medication the jail's doctor had prescribed for him. But if the pills played a role in slowing down his metabolism, they didn't keep his thoughts from racing about his case.

"They have these two witnesses," Seth told Bachman,

referring to the couple who had visited the apartment the same night Lizzi Marriot died. "If something happened to them, if they were gone, they wouldn't have much of a case left."

Bachman took this to mean Seth wanted these witnesses killed, and that he was looking for someone to do the job. Seth knew Bachman was going to be released relatively soon, in late December, and he asked his bunkie if he knew someone who could follow through. Bachman told Seth he might.

The assassinate-the-witnesses plot soon disappeared, however, in favor of a new scheme. Seth said he had an elaborate plan for escape, but he'd need Bachman's help when he got on the outside. Seth talked incessantly about the plan, and Bachman thought he might go crazy himself listening to it.

It wouldn't be hard, Seth told him again and again. All Bachman had to do was obtain some explosives, two guns, two getaway cars, disguises, fake passports, and a boat.

The plan was for Seth to wind up in the medical unit, which, by his measure, had the weakest security in the jail. (Bachman knew the medical unit was in reality one of the most secure places in the facility, but he'd quickly learned that there was no use in refuting Seth once he was on a roll.) Seth said that once he was in the unit, he'd bolt through the emergency exit, use explosives to blow open the fence, and then shoot his way out of the detention center with the guns Bachman would have procured for him. Once on the outside, Seth said, he'd need disguises and at least two cars to escape. He'd drive away to a boat that would take him and Kat out to sea, and then travel to a country with no extradition agreement with the United States.

The first time Seth told him about his elaborate plan, Bachman said he just rolled his eyes. It had a wild impracticality to it, just like his earnest fictional short story about kidnapping the president's daughter at an ATM. Bachman didn't even play along until Seth started talking about money.

Seth said he had about one thousand dollars in his personal bank account, the account that Kat would soon have access to. Seth offered to give Bachman all of it. He told his cellmate that, upon his release, Bachman was to parlay that one thousand dollars into five thousand dollars by buying drugs and then reselling them on the street. Bachman would then use the five thousand dollars to purchase the things Seth needed to execute his escape plan.

Seth suggested a hunting store that had a good selection of firearms and said pipe-bomb supplies could be purchased at Home Depot. As a show of good faith, he said, he'd have Kat deposit fifty dollars into Bachman's commissary account, which she did shortly after their conversation.

It might have been a crazy plan, Bachman thought, but it seemed like an easy thousand-dollar payday.

Kat had been calling Roberta Gerkin for days, trying to set up a meeting. Since Seth's arrest, Roberta had also been trying to get ahold of her.

Kat wanted to meet outdoors, while Roberta insisted they meet somewhere inside. Even after all that transpired, Kat could not let go of the idea that the psychic could somehow harm her. Everything between them was fraught.

Kat relented. When they finally met up in Portsmouth, Kat was visibly nervous.

Roberta asked her what had happened with the police, and what had gone wrong. Kat told Roberta that she and Seth had first made up a story that Lizzi never made it to the apartment, but the cops didn't buy it. Kat said she'd had to improvise a little. She said that, together, she and Seth had come up with a backup story in case no one believed them.

"I think it's going to be played up as a sexual thing gone bad."

Roberta pressed for more details, but Kat didn't seem to want to talk anymore. She told the psychic that it felt like Anay was trying to take over her body.

"It just sucks sitting here knowing that there's the *actual* truth." Kat shook her head. "Darkheart and I are probably the only ones who will ever really know, and that's it."

Roberta said that she needed to know what that truth was. The whole Lizzi incident was affecting her psychically, she claimed. People were pointing fingers. It wasn't fair to Roberta or to her boyfriend, Paul Hickok. The police had been questioning her. They thought she knew something, that she'd had something to do with it.

Of course they knew something. The couple the police were looking for was *not* the rope fetishists Darla and Eli, the ones who had seemed on the verge of having an orgy in the Lair. Those two never showed up that night. It had been *Roberta and Paul* who came over and saw the aftermath of the night's festivities. They were the couple summoned to Sawyer Mill in the middle of the night. It was Roberta's and Paul's names that Seth blurted out during his interrogation, and their names that spooked Kat so much during hers that she asked for a lawyer.

It had to be clear to Kat that anything Roberta said to police now would make them look bad. "Say you were never there," she commanded.

Roberta reminded Kat that she *had* been there. Roberta said the cops could prove she and Paul had been at the apartment. They had their cell phone records, paired with tower pings.

"Then say you never went *inside* the apartment." Kat told Roberta to say no one had answered the door, so she and Paul had just gone home, and to tell the same story to Seth's lawyers. It will help him beat the charges, Kat said. It would bring Seth home to her.

Kat said she was going to marry Seth so she could invoke marital privilege and not have to testify against him.

"It's a bad feeling," Kat confessed. "I would lie. I would lie for him."

That was all Roberta needed to hear. She ended the conversation and walked away, confident Kat had no idea that Roberta was wearing a police wire.

———

Around quarter of eleven on October 9, Roberta reached for her cell phone only to see that she'd missed two calls. They were from Seth's cell phone, both coming a minute apart. She had texted with Seth earlier that night and told him her psychic powers had been sensing trouble ahead for him, that he should be cautious. Might he have been ringing her to discuss her premonition? The phone buzzed in hand, the third call from his number in the past three minutes.

"Something's wrong!" It wasn't Seth. It was Kat. "You have to come over!" Kat gave no more specifics, but the urgency in her voice moved Roberta into action. She grabbed Paul, and the two of them rushed to the car. Five minutes later Roberta texted back, "We are on our way."

At 11:11 P.M., Roberta phoned, saying she was pulling up to the front door. Kat ran downstairs but in her haste forgot her keys and locked herself out of the building. With Seth's cell still in her hand, she called the apartment telephone and asked Seth to let them in. Kat told Roberta that Seth wanted her to park in the more secluded rear lot, and said he'd come down to meet them there.

When Seth appeared at the back door, Kat went to his side and whispered something. His eyes darted around the lot, and he grimaced when he saw Paul. Roberta said she took the look to mean he had not expected her to bring her boyfriend.

Seth looked directly at Paul Hickok and asked, "Can you keep a secret?"

"It depends on what the secret is," Paul later recalled replying.

The foursome walked up together and opened the door to the apartment. On the floor was the body of a young woman, her head disguised beneath a pair of plastic shopping bags. The woman was lying on her back, nude except for a pair of blue thong underwear.

Roberta and Paul would tell authorities Seth went to the futon next to where the body lay and sat with his head in his hands. Kat was slumped to the floor in the kitchen gulping little sobs with her back against the stove. They reported Seth kept saying over and over that he had "gone too far" and "things got out of hand."

Paul demanded to know what had happened. Seth told him he'd blacked out. "'When I came to, she was already on the floor with the bags over her head,'" Paul quoted Seth as saying.

Roberta knelt before the nearly naked woman on the floor. She took out a box cutter from her pocket and used the razor to cut through the knot on the plastic bags, then pulled them off. She saw the face of a woman she didn't know. The head was purple, and there was a very distinct ligature mark around her neck. Roberta and Paul both searched for a pulse but couldn't find one.

"You should call an ambulance," Paul said.

"It's too late," Seth reportedly said.

"They can help."

"It's too late."

Paul looked at Seth. "You need to do the right thing here and call the police."

Roberta interjected. "You can call the police," Kat would later remember her saying, "*or* you can take care of this yourself."

Seth nodded. "If something happens to me, you two need to take care of Kat."

"No!" Kat screamed suddenly from the kitchenette. "I can't lose him!"

Paul told police he thought he was giving Seth a shot to set things right and that he'd better take it.

"If you don't call the cops, then I don't know you," Paul said directly. "I don't ever want to see you again."

Seth said he thought he would call an ambulance, Roberta claimed, but then he went back to saying that "he'd gone too far, he'd gone too far."

Sensing the situation wasn't going to get any better, Roberta and Paul left the apartment. Neither of them called the police.

A few days went by. On Friday night, an officer came to the door of their Rochester apartment with questions about Lizzi Marriott. Roberta and Paul said they didn't watch TV, so they were initially unaware of the search for the missing college student. But when they finally heard the news that morning, they agreed they'd contact the authorities. They said Paul had just come home from work and they were about to call the cops when—in a stroke of serendipitous timing—the police arrived.

Roberta agreed to wear a wire and meet with Kat in hopes of eliciting some kind of incriminating statement about that night. She attempted the sting on three other occasions before Kat committed witness tampering by telling Roberta to lie to investigators.

Roberta Gerkin and Paul Hickok were now valuable resources for the investigators. They were also prime targets for someone looking to get away with murder.

CHAPTER SIXTEEN

Bishop's Vacation

Seth Mazzaglia's jailhouse plan was becoming increasingly intricate the longer he thought about it. He told Kat McDonough that, while his own statement to police was "damning," her story about queening could probably counter it.

"But to give us the clout we need," he wrote in a letter to her, "Paul and Roberta must leave or die appropriately."

Seth was remarkably candid in all of his letters. His phone calls were recorded, but whatever he put in writing was private. While corrections officials read all of the incoming mail, searching it for contraband like drugs or pornography, outgoing mail is rarely examined. Envelopes have a printed warning that say it has been mailed by an inmate and its contents have not been evaluated.

In his letter, Seth said he saw two options for getting

rid of Roberta Gerkin and Paul Hickok. The first would be Roberta committing suicide ("or is made to look as if she did"). Three to five days after her death, he wrote, a note would be released to the police and the media. Seth would compose it for Kat to transcribe on a computer. The note would "show Paul for the animal he is and puts blame where blame is due—on him and her."

Seth told Kat to have someone she trusted distribute the anonymous letters in case the police were following her.

The second option called for someone to run Roberta off the road. Once her car was wrapped around a tree or tangled in a guardrail, he wrote, "Someone gets out, stabs her to death, gets back in the car. All drive off."

Seth said that Eli, Darla's boyfriend, might help, but more likely he would have to provide Kat with some muscle recruited from inside the jail. Kat would then wait three days after Roberta's death to release a note implicating Paul in Lizzi's murder. That's when Kat would pretend to panic, go to Seth's public defenders, and get a bargained immunity deal to testify against Paul.

In addition to his hit man plans, Seth was also writing letters to Kat about his escape plans. The jailbreak was designed to coincide with the hit on Roberta. He used several chess-related terms as a code. He was "Bishop," Kat was "Queen," and Bachman was "Castle," although he later came to refer to him as "Murphy," as in Murphy's Law: *Anything that can go wrong, will go wrong.*

Seth named his escape plan "Bishop's Vacation."

Seth wrote that Castle/Murphy would fill Kat in on

the details of how to get it done, but he would need her to do some additional legwork. He directed Kat to look at the security and screening measures for trains, buses, boats, and cruise lines. She'd also have to find a way to get them both fake IDs and passports.

Together, Seth wrote, they'd have to choose a country to go to that allowed for immigration without asking too many questions. He liked the idea of New Zealand, but thought it had an extradition agreement with the U.S.

"I hear Australia fits this and is far safer than Singapore, Thailand, or Africa where I'd need a shotgun and luck to protect you from rapists and killers every week," he wrote.

Seth's instructions to Kat were to read all of his letters, make notes in code, and then hide her notes. She was told to then take his letters and "annihilate" them by tearing them up and flushing them down the toilet.

———

Seth sent Kat a six-page letter with the heading "Revised Version of the Night." In the margin, he wrote she was to memorize the letter and repeat its contents to investigators in her own words, then destroy it.

According to this revised version of the events of October 9, 2012, Lizzi came over, had some apple cider, and the three of them pondered what to do. Seth suggested either a movie, Dungeons & Dragons, or, "jokingly," strip poker. Lizzi thought about it and told Seth and Kat to get a deck of cards.

They played a couple of hands and everyone was losing

badly. Lizzi, the letter said, had her eyes on Kat the entire time. Once everyone's clothes were off, the stakes changed, and the person with the winning hand got to make a request. Seth's request was for the girls to make out. This escalated into soft fondling and fingering. Kat pulled out their box of tricks and, holding up some ropes, told Lizzi she could make requests involving the restraints. Lizzi's eyes lit up and the game was forgotten.

" 'You guys are into that stuff?' " Lizzi asked in the version Seth now described.

Seth wrote that he then demonstrated a single rope harness on Kat. He even drew in the margin a diagram of how this harness would have been worn: a cross-your-heart configuration that lifted the breasts. Seth said he'd slipped around Kat and grabbed on to the harness while he did her from behind, a game he called "light rodeo." In Seth's story, Lizzi was so turned on by what she saw that she'd asked to join in and had pulled a length of cotton rope out of the box and asked if they'd ever tried choking each other.

"I seem surprised," Seth wrote, his letter mixing present tense with past. "You looked to me to lead."

They'd told Lizzi they had, and that the act was called "breath play."

Lizzi said she'd heard her classmates talk about it, and that she'd always wanted to try it but it seemed too dangerous. Seth told Lizzi it was a good idea to engage in any new play slowly and carefully, he wrote, so Lizzi had asked if they could try it.

Seth wrote he'd told Lizzi that, in order to try breath

play responsibly, they'd have to use a safe word. Their safe word would be "teddy bear."

In the real world, Seth had never used a safe word with Kat. But in this elaborate jailhouse letter, he acknowledged it was a standard BDSM practice.

The revised version went on to claim that Lizzi was willing let Seth put the rope around her neck like a collar. He'd started off light, he wrote. He'd pulled the rope for three to five seconds and released it; when she recovered, he pulled again. After each tug, he asked if she was okay. She said yes each time. He asked if she wanted him to do it again. She said yes.

Seth's letter was rich with erotic detail. Lizzi's nipples were hardening and her skin was flushed, he wrote. In the margins, like stage directions, Seth kept a running description of Kat's reactions to everything going on in the narrative: when she was curious, when she was nervous, when she was excited.

Lizzi escalated the game, Seth wrote, and he detailed how she'd asked to wear a harness while Seth used the rope some more. The sex games went on and continued to get more extreme. The only break in the action was when Seth said he left the room in order to text Kat discreetly and to ask her whether they were going to his mother's to finish painting. This innocuous detail was likely added to explain one piece of evidence the prosecution might use against him.

The letter to Kat concluded with descriptions of how things became more and more elaborate, ending with a scene like the one Kat had described to investigators, where Kat sat on Lizzi's face as Seth penetrated her. Though, in this version, Seth mentioned checking in frequently to see if Lizzi was all right. Each time she said she was, he wrote, and each time she urged them to keep going.

"After a bunch of checks," he wrote, "we all agree it's safe and relax to enjoy. A bit later, we finish."

Kat dismounted and Seth pulled out. It wasn't until then that they'd noticed Lizzi's face was purple and swollen, her eyes rolling up and fluttering. She was having a seizure and her body rocked in a way that they'd confused with pleasure while they were having sex with her.

The pair used the knives from the box to cut her free. Lizzi was unresponsive but had a pulse and was breathing, Seth wrote. Afraid of how the situation looked, they panicked. Instead of calling the police, they called Roberta. Moments later, she arrived with Paul Hickok. Lizzi was alive, but the rope marks looked bad. Someone suggested calling 911 to save her, but Paul took charge.

" 'Too suspicious. Cops will blame us,' " Paul's dialog read in Seth's new script. " 'If we don't want to go to jail, we have to kill her and hide the body.' "

The group was in shock as Paul ordered Seth to grab the rope and finish Lizzi off. Seth wrote that he froze, and Paul said, " 'Fine,' " and did it himself.

Seth tried to grab his shoulder to stop him, but Paul delivered two quick punches to Seth's head, which knocked the third-degree black belt out cold on the kitchen floor.

While Seth was unconscious, he wrote, Roberta and Paul yelled at Kat to help them gather all of Lizzi's belongings. Paul wrapped Lizzi's body inside of the cloth tarp they'd been using to paint at Seth's mother's house while Roberta grilled Kat on what Lizzi's car looked like and where she'd parked it.

Kat was huddled in the corner, afraid of all these people in her home, Seth wrote. She overheard them conspiring to leave the Mazda at UNH in the secluded spot behind the horse barns.

Seth stirred on the kitchen floor and awoke just in time to see Paul hoist Lizzi's lifeless form over his shoulder. Reminding Seth he had the upper hand, Paul said, "If we talk, you die."

Then, in a more threatening tone, he said, nodding toward Kat, "If you talk, she dies." He and Roberta then took the dead girl and disappeared into the hallway.

Stunned, Seth and Kat drove around to clear their heads, Seth wrote. They cruised aimlessly southbound, finding themselves at the overlook on Peirce Island. That was the place they'd always liked to go to talk things over. They stayed until three in the morning and decided that, in order to keep themselves safe from Paul, they had to fabricate a tale to explain what happened to Lizzi.

The product of weeks of jail cell contemplation, Seth believed this story answered all questions and tied up every loose end in their previous statements. As with the other letters he'd sent, Seth ordered Kat to "rip + flush—burn—annihilate" the document.

250 KEVIN FLYNN AND REBECCA LAVOIE

———

In November 2012, the judge in Seth's murder case denied a motion by local newspapers to release court documents filed under seal at the time of his arrest. The prosecution opposed making the affidavits public, saying that releasing the information would give witnesses a chance to tailor their own statements and "aid potential suspects to avoid prosecution."

Clearly, investigators were not done with Kat Mc-Donough.

Seth's mood remained upbeat while he was in County and Kat was on the outside. The day of his cellmate Ryan Bachman's release was approaching, which meant Bishop's Vacation was approaching as well.

Kat wrote to Seth every day and visited him twice a week. She said she was still in love with him, and she had collected all the paperwork for their marriage. She thought everything that Seth did in jail was designed to protect her.

The police hadn't questioned Kat since the night of Seth's arrest, which made it easier for her to believe it when Seth would tell her that their hopeless situation was bound to work out. They would be that one couple in a million that made it through a challenge like this, Seth assured her. Darkheart and Skarlet had done it before; they would do it now.

"You'll be okay. We can do it with Mr. Castle's help," he wrote to her. "We can do it."

As the time drew closer to Bachman's release, Seth wrote to "Skarlet, My Love," giving her an additional set of instructions.

"It is a backup in case everything goes wrong . . . Trust my judgment, accept Murphy's help and all this will be rendered mute [*sic*]."

The letter explained certain rituals for how to "reset and recall past lives." If the escape plan didn't work, Seth wrote, they could return to the Veil together. Darkheart and Skarlet would commit suicide at the same moment, shaking free from their mortal coils and joining their family of personas in the Otherworld.

Seth wrote that their deaths and rebirths should ideally take place within seconds of each other, no more than an hour at the longest. But the rituals he set out could help Kat gather enough energy so the metaphysical tether between their spirits could be extended for three to seven days.

"The energy needed will be easy for you to gather— just potentially a bit unsavory in flavor."

There were two rituals, he wrote, one a "lesser" and one a "major," each providing different amounts of power.

The "lesser" ritual involved the seduction of her brother. Kat was to approach him while he was in front of the TV playing video games and straddle his lap. When he tried to speak, she was to take her bare breast from under her top and shove it into his mouth.

Writing about this bizarre ritual, Seth's prose read less like an instruction manual for black magic and more like a lusty romance novel or a *Penthouse Forum* letter.

" 'Please,' you say as the bulge in his pants chafes between your legs. He relaxes into the press of your flesh against his lips, his body."

He wrote that Kat should grind on her younger brother, then ride him until "his body tenses and his heat washes into your womb."

When she was done, Seth wrote, Kat was to lick the ejaculate from her brother's penis and say, "Happy Holidays."

The "major" ritual Seth detailed was more low-budget porno. It called for Kat to pose as a party girl from Craigslist and show up for a fraternity party at UNH. He even dictated her costume, writing that she should wear a low tank top, high skirt, dominatrix boots, studded collar, and no panties.

"Come in," the imaginary frat boy would say at the door. "Want a beer?"

"Nah—I'd rather just get rolling."

Kat would be escorted to a room reeking of cigarette smoke and booze, where ten guys would be waiting in a circle. She was to take off her clothes and dance for them. Next, she would pick one guy, and "blow him hard and fast." Once he was finished, Seth wrote, Kat was to go to the next guy in the circle, straddle his lap, and slip him inside of her.

"To another pair of guys you gesture and say, 'I still got 2 holes open.' "

Seth described in detail how the trio would forcefully take her. They would all climax, and Kat would turn to the others. "4 down, 6 to go," he wrote.

Dictating these rituals was not merely an exercise for Seth in writing prison pornography. It was the penultimate sexual power play over his Willing.

For what purpose would Darkheart goad Skarlet into incest and gang rape? It was a question that many would ponder months after he'd put pen to paper. Was it Seth's closing perversion? A final humiliation? A tactic designed to ensure her commitment to "Bishop's Vacation"?

Or perhaps it was designed to serve a different purpose: to steel Kat's resolve for the "final ritual" Seth would dictate from behind bars.

The one in which he would command Kat to kill herself.

————

Kat went so far as to prepare a suicide note. In it, she apologized for the grief she had caused.

"I thank you for all the kindness I have been shown, but my spirit comes from another pantheon and I grow tired of the human race. My love and I are going to try again in another life."

Kat asked that her mother and her friend Jill divide all of her belongings between them. She hoped that whatever money she had in her bank account would be donated to the ASPCA and that someone would be willing to take care of Raven, her cat.

————

Ryan Bachman was released from Strafford County jail on the morning of Christmas Eve 2012. Before he left, Seth gave him a package to deliver.

Bachman went directly to the Michaels store in Newington to find Kat. He knew what she looked like because Seth had pointed her out to him during a visit.

The store was full of last-minute holiday shoppers. "Castle" passed "Queen" the packet he'd been given by "Bishop." It contained instructions on where she should get "vacation" supplies. There were also magazine clippings of women in different hairstyles she should try out as potential disguises. The package contained everything she'd need to help Seth make his elaborate jailbreak.

Kat turned Seth's bank card over to Bachman as instructed. She was to wait for him to return once he'd parlayed the money into enough to fund the escape.

Bachman took the card straight to an ATM and drained the account of nearly one thousand dollars in twenties. He went directly from Newington to urban Lawrence, Massachusetts. Bachman then spent Christmas shooting heroin, courtesy of Seth Mazzaglia.

Not long after Bachman fled with the bank card, two detectives entered the store asking for Kat. When they found her in the aisle, they asked her to put her hands behind her back.

"Kathryn McDonough, you're under arrest for hindering apprehension."

They took her out of the store in handcuffs.

PART FOUR

DISCIPLINE

These violent delights
have violent ends.

—WILLIAM SHAKESPEARE,
ROMEO AND JULIET

CHAPTER SEVENTEEN

Gross Injustice

On Christmas Day 2012, Denise and Peter McDonough were at the office of attorney Ryan Russman trying to secure their daughter Kat's release. Her arrest had been a big story on a slow news day, her booking photo posted all over the place. In it, Kat was dressed in a black hoodie and T-shirt.

What little the press knew about the events of nearly three months earlier, on October 9, swirled around anonymous sources and innuendo: that Lizzi Marriott had died of suffocation or strangulation, that Kat was Seth Mazzaglia's live-in girlfriend, and that Seth's profile was all over a number of fetish websites. The papers were somewhat restrained in the way they presented it, but it wasn't a stretch to read a different headline between the lines of the newsprint: *"Coed Dies in Kinky Three-way Gone Wrong."*

Kat was to be arraigned via video link from the jail in Dover by a judge sitting on a district court bench fifty miles away. The prosecutor was seeking fifty-thousand-dollar bail, but Russman thought the amount would be knocked down to something more reasonable because Kat didn't have a criminal record. Her parents might not have to put up a lot of cash—maybe 10 percent of the amount, he said—but they'd have to put up their house as collateral for the bail bondsman.

The house? thought Denise. The mother of three later said she had finally decided she'd had enough with her marriage and had been planning on moving out. If there were a lien against their house, that would surely complicate divorce proceedings.

"What would the charges be?"

Everything was under seal, so they had no idea what the cops had on Kat. The state would want to know whether she'd lied to police, the lawyer explained, whether she'd destroyed evidence, or whether she'd told anyone else to lie for her. He went on to say that any charges against Kat would likely be felony level and come with the possibility of considerable prison time.

"Will she be charged with killing Lizzi?"

Russman didn't know and wouldn't fully know until he'd seen the paperwork . . . which could be weeks away if it were still held under seal. The charges presented at arraignment might not be the only ones filed, he explained. A probable cause hearing, which nearly all defendants waive, would be scheduled. The state would likely take the case to a grand jury. There, the lawyer said, the prosecutors could seek indictments on whatever new charges they wanted. A grand jury might fail to indict, but it was unlikely.

What authorities might learn about Kat's role in Lizzi's death would greatly shape the charges she'd ultimately stand trial for, Russman told the McDonoughs. Prosecutors could ask the grand jury to indict Kat for conspiracy to commit murder. If there was evidence that Seth was taking the fall for something Kat had done— or had done something at Kat's direction—she could face her own second-degree murder charge.

On December 26, Kat McDonough awaited her turn in front of the video camera, just as Seth had nearly three months earlier, while her parents, grandparents, and other relatives waited anxiously forty miles away in the Derry gallery for her appearance on the video monitor.

Kat was one of several detainees facing arraignment that morning. The county attorney introduced the judge to the parade of prisoners, who ran the spectrum of legal entanglements: drunk driving, shoplifting, domestic violence, outstanding warrants. The judge took pleas on the misdemeanors and pushed them into the system. Bail was discussed for those with felony cases that would be kicked up to superior court.

The gears of the machine stopped as the county attorney relinquished his place at the table and made way for a homicide prosecutor from the New Hampshire Department of Justice. That's when Kat, wearing a red county-issued jumpsuit, was called upon.

If this were the Disney musical based on Kat's life, this moment wouldn't have been the showstopping dance number. It wouldn't even have been the "woe is me" solo tune. It would have been Kat sitting alone on an empty stage, still and silent as the floodlights dimmed and died. Then the spotlight would have come on with a *clunk*, so bright she would shield her eyes, while sudden screams of disharmonious notes from the orchestra pit swelled.

It was a moment of reckoning, the first of several to come.

The man standing in front of the judge was Assistant Attorney General Peter Hinckley. He told the court that Kat McDonough faced two charges of hindering apprehension or prosecution, and conspiracy to commit hindering apprehension or prosecution. He said Kat had lied to the cops about where she was on October 9.

"Ms. McDonough made an intentional attempt to disrupt the criminal process," Hinckley said. "Lizzi Marriott's body has not been found in no small part because of Ms. McDonough's participation in the alleged conspiracy."

The bail amount was reduced to $35,000 in cash or corporate surety bond. If Kat were to make bail, there were two conditions placed on her release: She must refrain from any contact with Seth Mazzaglia, and she must live at home with her parents.

When questioned by the press, Bob Marriott said his

family was pleased to hear of Kat's arrest, that it was a good sign that the process was moving forward. When asked what he knew about Kat McDonough, he said, "I never heard of her name before Lizzi went missing."

Officials assured the Marriotts that the investigation was still ongoing. They were still looking for more charges against the accused, still seeking to learn if others were responsible. They were also still searching for Lizzi's body.

In their hearts, the Marriott family hoped for much more than the justice in front of them.

———

The McDonoughs began putting together the resources to pay Kat's bail, although they were unsure if they could get the money or even if Kat was willing to come home if they did. Denise decided that if her daughter did make bail, she would also stay in the house after all, to make sure Kat was taken care of.

Kat agreed to the bail terms of living at home and being chaperoned by her parents if she went out of the house after six P.M.

Out of earshot of Denise, family friends in the theater community listened to Peter talk of how disappointed he was in his daughter. He was taken aback by the sexual nature of her secret lifestyle, calling it "sinful." The people he talked to later claimed that Peter openly wondered whether it would be best to leave Kat in jail.

Denise, however, was happy to finally have her daughter—her best friend—back in her life. Things were quieter than they had been before Kat moved out. Everyone seemed to be walking *around* Kat, whose eyes were always looking at the floor or away from whoever and whatever was in front of her. Her father was less confrontational. The things he said that had once been sharp enough to catch her delicate feelings were shrugged off, left unchallenged. Kat no longer took the bait.

Denise took Kat with her to her pottery studio to help out and so she could keep an eye on her daughter. When there wasn't anything to do, she would let Kat paint on canvases or ceramics. As a girl, it had always been one of her favorite activities, but now, as Kat sat in a corner of the studio with a brush in her hand, there was no joy in her eyes.

Kat stared blankly at the pieces she slopped with acrylic. Denise thought she looked like she was moving her arms like a marionette and wondered if maybe that was because, for so long, someone else had been pulling her strings.

Kat was forbidden from talking about the crime with anyone, including her parents, lest they run the risk of being subpoenaed themselves, but Denise held out hope that her daughter would open up about her relationship with Seth.

It was only a matter of days before Kat's darkness began to lift, and she finally spoke to Denise.

"Oh my God, Mom. The things he did to me . . ."

Denise was overwhelmed when she heard what Kat's life had been like with Seth—although she wasn't completely surprised. She'd been afraid of what kind of power a grown man could have over a teenager with daddy issues. And the way she'd observed Kat behave once she'd moved in with Seth bore many of the hallmarks of abuse. But she was horrified to learn the abuse had been sexual, emotional, and psychological.

Given the complexity of Kat's case, Ryan Russman referred the McDonoughs to a colleague better suited for such a challenge.

Attorney Andrew Cotrupi was aware that the state didn't have the body of the victim, and the physical evidence they'd collected was worth almost nothing without context. The state was technically required to indict a defendant within ninety days or drop the charges if there was no probable cause, though the ninety-day maximum since Seth's arraignment had passed, and prosecutors still hadn't produced an indictment against him. Instead they'd asked the judge for an extension, citing the time-consuming complexities of their investigation. Prosecutors had so far received two extensions, the latest giving them until April 2013 to indict.

Cotrupi believed that if the state was postponing an attempt to get an indictment, it was because they didn't want to risk a grand jury shooting down whatever case they'd stitched together so far. It had been decades since the New Hampshire Attorney General's office had lost a homicide case, but this could very well be the one that broke the streak. But there was no way prosecutors wanted to pursue a conviction on second-degree murder against Seth; they wanted an indictment for first degree.

Cotrupi also knew something the state did not yet know, which was that Kat had given a videotaped statement that could raise significant doubt with a jury about Seth's culpability. Without Kat recanting this statement in front of the jury, an acquittal for Seth was a strong possibility. Kat was now the most important component of the state's case—maybe the only case they had. Plus, Kat was in possession of key physical evidence the state didn't previously know about. While negotiating with prosecutors, she'd turned over an envelope filled with hundreds of bits of paper. The pieces were what remained of Seth's jailhouse letters to her.

Kat had torn them up, but she'd never burned or flushed them as Seth had commanded. She'd instead hidden them in a windowed envelope. Unbeknownst to prosecutors, the remains of these letters had been in police storage after the seizure of Kat's things.

Cotrupi, Kat, and Denise had been allowed to search the items, and Kat knew exactly which box the envelope had been in.

The letter containing Seth's instructions for her suicide rituals was still in one piece, wrapped up inside Kat's sleeping bag. When Denise read its contents, she'd reflexively made a sign of the cross over the letter, as if to exorcise the devil from it.

The attorney general wanted to turn the heat up on Kat, to force her into a cooperating-witness role by giving her more stick than carrot, but Cotrupi knew that most of the state's bluster was bluff. Kat was too important to their chances of getting a conviction against Seth. He knew the state couldn't charge Kat with more, regardless of her actions before and after Lizzi's death, because in New Hampshire, neither the charge of accessory to murder nor of conspiracy to murder are prosecutable offenses.

Instead, the state would seek a felony charge of witness tampering for Kat telling Roberta Gerkin to lie to the cops (which they had on tape, because Roberta had agreed to wear a wire). Adding that on meant Kat could face up to eighteen years in prison.

It was a high-stakes game of legal poker. But Cotrupi knew his client held all the cards.

It was three P.M. on Valentine's Day 2013, a year after Kat McDonough ran away from home to move in with Seth Mazzaglia. Kat and her mother walked into a closed courtroom at the Strafford County Superior Court in Dover. Attorney Andrew Cotrupi was with them.

The trio was spotted by a curious reporter who happened to be at the clerk's office waiting for a decision on another matter connected to the case. The reporter found Kat and Denise—but not Cotrupi— sitting on a bench in the otherwise empty courtroom. When asked why she was at court, Kat simply said, "My lawyer told me I can't say anything."

The journalist checked the court docket. At three P.M., an ex parte meeting with a judge had been scheduled. The listed attendees included none other than the state's attorney general, Michael Delaney. Another participant was Andrew Cotrupi. The only information on the docket was a note that the meeting concerned a "grand jury matter."

The following day, Kat was spotted again at the courthouse, her visit coinciding with what reporters knew were grand jury proceedings. Neither Corrupi nor Assistant Attorney General Peter Hinckley answered questions as they left.

In early April, Kat was indicted on a single charge of witness tampering as well as on two counts of hindering prosecution. Strung end to end, convictions would put Kat behind bars for up to twenty-one years, but no one was talking about her serving that much time. She'd obviously struck a deal with the state.

The terms of Kat's plea bargain did not sit well with Lizzi's family. They understood that Kat was going to be the cornerstone in the state's case against Seth, but the Marriotts were enraged that these three charges were all that prosecutors could lay on her.

They couldn't believe the limits of New Hampshire law, which prevented Kat from being charged with conspiracy after the fact, nor was there enough evidence to convince a jury that Kat had known Lizzi was going to be murdered when she lured her former coworker to the apartment. Kat also couldn't be charged for dumping Lizzi's body in the river. In New Hampshire, abuse of a corpse is only a misdemeanor.

Weren't there others involved? the Marriotts asked. *Wasn't there a couple that knew Lizzi had been killed but did nothing?*

In New Hampshire, the prosecutors explained, there

is no legal duty for a person who witnesses a crime to report it, even if that crime is murder. And Roberta Gerkin and Paul Hickok had been cooperative with investigators since they'd first surfaced as key figures in the case.

The Marriotts were in no mood to speak to reporters after Kat's indictment was announced. The family's lawyer released a statement blasting Kat for betraying Lizzi's friendship, stating that the Marriotts were hopeful more information would come to light allowing stronger charges to be filed against Kat.

"It is the family's opinion that Ms. McDonough, or any other individuals who are ultimately found to be involved with Lizzi's homicide or the conspiracy to frustrate the investigation of the homicide, bear both a moral and legal responsibility for Lizzi's death as well as the family's ongoing anguish over their inability to provide their daughter with a proper burial."

———

A week later, on April 22, 2013, the court published Seth Mazzaglia's grand jury indictment for first-degree murder. There were two first-degree charges, each offering alternate theories of the crime. One accused him of strangling Lizzi Marriott, and the other said he used physical force to strangle her before, during, or after a sex act. It would be up to a jury to decide if he was guilty based on which of these two theories they believed.

A first-degree conviction meant life in prison without the possibility of parole. There was also a lesser charge of second-degree murder included in the indictment, stating Seth showed "extreme indifference to human life." That would likely mean twenty-five years to life. There were also some lesser charges associated with the cover-up.

This time, the Marriotts were satisfied with the results of the indictment. But they also knew the arrest affidavits under seal would be released to the press, and Seth's assertion that Lizzi died in a consensual sexual liaison would become public. In a lengthy written statement, the family called Seth's ploy "as predictable as it is reprehensible." They said Seth and Kat's own actions proved Lizzi wasn't a willing participant.

"If Lizzi's death was truly accidental, it defies common sense, and the smallest speck of human decency, that Mr. Mazzaglia would then place her body in the Piscataqua River with the intent that it never be recovered."

————

On July 24, 2013, Kat McDonough pleaded guilty to all the charges against her, waiving her right to a trial. The terms of her plea dictated that most of her ten-and-one-half-to-twenty-one-year sentence would be suspended if she testified against Seth at trial. For her role in the death of Lizzi Marriott, Kat McDonough would serve just one and one-half to three years in prison. With Seth's murder trial still months away, Kat would already have served a large portion of her sentence by the time she'd take the stand.

In the days leading up to her sentencing, Kat was increasingly short-tempered around the house, anxiety about her pending incarceration showing through.

"This is something you need to do," Denise would scold her daughter gently. Kat would breathe deeply and agree.

Kat's mother and grandmother took her shopping for a dress to wear at the sentencing hearing. They wanted her to look serious and appropriate but feminine. They selected a simple burnt orange dress paired with a light gray cable knit cardigan, and discussed taming Kat's curly hair with an army of bobby pins. The whole endeavor felt like selecting clothes for a funeral.

At the sentencing, the Marriott family got their chance to confront Kat. Nearly two dozen of Lizzi's loved ones showed up, many wishing to give victim impact statements in open court. They declared Kat's sentence "wimpy" and a "gross injustice."

Both of Lizzi's grandmothers testified.

One said, "My sleeping hours are nightmares, and my waking hours are worse."

The other told Kat she must do something positive with her life after prison because she owed that much to Lizzi.

Brittany Atwood wept during her statement, saying she'd been haunted for months by the belief there was something she could have done to stop Lizzi's murder. She said her girlfriend was too pure to have seen the evil in Kat.

"No one will ever compare to her. No one will ever make the same impact on this world like Lizzi did."

Bob Marriott slumped behind the podium, trying to keep his emotions in check. He said he ached because he could not say good-bye to his baby. No matter how many times he talked to Lizzi from the overlook on Peirce Island, it would never be the same thing.

"You had the chance to do the right thing," he said to Kat during his statement, "to try to help, to do something heroic. Your failure in that moment is why Lizzi is not here to live out her life."

Even Judge Marguerite Wageling expressed wonder at the brevity of the negotiated sentence. In response, prosecutor Peter Hinckley told the court the plea was a result of mitigating factors, including the "manipulative" nature of Kat's relationship with Seth.

Before deputies cuffed her, the judge read Kat the riot act.

"But for your cowardly and selfish actions, Elizabeth Marriott would be alive, and this family would have the body to lay it to rest," she said from the bench. "But for you, they would have that peace, and you will carry that around in your conscience for the rest of your life."

Although she walked away from her sentencing and was taken to the state's prison for women, this was not the closing curtain on the story of Kat McDonough. The next eleven months would set the stage for the final drama, with Kat playing the lead. And as with any piece of theater, the success of the show would depend on a great performance from its star.

CHAPTER EIGHTEEN

The Gauntlet

Opening arguments for *State v. Seth Mazzaglia* were scheduled for May 2014, nearly ten months after Kat McDonough's sentencing.

The attorneys whom the tarot cards had convinced Seth to choose were public defenders Joachim Barth and Melissa Lynn Davis. In a small state where just two dozen homicides occur each year, only a handful of lawyers can claim extensive experience in defense at murder trials. But since very few homicide defendants in New Hampshire bankroll private attorneys, Seth's initial impression that his team was green and untested wasn't accurate. He was right, however, when he guessed Barth and Davis would fight doggedly on his behalf.

The ace up their sleeves was the videotaped statement from Kat, in which she said she'd been the one who smothered Lizzi during a consensual sex act. Seth and Kat may have believed they fought side by side in other worlds and other dimensions, but in this trial, they were destined to be adversaries.

The only possible conclusion was for one of them to carry the blame for Lizzi's death. The lingering trouble for the defense was that, at least for the moment, there were recordings of both Seth and Kat taking responsibility for the crime. They had to bring the number of confessions in play from two down to one.

Barth and Davis filed a motion to suppress Seth's confession. They argued Seth wasn't read his Miranda rights until 1:40 A.M., about nine hours into his interrogation. Key to the constitutional argument was whether the suspect believed he was "in custody." Although Sergeant Joseph Ebert repeatedly told Seth his interview was voluntary, Seth's legal claim was that he felt he wasn't free to leave to see his parents or his girlfriend and had been coerced into talking.

The defense also wanted any evidence discovered as a result of Seth's interrogation suppressed as well. If the confession was illegal, they argued, then any evidence obtained from it would be fruit from a poisoned tree.

The state responded with transcriptions showing the dozens of times that Ebert had asked Seth whether he understood that he could walk out of the interview. They highlighted the hours of cordial and noncoercive conversation they'd had—Ebert's "good cop" technique.

There were exigent circumstances, as the police were searching for a missing person, the state claimed. Prosecutors also underlined the many times Seth bragged about his own law enforcement training, that he'd even noted that the very interview room in which police first talked to him was where he'd learned about Miranda rights.

After two days of hearings, a judge gave the defense a partial victory. He ruled that investigators had not read Seth his Miranda rights in a timely manner, as is required by the Constitution. All of his statements about throttling Lizzi with a rope during his orgasm would be inadmissible, as would his confession about how Lizzi's body was dumped into the river and how the rest of the evidence was disposed of. His surrogate apology to Lizzi's parents was also suppressed.

The ruling did not suppress the entire interview, however. The judge essentially stopped the clock about three hours into it. The judge determined the state could use everything Seth said up until 7:20 P.M., just before they left the Newington police department to drive to Seth's Dover apartment and Peirce Island. This meant prosecutors could still use Seth's map as well as his statements that he'd put Lizzi in the river and his disclosure of the location of her SUV.

Although the majority of Seth's interview was suppressed, the evidence collected after it was not. By 7:20, Dover police had already secured the apartment, UNH campus police had found the Mazda, and the trio of detectives knew Peirce Island was the likely place the body had been dumped. There were also the independent statements from eyewitnesses. Even after stopping the clock, the judge ruled that all of that evidence would have eventually been recovered through the course of the investigation.

The defense also filed an unusual second motion. They planned to argue that Seth had been trying to protect his girlfriend from prosecution, and there were select statements he'd made after 7:20 they wanted to use at trial. Assistant Attorney General Peter Hinckley bristled, arguing if a statement is inadmissible for the prosecution it should be inadmissible for the defense.

The judge disagreed. His ruling allowed the defense—and only the defense—to cherry-pick which of Seth's late-evening statements the jury would hear.

————

After the case had bounced around from court to court for various hearings, the judge for *State v. Mazzaglia* was assigned. It would be Steven Houran.

On the eve of the proceedings, both sides argued over whether Houran should admit sealed evidence about the victim, Lizzi Marriott, into the trial. The nature of the evidence was not disclosed in open court, but the public defenders argued that what it implied about Lizzi's behavior or character was critical to their case.

In this final battle over what was in and what was out, Houran sided with the prosecution, determining the evidence about Lizzi was irrelevant and prejudicial. The nature of that evidence has never been made public.

————

Jury selection began on May 14, 2014. When Seth appeared in court, he looked very different from the photos that had been plastered in the press a year and a half earlier. His weight always seemed to fluctuate, but even when he'd been in court three months earlier he'd looked fit, almost chiseled. As his trial began, Seth now looked bloated, like a version of himself that had been left in the sun to melt.

His features were rounder, his eyes sunken. Instead of a suit, Seth walked in wearing a dress shirt and tie beneath a black vest—the same kind of vest he'd insisted on wearing on stage. Whatever look he thought it afforded him, it wasn't working. Among the press corps, there were whispers that Seth looked like a steakhouse waiter or a parking valet.

There was no set time frame for jury selection, but voir dire—the questioning of potential jurors—went on far longer than anyone expected. It took two weeks to find twelve jurors and four alternates. Hundreds of prospects came through the courtroom and were dismissed one after another. There were reservations on both sides about finding a jury that could honestly weigh the evidence without being influenced by the salacious facts of the case.

Those present got a preview of each side's trial strategy by listening to the lawyers' voir dire questions. Assistant Attorney General Peter Hinckley quizzed prospective jurors on whether they might prejudge Lizzi Marriott for choices she made in her life. He also asked whether they might understand why someone like Kat McDonough could give two different versions of how a crime occurred. On the other side, defense attorney Joachim Barth asked potential jurors if they could understand why someone who was innocent might lie about a crime in order to protect someone else. He also wanted to know whether potential jurors believed someone whose sexual preferences included pain would be inclined toward violence in other aspects of his or her life.

Judge Houran asked prospective jurors whether they could sit through a trial in which BDSM would be a prevailing theme. Most told him they could. Houran also asked whether they had been exposed to media coverage of the case or had been influenced by it. There were many who answered yes to one or both questions.

———

Unsurprisingly, interest in the trial was enormous among the press. Those seeking media credentials included a half dozen television stations and the prime-time network news magazines *48 Hours* and *Dateline NBC*. At least five daily papers and the Associated Press sent reporters— sometimes multiple reporters—and requested access for their still photographers. The demand was so great that Houran ordered the media to form a pool.

Each day the papers would take turns providing a photographer, who would share his or her pictures with all of the outlets. There would be a single audio/video feed from the courtroom for each of the TV crews to plug into, and one of the network shows that had a robotic two-camera rig offered to run the feed. A live stream of the proceedings was hosted on at least twenty websites, and reporters live-tweeted the trial "gavel to gavel" from the gallery. Space was made in a nearby office for an ad hoc media center, where journalists could tap into the video, edit tape, or do their writing. It was large enough for two dozen people, which cleared space for even more media in the courtroom.

Houran's orders to the media included some standard protocols, such as permitting no pictures of the jury and allowing no interviews to be conducted inside the courtroom except during recesses, after he'd left the bench. There was also another, more unusual order imposed on the media. The judge prohibited any video or still photography of the Marriott family in court or even outside the courtroom in the hallway, nor were reporters allowed to ask the Marriotts questions at all until the trial was concluded. Houran said the order was designed to preserve the family's privacy.

The order rankled some in the media. There was a large chasm between taking someone's picture and harassing them. And if a family member did something notable, for instance if someone had to be removed from the courtroom for shouting epithets or fainting, the press felt that should be fair game for coverage.

The reporters complained to each other that Houran was making a special exception for the Marriotts based on sympathy and not legal reasoning. What legal expectation of privacy was *any* spectator entitled to in an open courtroom? Why *this* victim's family and not others?

The reporters knew they could appeal the judge's

order, but they also understood how raw all of the emotions were, so no one had the stomach to do it. There would be no victory in winning—or even making—that argument, especially not in the eyes of the public.

The result of the order was that each morning, the still and video photographers gathered in the hall to take shots of Seth exiting the elevator and walking into courtroom 2 at the Strafford County courthouse, then would stand silent and frozen as the Marriott family entered the hallway and marched somberly to the same door.

―――――――

In courtroom 2, the podium in the well of the court from which attorneys examine trial witnesses usually faces the bench, but it is spun 90 degrees twice during the trial, so that lawyers on each side may directly address the jury during opening and closing arguments. Peter Hinckley walked to that podium with a stern look on his face. It was an expression the AAG wore daily, and it fit him better than his suit jackets, which were all too large at the shoulders to begin with and would become even more so as he lost weight during each trial; colleagues noted that he'd get wound so tightly that he'd eat nothing all day.

If there wasn't a reason for him to leave the courtroom during a recess, Hinckley wouldn't; he'd just pace around the well and in front of the empty jury box with his hands folded across his chest. To onlookers, it seemed like the whole weight of the world was upon him. He later told colleagues that, during this trial, he felt like it truly was.

Hinckley, a veteran attorney out of Boston College Law School, was known in legal circles for his straitlaced demeanor. He was also somewhat shy, an unusual trait in a homicide prosecutor. It seemed some kind of cosmic joke for him to draw a case that centered on BDSM culture, something he told colleagues he knew little about. As he prepared to conduct his research, Hinckley was unsure how the State of New Hampshire would feel about his spending taxpayer dollars on an encyclopedia of alternative sexual practices.

Jury selection had taken nearly two weeks, so the trial began on May 28, 2014. During his opening argument, Hinckley's tone was intense, impassioned, and at times angry. He called Seth Mazzaglia a monster. His descriptions of how Seth killed Lizzi Marriott were explicit and brought the Mazzaglia family to tears.

He did his best to frame the graphic details the jurors would hear about not as acts of sex, but of abuse, fifty shades of domestic violence.

"This case is not a romanticized, fictionalized novel some of you may have read. This was the exercise of power and control."

Hinckley explained that Seth dominated every part of his girlfriend Kat McDonough's life. She was a "loyal and obedient Slave" in their world of "sex, dominance, and control," he said. Seth manipulated Kat to get anything he wanted—even insisting under threat of sexual violence that she bring another woman into their bed.

That's where the victim came in, Hinckley said.

"Lizzi was attractive, she was what he had been looking for. The defendant and McDonough schemed about how they could exploit her sexually."

In his opening statement, Seth's defense attorney, Joachim Barth, sketched a very different picture for the court. His story did not revolve around Seth, but around Kat, and what Barth said were her psychological problems.

"She had five voices in her head," he said, and she gave in to the one called Charlotte.

The defense attorney claimed it wasn't Seth who had introduced Kat to BDSM; rather, that she'd come to the relationship with those desires. He said it was Kat, not Seth, who had been obsessed with bringing women into the relationship. It was Kat, not Seth, who had lured Lizzi to the apartment. It was Kat, not Seth, who had smothered Lizzi by sitting on the victim's face for her own sexual gratification.

Barth said Seth's only crime was hindering prosecution by lying to police about what had really happened that night, but that he had done so to protect the woman he loved.

After the opening arguments, court recessed for the day. The press corps and court staff couldn't help but talk about the shockingly explicit nature of both opening arguments. Said one court staffer to a writer: *Never in all my years have I heard anything like that.*

The journalists got to work on their stories, trying to figure out the right balance to strike while reporting on this trial—a conversation that would take over the state's newsroom editorial meetings in the weeks to follow.

The jurors had also been given their charge. But their decision wouldn't be as simple as weighing in on Seth Mazzaglia's innocence or guilt. They had to figure out whether Lizzi Marriott had been killed by Seth—or by Kat McDonough.

————

On the first day of testimony, Lizzi's aunt, Becky Hanna, appeared on the stand to introduce the note her niece had left for her on October 9, 2012. This was the note in which Lizzi had said she was meeting a friend and would be home before midnight. Becky couldn't get through her brief testimony without bursting into tears.

The state also called a neighbor of Seth and Kat's from Sawyer Mill, who testified that she'd heard a chilling scream through her half-opened window around ten thirty P.M. that night. She remembered the time, she said, because it came in the middle of *Little House on the Prairie*. Afterward, she'd heard the sound of a man barking commands. The neighbor testified that she hadn't thought much about the disturbance at the time, however, because it was Halloween season.

Also called to testify on the first day was Brittany Atwood. She described her slain girlfriend as bubbly, goofy, and "experimental." The prosecution asked her to tell the jury about the text messages she'd received right before Lizzi disappeared.

During cross-examination, the defense landed some of its first punches. Attorney Melissa Davis got Brittany to admit that Lizzi's moving to New Hampshire had put a strain on their relationship. She also got Brittany to concede that she had been jealous of Lizzi's friendships with Kat McDonough and Nate McNeal. Davis questioned whether Brittany's relationship with Lizzi was as strong as she'd thought.

"She was also 'experimental,' " Davis said, using Brittany's own word, "so if she wanted to try something, she was going to try it."

The defense was trying to make the case that perhaps Lizzi Marriott was just the kind of "experimental" girl who'd cheat on her girlfriend by taking part in a three-way.

The state then called Ryan Bachman, the inmate Seth had dubbed "Castle" in the plan he'd called "Bishop's Vacation." Bachman described the elaborate escape plan for the court and admitted using Seth's money to buy drugs.

Bachman had been arrested again only days after his release, and when he was sent back to the Strafford County jail, he had been put back in the same cell with Seth. His bunkie had wanted to know how the money-for-drugs scheme was coming, as he'd still hoped to procure guns, cars, and explosives.

Bachman testified that he'd told Seth the money he'd actually blown on heroin had been stolen.

———

It wasn't until the fifth day of testimony, June 3, that the state called its star witness. Kat McDonough arrived at Strafford County Superior Court early in the morning wearing her orange state prison top and khaki pants, her curly hair tied back off her face, exactly as she'd described how Violet—the maternal healing persona she called upon to stay calm—always wore her hair.

Before she took the stand, security staff held Kat in an empty room down the hall that had been used as a juvenile court.

Plugging into the network video feed, the assembled TV camera crews had almost nothing to do all day except take pictures of Seth getting on and off the elevator on the second floor and walking to courtroom 2. The only thing that ever changed about the scene was the dress shirt he wore beneath his black vest. One day it would be white, the next it would be blue, and then back to white again. The trip from door to elevator was about twenty paces, not nearly long enough for anything visually interesting to occur.

The distance between Kat's holding room and courtroom 2 was much longer, allowing the cameramen to form a sort of gauntlet along the hallway. The first time she and her security detail made the journey, Kat—still in handcuffs—nearly sprinted the distance as halogen lights and rapid-firing shutters tracked her journey. But, after a while, as the scene played out over and over—every morning, every lunch break, then end of every day—Kat made the trip at a regular pace, her head bowed to avoid eye contact with anyone on the sidelines.

Kat took the witness stand and was sworn in by Hinckley. Now the real case would begin. In so many ways, it was not Seth Mazzaglia who was on trial; it was Kat

McDonough. Twelve people would need to take the word of a young woman who had lied easily to her parents, to police, and to attorneys. The jury's verdict was still weeks away, but the court of public opinion turned on her almost immediately.

CHAPTER NINETEEN

Star Witness

"Miss McDonough, who killed Lizzi Marriott?" asked Hinckley.

"Seth Mazzaglia."

"How did Seth Mazzaglia kill Miss Elizabeth Marriott? Please tell these jurors."

"He strangled her with a rope."

"How do you know what Seth Mazzaglia did to Elizabeth Marriott?"

Kat did not hesitate. "I was there."

"I'm at the outer door :D"

The text came from Lizzi at 8:51 P.M. According to Kat's testimony, Seth had just gotten out of the shower. He reminded his girlfriend that Darkheart and Skarlet were their sexual personas of the evening, and that it was her job to get something going. Strip poker was on the menu, he told her, and she should wear something alluring. Kat was already wearing a plain top, so Seth had her take off her bra.

Kat headed to the ground floor. When she opened the back door, she found Lizzi in her black *Avenue Q* sweatshirt sending a text to her girlfriend.

Seth welcomed Lizzi as she came into the apartment. The room was relatively neat, save for the mixture of painting supplies he'd collected for the work at his mother's house. Seth had turned on a floor lamp with a red lightbulb in it, so the room was dim.

Seth asked what Kat and Lizzi felt like doing that night. He suggested that they could either spend some time creating Dungeons & Dragons characters or watch a movie they'd rented.

"Or," Kat offered in a joking tone, "we could play strip poker."

Lizzi laughed, Kat claimed, and said, "That would be fun."

Kat admitted she didn't know how to play poker, so Seth explained the rules. The player with the best hand got to keep his or her clothes on; the two losers had to throw an item of clothing in the pot. Kat went into the bathroom to put back on the bra she had just taken off, as she wasn't wearing very much to start with.

According to Kat, the three of them sat on the floor in front of the futon, the movie playing in the background. The cards were dealt to all. Bad cards were discarded, and the trio picked up two or three new ones to replace them. They flipped their hands and everyone laughed at Kat and Seth for losing the first round. Kat took off her glasses and placed them on the floor in the center of the circle.

More hands were dealt, won, and lost in rapid succession. Kat tried to delay the inevitable by surrendering bracelets and her mismatched socks. Another low card fell, and Kat had to throw her top into the pot. Seth stood up to remove his pants, and the girls squealed at his supposed embarrassment. Lizzi lost fewer hands than either of them.

Kat said that Lizzi bragged, "I'm a lucky person. If there's another me in another dimension, *that* me has all the bad luck." She said that Lizzi's mood remained light and playful the entire time.

Kat was bare breasted before Lizzi finally lost her shirt, revealing her brassiere. Kat admitted to feeling conflicted. She was losing her clothes quickly, and she knew Seth wanted her to "make something happen." Her friend Lizzi was having fun, but she seemed oblivious to any sexual tension they were trying to create.

At 9:54 P.M., Kat's cell phone buzzed. It was a text message from Darla, her friend who was supposed to come over later in the evening to learn some fetish rope play:

"I'm at my grandpa's tonight."

Kat knew Darla's grandparents had been sick and that her family had been taking turns providing care. To be certain that this meant Darla and her boyfriend wouldn't be coming over later, Kat texted back, "So no hang out?"

She waited for a response but didn't get one, so finally

said, "Seth, our friends don't need us to pick them up at the airport."

It was the signal they'd arranged that there would be no bondage demonstration with Darla and Eli later that night. Seth's face pinched, Kat testified, but he quickly returned his attention to the game at hand. "That means you can stay later if you want, Lizzi."

———

Peter Hinckley moved steadily through the questioning, not rushing anything. His pacing matched Kat's responses, which were measured and flat. Few people watching in court or on television had ever met her, had ever seen her theatrical effervescence. Her whole affect on the stand formed the jury's (and the public's) opinion of what kind of person she was.

It was hard to get a read on her.

———

Continuing her direct examination, Kat recalled that both she and Seth were soon completely naked. Lizzi still had on a pair of blue thong panties. With nothing left for two of the players to offer, Seth suggested a change in the game.

"How about something happens to the next person who loses?"

Kat had the next low hand and turned to Seth to ask for the consequences.

"Kat, why don't you kiss Lizzi?"

Lizzi looked back and forth between them. "I'm not comfortable with that," she said.

Seth gestured to his naked girlfriend. "Come on," he invited Lizzi. "Just make out a little bit with her."

Lizzi said, "No. I'm in a committed relationship."

Seth nodded and said it was cool, but Kat read his body language and said she knew he was upset.

He stood up, put on a robe, and went to get the women glasses of apple cider. Kat and Lizzi sat on the floor, their backs to the futon, and watched the movie while still in their states of undress.

Seth texted Kat from the kitchenette. "We painting tonight?"

On its face it was a reference to the painting they'd been doing at his mother's house, but Kat understood it to be a coded message: *Are we having sex with Lizzi tonight?*

She texted back. "Your decision I guess. If you have a plan." Afraid of Seth's reaction if things didn't go as he hoped, Kat was on edge. She added to the text the word, "Nervous." That was at 10:29 P.M.

Seth got on the futon behind them. Kat knew the move he was about to make.

"Lizzi, is it okay if Kat and I have sex now?"

It was the line he'd used several times before, and each subsequent time he'd used it, the sexual encounter had gotten hotter. The last two girls he'd used it on eventually joined them in bed. Lizzi was already topless. This had all the hallmarks of an epic night. Maybe this time he could be the one getting all of the attention.

Unlike all the previous times he'd used this line on people, Lizzi didn't acquiesce. Instead, she scowled. She didn't want them to do that in front of her, she said.

Seth protested, saying, "My girlfriend is here and I want to fuck her."

Then he asked Lizzi to join them, his voice rising, saying there were things that Kat could do to her that he couldn't.

Lizzi repeated firmly that she was in a committed relationship. She wasn't interested.

Seth appeared to let it slide, but again, Kat testified, she could tell he was angry. He was always the Master and was unaccustomed to people saying no to him.

Kat stared at the television, now hyperaware of her nakedness. She crossed her arms, casually trying to cover her breasts. She wondered what Seth was thinking. She could hear him moving around on the futon but didn't want to look back at him.

It was then Seth struck, looping one of the white cotton ropes they'd used for sex play around Lizzi's throat, crossing it behind her neck and pulling as hard as he could. Kat testified that Seth was wearing a pair of black leather gloves he'd worn the previous winter.

On the stand, Kat described how, as the cord wrapped around her throat, Lizzi let out a short shriek that was quickly cut off by the rope. Seth pressed his knee into Lizzi's back as he pulled tighter and tighter. Her whole body froze. Her legs stretched out straight, then began to turn inward. Her arms curled up to her chest.

Instead of helping the struggling woman beside her, Kat claimed she merely turned away from the attack and watched the images on TV. Kat testified that she'd been unsure what to do. So her response had been to do nothing at all.

Eventually, she got up from the floor and walked to the window overlooking the river. It was the place in the apartment she said she'd go to when she felt lonely or depressed. She pulled the curtain closed. She looked behind her to see if it was over. It wasn't. Seth was still pulling tightly on the rope as Lizzi convulsed. He nodded toward the other window, and Kat pulled the curtain on that one too.

Kat testified that the strangling seemed to go on for hours, although it probably lasted about ten minutes.

After Seth stopped pulling on the rope, she testified, Lizzi remained slumped in the seated position against the futon. He laid her on her back on the floor and asked Kat to check for a pulse. Both of them had completed the EMT-B course and knew how to administer first aid. She tried the ankle, then the wrist. No pulse. He told Kat to try Lizzi's neck. Still nothing.

Seth's father, Joe, lived in the same building and was likely in his apartment at the time. Instead, Seth decided to reach out to someone else for help.

"Call Roberta," he instructed Kat. She didn't have Roberta's number, so she used Seth's cell phone. It was 10:47 P.M., eighteen minutes after Seth had sent the "painting" text from the kitchen. When Roberta didn't answer, Seth demanded Kat call again. Roberta still didn't pick up until the third time she called. Five minutes later, Roberta texted they were on their way. Kat said that, at that point, she walked into the bathroom, the only place in the apartment where she couldn't see the living room floor. She considered leaving the apartment, but felt she had no one else, no place to go. She was in love with Seth. There was nothing else in her life. It was him or it was nothing.

When she returned to the living room, Kat testified about the monstrous thing she saw. She said she saw Seth on top of Lizzi Marriott, raping her dead body, and as he thrust, he barked insults and profanity.

"Say no to me? I'll show you . . . you fucking bitch . . . fuck you."

Seth grunted as he ejaculated inside of Lizzi Marriott's body.

———

During her long narratives testifying for the prosecution, Kat's voice was timid but steady. But when Hinckley reminded her, his star witness, that she had done nothing to aid Lizzi as Seth strangled her, Kat's voice began to tremble.

The assistant attorney general and his witness tried to plow ahead. It was better the jury heard it from Kat—not from the defense—that she failed to act, failed to save Lizzi's life. As she talked about the murder and answered questions about why she hadn't intervened, Kat doubled over and cried uncontrollably, prompting Hinckley to call for a recess and the removal of the jury from the courtroom.

When her testimony resumed, Kat said Seth stumbled toward the bathroom to clean himself off. He told Kat to grab the rope, now hanging loosely around Lizzi's neck, and pull it tight again. Maybe he wasn't positive the girl was dead. Maybe he just wanted Kat to take some active role. Maybe he needed her to put her own hands on the murder weapon. Kat was crying. She couldn't refuse one of Seth's orders.

Up close, Kat could finally see Lizzi's face, swollen and discolored. She protested, Kat testified, but said Seth demanded she also throttle the corpse of her friend—the young woman who'd been giggling about her good luck at cards not thirty minutes before. She claimed to have held the rope for about ten more minutes but hadn't pulled hard.

When Seth emerged from the bathroom, Kat said he told her to find a plastic grocery bag. Kat found two in the kitchen and tried to hand them to Seth, but said he wouldn't touch them. He told her to put them over Lizzi's head and to tie them shut at the bottom, Kat testified, so that Roberta wouldn't see the dead girl's face.

Roberta Gerkin had testified two days before Kat had, telling the jury how she and Paul Hickok had responded to Kat's desperate call and found a lifeless woman with two plastic bags on her head lying on the apartment floor. Roberta said Lizzi's face was purple and there were marks around her neck, but in her opinion the marks were made by the bags and not a rope. Other than this detail, Kat's retelling of the visit substantially matched Roberta's. Kat told the jury that Paul advocated that they report Lizzi's death, but she felt Roberta would have tried harder to convince Seth to cover it up if Paul had not been with her. The couple left the Lair without providing any assistance to them (other than their temporary silence).

If they were going to "take care of this" themselves, they had to start covering their tracks. Kat said she picked up her cell phone and sent a text message to Lizzi's number. They needed to make it look like Lizzi had never been to the apartment.

"Hey dahling i expected you at 10? i passed out and lost track of time. you still coming?" It was another step in Kat and Seth's efforts to cover up Lizzi's murder.

At this point, Kat said, Seth came over to console her. He curled his arms around Kat and told her that all of this had happened because of Doomsday.

"'We're in this together now,'" she quoted him. "We have to figure out how to get rid of her body."

They both pulled out the blue latex gloves Seth had used to clean the apartment, and Seth also put on the black leather gloves he'd worn to strangle Lizzi.

Kat testified that they then gathered all of Lizzi's clothes and put them in plastic shopping bags, setting her car keys aside. Then, she said, Seth took the painting tarp and wrapped Lizzi's body inside of it. Kat—remembering how her brother had traced her movements via her cell phone at New Year's—shut off Lizzi's phone. She and Seth also both switched off their cellphones, afraid they might ping a tower.

The rolled-up tarp still looked suspicious, so Kat told the jury that it was her idea to use her suitcase from summer camp, the big one with the extendable handle. They folded Lizzi's body up, but couldn't close the case completely, so Seth held the sides together as best he could while Kat wrapped it with duct tape.

Kat used Lizzi's key fob to locate her Mazda in the back parking lot. Relieved to see it was an automatic—she didn't know how to drive a stick—she pulled the car up to the back door and opened the Mazda's tailgate, then helped Seth put the plastic bags and the bulging suitcase into the back of the SUV.

Kat took the wheel with Seth sitting in the passenger seat, and they left Sawyer Mill.

Seth didn't want to take the highway, where the E-ZPass toll system and cameras might track them. Kat was worried because the car was low on gas. They pulled into the parking lot of the Wentworth-Douglass Hospital to consider their next move, and Kat testified that it was her suggestion to take Lizzi's body to Peirce Island. She knew the current was fast, and her mother had told her never to go there at night because "that's where the bad people went."

———

After spending her first day on the stand describing her intimate, abusive relationship with Seth—complete with graphic descriptions of their BDSM sex life—and telling her recollections of October 9, Kat returned the next day to explain what happened next. She appeared in court wearing the same prison uniform, the same plain glasses, her hair pulled back in a bun.

———

They arrived at the island after midnight, Kat told the court, and parked as close as they could to the overlook in the unpaved lot by the dog park—but they still had a long way to go. There was just enough moonlight for them to see what they were doing. Together, they wrangled the suitcase from the car. Seth extended the handle and pulled. It wobbled as he dragged it over the dirt parking lot, then stopped when the wheels hit some grass. Seth heaved, but the wheels wouldn't spin in the turf. They tugged together, but the cumbersome bag would only lurch and then stop mere inches away.

"This isn't working."

Seth suggested they take Lizzi's body out of the suitcase and drag her on the tarp. They unwrapped the duct tape, and let Lizzi's body tumble out of the carrier. Kat described how Seth laid Lizzi out on the cloth and grabbed a corner, hoping her body would slide over ground; but it soon became clear that he would just end up yanking the tarp from beneath her uncooperative body.

Eventually, Seth picked the body up and flung it over his shoulder in a fireman's carry. His feet were moving slower and his breath was coming faster.

When they got to a dirt path, Seth told Kat to reopen the suitcase. They again folded Lizzi's limbs inward and he resumed dragging the bag, dragging it past their once "magic tree," dragging it toward the water. Without any duct tape holding it shut, Kat said, Lizzi's body fell out again and again.

Kat testified that, when they were nearly to the overlook, Seth let go of the suitcase handle and put his hands on his hips, gasping for air.

"'I can't do it anymore. You have to pull it,'" she said he told her, so Kat tugged the suitcase the last few feet from the trail to the end of the semicircular railing on the overlook.

The light from the naval shipyard on the other side of the river was just enough to illuminate the shapes around their destination. Behind them they'd left a tortuous, irregular set of drag marks in the dirt. Delaying the inevitable, they sat down on the granite benches, the same place they'd once come to hold hands and dream of their future.

Kat testified that Seth stood up first. Sweating and wheezing, he picked up Lizzi's body, lifted it to the top of the waist-high railing, and heaved it over the side.

Instead of the splash they expected to hear, there was a thump.

The overlook had not been built at the very edge of the cliff. It was set back about three feet, with just enough turf on the other side of the railing to walk on. Seth and Kat peered over the rail only to see Lizzi's body resting on the lip above the twenty-five-foot drop into the Piscataqua.

"'Go and push her the rest of the way over,'" Kat said that Seth demanded. "'You're smaller than I am.'"

Kat swung a leg over the railing and got on her knees. She shoved as hard as she could, but she had neither the strength nor the leverage to move Lizzi's body.

"Come help me," she asked Seth, but he said he was too tired to climb over the rail.

Kat pointed out that there was no need to climb. "'Go to your left. You can walk around the fence,'" she recounted on the stand.

Seth walked around to where Kat knelt, and together they rolled Lizzi's body over the precipice.

There was still no splash.

They looked over the cliff and in the moonlight saw Lizzi's lifeless form on the rocks below.

———

In the courtroom, Seth watched his ex-girlfriend explain her actions on the night of October 9. The defendant wore little or no reaction on his face. The only indication that something was churning inside his head could be seen under the table. With the ball of his foot firmly planted on the floor, Seth bounced his right leg up and down. He seemed to never stop.

Kat testified that the river lapped hard against where Lizzi lay, but it wasn't nearly strong enough to pull her partially submerged body away from the shore.

When they'd visited the island during the day, the water on the Piscataqua had been coming in from the ocean and was eight feet higher than it was this night, as the river was flowing outward. They'd never seen the cascade of rocks hidden just beneath the surface of the high waterline. At first, they contemplated leaving Lizzi there and letting the next high tide take her away, but then Seth said they had to make sure she went into the water, Kat testified, because his DNA was inside her.

Seth and Kat climbed up to the overlook and walked back to the parking lot, where there was a path to the shore. The beach was rocky, with no sand, just gray river stone and washed-up shells. They doubled back on the lower rocks of the shoreline, hoping to reach Lizzi's body. Some of the boulders along the way were the size of furniture, covered in lime- and rust-colored seaweed.

They shimmied along the shore until reaching a U-shaped break along the boundary. The crevasse was filled with water, and the only way to get by was to climb across a slab of rock to the other side. Kat said she found a fingerhold and hoisted herself across, then turned and summoned Seth to follow.

But, she testified, he refused. "'I'm too tired. I can't make it. You go on and do it,'" Kat quoted him as saying. He told her he'd go back to the overlook and direct her from above.

Kat made it to Lizzi's body and waited for her boyfriend to reappear. When Seth reached the overlook, Kat pointed out a way he could scale down to where she was, but again, Seth said he couldn't do it.

Left alone at the bottom of the cliff, Kat tugged on Lizzi's body, but she could only move it an inch or two. She kept pulling, and as she yanked, Lizzi's thong underwear balled up and came off her legs. Kat grabbed the panties and put them into her pocket. All Lizzi was left wearing was her necklace. Kat testified she thought it was a kind of crucifix, but it was actually a starfish.

Lizzi was half floating now.

"It's too bad we don't have a rock to weigh the body down," Seth said from above.

Kat began covering the body in seaweed to hide it. She told the court how surreal she thought the whole scene was. A few hours beforehand, she, Lizzi, and Seth had all been laughing together, and now Lizzi was dead, her body refusing to go into the water.

Kat began pulling and pushing again and, gently, Lizzi made her way to the ocean she'd loved. Finally the current won, cradling Lizzi and finally pulling her into the briny deep.

———

As prosecutor Peter Hinckley walked Kat through how she'd pushed Lizzi's body into the water, Kat began to sob.

Hinckley, who had been walking the line between maintaining his star witness's credibility while acknowledging her culpability, asked Kat if she was aware that Lizzi's body would never be recovered.

"Yes," Kat barely squeaked out the word.

"Tell these jurors: Do you have any remorse for what you did to Lizzi and her family?"

She answered. "There's so many things that she's never going to be able to do. So many things in her life that she missed out. I mean I'm only twenty, but I still look back and think that even now there's so much I've yet to do, so much of life left. She never got to get married. She never got to have kids. She never really got to live her life yet."

Kat was sobbing again.

"It was because of us that she never got to live her life. This isn't something we can fix. She can never come back."

The judge called for an early lunch break to give Kat some time to compose herself.

———

Finishing her direct examination, Kat said she and Seth drove away from Peirce Island in Lizzi's car, the needle on the gas gauge hovering just above E. They stopped at a hotel parking lot and threw the suitcase into a Dumpster. Seth placed Lizzi's iPhone and TomTom GPS unit under one of the Mazda's tires and had Kat drive over them. He collected the pieces and threw them from the SUV's passenger window as they crossed the General Sullivan Bridge over Little Bay. Then they threw the bag containing Lizzi's clothes, her panties, and the rope Seth used to strangle her into another Dumpster near a volunteer fire department. Those items were never recovered.

Coasting on fumes, they parked the Mazda Tribute in a UNH parking lot near the equestrian center on the far end of campus. Seth, still wearing gloves, wiped the car's interior and exterior with a towel. Now on foot, they carried the tarp and dropped it in yet another Dumpster they passed on campus. The pair then walked the seven miles from Durham to their apartment in Dover.

They arrived home at six A.M., just before sunrise. Seth told Kat to remove all of her clothing and shoes and put them in a trash bag. He did the same. He carried the bag to the Sawyer Mill Dumpster, confident he had removed all traces of Lizzi from the apartment.

A day later, they would find Lizzi's *Avenue Q* sweatshirt in the living room and quickly throw that away as well. They would also go through their phones deleting text messages, including Lizzi's "I'm at the outer door," Seth's "We painting tonight?" and Roberta's "We are on our way."

Kat testified that, when they finished their walk from UNH to the apartment, they both took showers and fell into restless sleep. When Seth awoke, he made breakfast and served it to Kat on the futon. After she ate, Seth said he wanted to have sex.

They removed their clothes. Seth instructed Kat to climb on top of him, her favorite position. Kat knew what the gesture meant. It was her reward for a job well done.

CHAPTER TWENTY

Without Tears

Seth Mazzaglia's defense attorney Joachim Barth prepared for his cross-examination of Kat McDonough thoroughly and intently. After reviewing her video statement and her testimony to the grand jury, his attack on the witness wasn't just legal theatrics. Deep down, Barth truly felt Kat wasn't telling the truth on the stand, and he hoped to convince the jury to feel the same way.

Barth used the French pronunciation for his first name and went by "Jacque" for short. Barth was married to Tina Nadeau, a respected former homicide prosecutor and legal advisor to the governor, and now chief justice of the state superior court system. Her father, Joseph Nadeau, was a retired state supreme court justice.

Statuesque and fit, Barth was a keen, professorial litigator, but he wasn't bookish around the clock. At home he raised livestock, and before leaving for court each day, he would venture into his backyard to feed his pair of four-hundred-pound hogs. When asked by friends if he'd named the hogs, he'd answer, "Yes. Delicious One and Delicious Two."

The defense's decision to have Barth—rather than Melissa David—cross-examine Kat was risky. General wisdom dictates juries can be turned off if male lawyers are seen as antagonistic toward female witnesses. But as first chair on the team, it would've been hard for Barth to play spectator during Kat's cross-examination. There was too much riding on what she might say.

Seth Mazzaglia, on the other hand, had no choice but to play spectator for this critical part of his defense. There was little to no expectation Seth would testify, lest he open the door for the prosecution to poke around and elicit threads of his suppressed confession. Throughout the trial he'd sat silently in his parade of rotating blue and white shirts and black vest, bouncing his leg under the table as if to expend his buildup of nervous energy.

The only time the media and gallery heard Seth speak was on the trial's opening day, when in a surprisingly light voice that belied his gruff exterior, he'd acknowledged for the judge his understanding of the consequences of his legal defense.

There were certain things that Seth couldn't make go away, such as his lies to police and his knowledge of Lizzi's watery grave. At trial, his position was that Kat had smothered Lizzi, and all of the steps he took after that were to protect her. The rub was that by saying that, Seth was incriminating himself on a host of lesser hindrance charges. Even if the jury found him innocent of murder, he'd still likely be sentenced immediately for those crimes. It was a calculated risk: admit to being the accomplice instead of the mastermind.

———

Assistant Attorney General Peter Hinckley's direct examination of Kat McDonough had lasted a day and a half. Joachim Barth began questioning her on June 5, day six of the trial, after the court's lunch recess. He started jabbing at her right away, reminding Kat how she'd come to the public defender's office two days after Seth's arrest and told them Lizzi had died lying on the floor wearing a harness while Kat smothered her friend with her vagina.

"You described in detail that you were literally on her face for ten to fifteen minutes."

Kat acknowledged that she'd said that.

Barth said, "You have since changed your story. You have changed your account of what happened. You made that change while actively engaged in your immunity agreement."

He pointed out that Kat's agreement to testify against Seth reduced her prison sentence by decades.

"I had no idea I was getting a one-and-a-half-year deal," she said.

This would be the predominant theme of Barth's cross: Kat McDonough was a habitual liar and was motivated only by saving her own skin.

"The police asked you for your integrity and your honesty, didn't they?"

"Yes, I believe they did," Kat said.

"And you continued to lie to them."

"Yes," Kat replied flatly. "And that's why I'm now serving a prison sentence."

"In fact, you told them that perhaps you had an explanation for what happened to Miss Marriott."

"Um," Kat looked down, as if taking her time trying to recall. "I believe Seth said something to me that maybe it could be blamed on a fraternity. I believe I may have said that."

Barth spoke to Kat loudly, carefully, and pointedly, doling out each question in parts—one phrase at a time. In contrast, Kat was soft-spoken. It took her an eternity to answer each of his questions. After an "um" or an "I don't know," she'd pause, as if considering how each question was phrased, testing the likelihood she was stepping into a trap. Then she'd answer slowly, in fragments that sometimes didn't fit together. Their exchanges were excruciating to follow, like an out-of-time duet between a tuba and a piccolo.

When Barth wanted to make a significant point during cross, he did what all lawyers do. He'd asked some basic, leading foundation questions, reestablishing the narrative for the jury's sake: *On this night you did this, correct? You said you were here, were you not? The next thing that happened was this, correct?*

These questions were designed to lead to the actual point he planned to hit home, little queries that could be answered, *Yes, yes,* and *yes.* Kat, however, would pause and ponder each question, breaking Barth's intended rhythm. In her halting style, she'd respond, *It might have been that or the week before,* or, *That's not what I said,* or *I don't remember what happened after that.*

Kat's obfuscation required Barth to ask if reading her police statement or grand jury testimony would refresh her memory, prompting countless trips to the stand to present transcripts with the hope of moving things along. It seemed that if Barth were to ask Kat whether it were Tuesday, she'd likely take two minutes to explain that she didn't own a calendar. Her reluctance to answer anything stymied Barth from creating a solid, damning story from her testimony.

"Did you have the capacity to look police officers in the eye and lie to them while you were projecting confidence?" he asked.

Kat seemed genuinely unsure of what he meant. "I don't know."

"Do you have the capacity to look these jurors in the eye and lie to them while you project meekness and sub-missiveness and remorse?"

Kat turned toward the panel. "I'm not lying to them."

Later, Barth would state as a matter of fact, "You consider yourself a good liar."

"Not necessarily," she replied slowly, "seeing as I got caught lying."

———

The swings at Kat's character and credibility weren't un-expected. In fact, AAG Hinckley had prepared the jury for that during his direct examination. He reminded his star witness again and again how she'd done nothing to render aid to Lizzi Marriott and had instead lied repeatedly to police, to friends, and to Seth's defense team. Hinckley was attempting to inoculate Kat against the accusations he knew the defense would make in cross. The message to the jury was that they didn't have to like Kat McDonough or approve of her actions to believe her testimony.

Like a prizefighter, Barth jabbed at Kat repeatedly to see if the challenger could stay on her feet. To the reporters in the gallery, Kat was hanging tough. The questioning had gone on for several days and she hadn't yet lost her cool. She answered (if somewhat timidly) all of Barth's queries about whether she'd lied and why she lied. She'd been figuratively bruised, but she hadn't yet fallen away from one of his punches.

"Ms. McDonough," Barth asked suddenly, as he removed his reading glasses, "do you believe in dragons?"

The courtroom was silent. It was obviously a question designed to make Kat look crazy, an easy enough trap for her to avoid. Yet she fumbled her answer.

"I can't say . . . there has never been a creature that *wasn't* a dragon. Or that the *essence* of such a creature never existed . . ."

Barth then asked Kat whether she believed in ghosts, and then whether she believed in aliens. There was an audible groan among the journalists. Barth had finally landed a punch that knocked Kat against the ropes, and the jury might be ready to see her in a new light.

Barth's focus had shifted, and he was now singularly drilling down into the bizarre fantasy world that Kat claimed she and Seth shared.

He probed their sex life. *Weren't you the one*, Barth asked, *who wrote all of those online ads looking for a Slave? Isn't it true that, as a bisexual woman, you couldn't be satisfied by Seth the way you demanded? Haven't you admitted to this jury that you were aroused by being tied up? Wasn't it you who kept Post-it notes of new fetishes to research? How do you explain your letters in which you beg Seth to beat you for your own sexual pleasure? Isn't that why you call yourself "The Willing"? Didn't you identify yourself as a "Switch"—meaning you took turns being the dominant one? Would Seth have really let you carve an X into his back if you truly were a "Slave"?*

The defense attorney then picked apart Kat's personas. *Hadn't you already created Scarlet and James before you came to the relationship?* he asked. *And weren't Seth's "alter egos," Wild Card and Cyrus, simply the names of characters that your boyfriend had been using in role-playing games and video games? Wasn't Seth's world domination plan just one of the fanciful short stories he had been writing on his computer? Isn't it possible you took all of this fantasy talk too seriously? Weren't you the one who really believed everything beyond the Veil was true?*

Barth opened one of several three-ring binders filled with printouts of the couple's Facebook instant messages. He turned to one of Kat's messages to Seth, written on the day she'd described Skarlet, Anay, Violet, and Kitty fighting over her soul while she folded shirts at Target.

"At this point the voices in your own mind are literally arguing amongst themselves," Barth said accusingly.

Kat replied in the same quiet voice she'd had on the stand all along. "I had created the characters, but I began to wonder. I was really confused at the time."

Barth dug into the conversations Kat had with Roberta that were secretly recorded.

"Didn't you acknowledge to Roberta Gerkin that on the night of October ninth, while you were in your apartment, you were affected by one of your inner voices?"

On the wire, Kat told Roberta she felt like Anay was taking over her body. On the stand, Kat said she didn't remember saying that, but added that much of what she told Roberta was made up.

"You don't remember," the attorney said with disapproval, "but you *do* remember that it wasn't true."

Kat conceded again that almost everything she had said to Roberta was a lie.

———

As the cross-examination continued into a second week, Kat would rush past the hallway cameras each time she entered and exited the courtroom. For most of the fifteen-minute midday recesses, she was left to sit alone in the witness box while the judge, the jury, and most of the spectators left the room to stretch their legs.

On occasion, the witness advocate from the attorney general's office would engage Kat in small talk. The rest of the time, Kat sat silently staring at her hands and taking care not to look at the defense table.

Seth wasn't allowed to leave the room during the recesses either. He stood up and stretched his legs and browsed through his lawyers' notes, also careful to avoid looking Kat's way. The last time Seth and Kat had actually spoken, their conversation had been about jailhouse weddings and escape plans. It was clear now that neither of those things would ever happen.

The defense wanted to go over the timeline of October 9, 2012. Barth stated that the text message proved Lizzi arrived at Sawyer Mill at 8:51 P.M. Kat agreed to his assertion. *They decided to play strip poker then? Yes. Seth explained the rules? Yes. Seth dealt out about twenty hands?* Kat looked at Barth in puzzlement, and said she didn't know if what he did was "give out hands." *Seth dealt hands, correct?* Kat still claimed ignorance.

"My question is pretty simple," Barth said, his patience wearing thin. "Seth dealt hands?"

Another searching pause. "I don't know if it's a 'hand,' " Kat said. "Seth dealt out a pile of cards to each of us."

Barth finally exploded in frustration.

"When you do this," he almost shouted, "are you trying to buy more time to answer questions or are you seriously answering my questions in this way because you need to?"

Barth took a breath and got the questioning back on track. Kat slowly attested to the facts she had previously provided, and agreed that they'd played around twenty hands of strip poker. The game went quickly, she said, taking only half an hour.

When Lizzi refused to make out with Kat, the game stopped and they watched the movie for about ten minutes. Kat claimed Seth choked Lizzi for an estimated ten minutes, and then he ordered Kat to choke Lizzi for another ten minutes. After that, she called Roberta at 10:47 P.M.

"You are missing approximately *an hour* in the evening of October ninth at your apartment," Barth pointed out.

"Um." Kat remained speechless for a while. "I don't know. Like I said, I wasn't really looking at the clock. Those were just time estimates."

"We have the benefit, Ms. McDonough, of knowing when she arrived by virtue of her text message at 8:51 and your phone call to Roberta Gerkin at 10:47. According to your claims of activity, you are missing *an hour* of activity on the night of October ninth."

Barth circled the podium to provide this long-awaited coup de grâce.

"Do you remember how long the activity you described to us, the sexual activity, took when you made your statement to *us*?"

"No. I just made it up.".

Barth said, "You claimed the sexual activity took approximately one hour."

———

The defense then played the video of the statement Kat made at the public defender's office. Her devil-may-care demeanor on the screen was in stark contrast to the mousey court performance the jury had watched over the past week. The image of Kat getting on her knees and pantomiming queening, flatly describing how she'd smothered another human being, seemed particularly damning.

Building on the doubts about her credibility, Barth used the tape to show Kat's lack of remorse over Lizzi's death.

Barth flipped back through the pages of Kat's grand jury transcript and pulled out a detail she'd omitted during her direct testimony. She told the grand jurors that, as she watched Lizzi float away, she said, "Welcome to Davy Jones's locker." Hearing this for the first time, reporters found the quote to be flip and uncaring and another example of damning details left out.

"You made a comment about her going to Davy Jones's locker," Barth said contemptuously.

"Yes, because . . ."

"Because of your affinity for *pirates*." His voice was dripping with incredulity.

"Not just pirates. I like the ocean. I like sailors."

Barth spun back to the many different ways Kat had told the story of Lizzi's death, challenging her on why she seemed to so easily remember some details about that night and not others.

"Like right now, I can't get it out of my mind," Kat said, her voice quivering for the first time since Barth began his cross. "And the other details of the night are not easy to remember, 'cause all I can think about is what it was like for him to strangle her right next to me. It's all I can think about. I'll try to remember all of the facts the best that I can, but . . ."

Kat's face contorted suddenly and turned red as she sobbed.

"Days after this event, you appeared in our office and you didn't look this way," Barth said.

Kat didn't respond, so he continued, "You didn't cry."

"I've been crying for days straight."

"You went through detailed claims," Barth exclaimed. "You talked about taking her body out. You did not flinch."

Kat's voice cracked again. "It's because I was making up a *story*. There were details, but a lot of it was just a story. It wasn't *real*. I was able to push those images aside and just think about keeping up with the fake story I was telling you."

Kat looked out into the gallery where the Marriotts sat.

"I mean, right now, it's just, *this* is when it's really being told. This is when everyone's finding out. This is when her family really gets to find out. And this is when I'm sitting in the same room as *him*."

Kat sobbed some more. Barth approached the stand briefly then walked away. With his back to the witness, he asked, "You cry without tears, Ms. McDonough?"

"What?" The question took everyone in the courtroom by surprise.

"You cry without tears?"

All eyes turned to Kat's red face.

"I don't know," she said. "Sometimes." Kat reached for a handful of tissues and wiped her face.

A moment later, Barth looked at her closely and said it again.

"You still do not have tears?"

"I do. I don't know what you are talking about," a perturbed Kat replied.

The exchange was the sound bite for the evening news. Whether it raised doubt in the minds of the jury that moment is unclear, but it certainly raised doubt about Kat's sincerity in the court of public opinion.

———

Even before the "no tears" incident, there had been a growing public antipathy toward Kat McDonough. Despite extensive testimony that Kat had been in an abusive, manipulative relationship with Seth—that she was literally his sex slave and forced to do his bidding—there was a growing chorus of doubt as to whether Kat was in fact his unwilling partner. That doubt was amplified by the shared notion that Kat was unlikeable, something not aided by her flat and sometimes off-putting demeanor on the witness stand. For months, news reports had said Kat "lured" Lizzi to her death, that she'd presented her "gal pal" as an "offering" to her "master" for their "sexcapade."

Kat's plea deal had been light, perhaps *too* light, for someone who had at minimum pushed a dead body in the river and then lied to police about it.

The extent of the media's and the public's backlash against a cooperating witness was unprecedented in New Hampshire.

In more than one local newsroom, reporters argued as to whether the state's star witness was a victim or a stone-cold liar. A local TV station ran an entire story posing the question: "Is Kat remorseful enough?" A newspaper printed a sidebar on whether Kat's sweet plea deal could be invalidated. Trial coverage from online streaming services featured criminal profilers who dissected her body language and word selection on the stand—giving her failing grades across the board.

Plenty of accomplices had fingered a killer and confirmed for trial-watchers the presumed guilt of the man or woman on trial. Kat was not afforded the same trust.

The online comments were incendiary. *She's a liar. She's a pervert. She's faking her tears. Throw the book at her. She should register as a sex offender. She's hiding something. You sex slave slut puppy #gotawaywithit. u r sum freaking creepy liar psychopath.* And more than one commenter gleefully pointed out the worst of Kat's character flaws: She was an actress.

To be fair, there was a lot about Kat's story that didn't add up for the average observer. The missing hour in the timeline was troublesome. Her conduct in the video was indefensible.

Kat's flaky belief in dragons and spirits, tied together with her known history of lying, also did not instill confidence. The things she claimed about Lizzi also seemed hard to square. Why would Lizzi agree to play strip poker with virtual strangers? After firmly refusing multiple invitations to have sex, why would Lizzi then remain topless while watching a movie? Why would she stay at all?

At watercoolers and across dinner tables, the debate raged on. Many doubters skimmed over the evidence; instead, they said, there was something *not quite right* about Kat's story, something they couldn't put their finger on.

Some journalists even debated the veracity of Kat's domestic abuse allegations against Seth.

"But she was only seventeen when they met," argued one reporter, who'd been watching the live stream at her desk.

"I don't care how old she is," said her colleague, his computer also streaming video of the trial. "She's clearly a pathological liar."

One thing *was* clear: None of the Kat blowback translated into a groundswell of reasonable doubt for Seth Mazzaglia. There was debate about whether Kat was a coconspirator but next to none questioning Seth's culpability.

In fact, as the trial went on, Seth became more a target of public ridicule than debate. There was even a parody Twitter account created for Seth's vest, called Stretched to the Limit. The account's writer live-tweeted along with the trial, creating posts in which Seth's sweaty, bulging vest begged for mercy, cried for its popped buttons, and begged Seth to again play strip poker just to give it some relief.

Also posted online was this O. J. Simpson–inspired quip: "If the vest needs alteration, the defendant needs incarceration."

———

Kat McDonough spent ten days on the witness stand, longer than any witness the New Hampshire legal community or press could remember. But ten days of Kat McDonough also meant ten days of Joachim Barth.

The public defender's frustration with Kat as a witness became more and more apparent. It began to filter into the line of questioning, diluting what Barth had likely planned as a linear and more conventional cross. As the cross-examination wore on, the press began to wonder whom the jurors would be happier to cease listening to.

"Do you think there is a difference between the way you answer my questions and the way you answer questions from the state?"

"Some of yours have been a little open ended and confusing."

"Isn't it that you answer my questions differently from the state, because you are afraid to [admit] to a lie and then your plea deal would fall apart?"

"The way you talk confuses me sometimes."

By all accounts, Barth made the trial about Kat Mc-Donough and not about Seth Mazzaglia. He did everything he could to impeach Kat's credibility and the notion that she had been a prisoner in her relationship. He framed the safety of her plea bargain as a driving motivator for her to lie, thoroughly ripping apart the version of events she gave on the stand and playing Kat's videotaped statement for all it was worth.

He used her own words to illustrate her ideas about past lives and her fetish for kinky sex. He took every opportunity to present Kat as unfeeling and insincere and as a skilled liar.

At the end of his cross-examination, Barth said, "In addition to your challenges of truth and reality, you have no appreciation for Ms. Marriott's life."

Kat's mouth opened, but nothing came out. Before she could form an answer, Barth showed her his back and said with disgust, "Ms. McDonough, I don't have any further questions for you."

That's when Kat finally told off her inquisitor.

"I don't see how you can say that. You don't know me," she said. "You don't know what I have been through. You have your ideas, but I have spent so much time trying to understand this. I have spent all this time not being able to say anything to anyone because I had to keep quiet because this was before the trial. Of course I think about her, but I haven't been able to say anything yet. This is just the beginning where I can actually explain what really happened to her."

CHAPTER TWENTY-ONE

Closing Act

Police never found the suitcase, the rope, the tarp, or Lizzi Marriott's clothes, all of which had been scattered in trash receptacles around the Seacoast. The Dover police did, however, secure the Dumpster at Sawyer Mill, which hadn't been emptied between the search and the morning after the murder.

Investigators recovered bags containing all of the clothes that Seth Mazzaglia and Kat McDonough threw out that day—their own shirts and pants and even their shoes. There was also the pair of black leather gloves that Kat described Seth as wearing during the strangulation. In a different bag, they found Lizzi's *Avenue Q* sweatshirt.

Police sent a used condom from one of the bags to the lab for testing. There was no way to tell how long ago the condom had been worn, but DNA on the inside belonged to Seth. There was also DNA on the outside of the condom. While technicians could definitively prove Lizzi was not the source of that DNA, the best they could do was report they were "unable to exclude" Kat as its source.

Also tested was a pair of men's underwear. Inside, technicians found three DNA samples: one from Seth, one from Kat, and one from Lizzi, proving Seth's penis had been inside both women.

FBI experts examined the blond hairs found on the shoreline rocks on Peirce Island. The match to Lizzi was strong, but not conclusive. Those hairs were consistent with ones collected from a hairbrush belonging to Lizzi, but the lab couldn't scientifically exclude the possibility that they'd come from someone else.

Inside the apartment, cops recovered the couple's box of BDSM supplies. It contained several different kinds of restraints—a chain, a belt, and several collars—a leather bra, a knife, and a collection of wrapped condoms. Despite the allegedly frequent use of a rope in the couple's sex play, none was found in the box or anywhere else in the apartment.

Investigators found one other thing of note inside the Lair: a dry erase board on the refrigerator. In black marker was the note, "Ran @9, home @10, Kat not home till midnight. Called Roberta to see if Kat was okay." Next to the board was Dover Officer James Yerardi's business card.

The cop who'd searched Lizzi's car at the UNH parking lot said he'd found accessories for an iPhone and a TomTom GPS but not the devices themselves. A further examination of the Tribute revealed it had been wiped down, but a fingerprint belonging to Kat was discovered on the underside of the door handle.

Kat's torn letters about Seth's escape plans were introduced into evidence. Crime technicians had spent hours painstakingly piecing the shreds back together. These letters described Seth's "revised" version of events and his prison escape plan. Also submitted were the "ritual" instructions he'd mailed to his fiancée, which she had hidden in a sleeping bag.

The jury read Seth's text to Kat at camp, the one in which he graphically described the violent acts he would inflict as punishment on her for failing to secure him a sex surrogate during her two-week absence. The message was still on Kat's phone months later when they seized it. In the text, Seth had promised to make a friend die "of orgasms" while Kat watched.

Jurors heard from the dog walker who'd discovered the drag marks on Peirce Island. They also heard from a Portsmouth harbor pilot who explained the tidal charts, showing the currents were heading out to sea at the time Lizzi was pushed into the river.

———

After Kat's marathon testimony on the stand, prosecutors Peter Hinckley and Geoffrey Ward worked in earnest to shore up the case against Seth Mazzaglia.

The witness who followed Kat was a sexual abuse and domestic violence counselor. Dr. Scott Hampton was the director of an advocacy group, Ending the Violence, and had appeared on *The Oprah Winfrey Show*. He could not speak directly to Seth and Kat's relationship, but he explained how the cycle of violence begins and the reasons that it's difficult for victims to get out of it. Walking away, he said, means losing the world as they know it.

AAG Ward asked if a person who is a victim might still help her abuser if she saw him commit a crime. Hampton said yes; there was no upside for her to do otherwise.

"She would say, 'It's my fault.' If I bail out, I have to admit ultimate failure, and lose my relationship."

Dr. Hampton testified that witnesses to traumatic acts often remember the incidents in a variety of ways, which doesn't mean they're being purposely deceptive. When asked how to tell when an abuse survivor is telling the truth, Hampton answered that such witnesses are most truthful when they feel the safest, when they get the sense there will be no repercussions for telling their story. Hampton said those witnesses might feel safest if given immunity.

———

Catherine Fish, Seth's long-time girlfriend who'd alleged brutal abuse at his hands, was on the prosecution's witness list, but was never called to testify.

———

When Paul Hickok was finally called to the stand, his version of that night backed up the testimony of both Kat and Roberta. He recalled seeing Lizzi's partially nude body on the floor and that he'd urged Seth to call for medical help.

When asked why neither he nor Roberta had reported the incident to police, he said, "The biggest reason that we didn't do anything was to give him the opportunity to do it himself."

Barth asked Paul where Kat was when he and Roberta were looking at Lizzi's body. He responded that she was sitting on the floor in the kitchen, her knees pressed to her chest.

"She seemed to be crying from time to time."

Barth then asked Paul if he'd seen any tears on Kat's face when she cried. Paul testified that he had not.

———

While the Marriott family stoically walked past the press every day, Seth's mother, Heather, sat virtually unnoticed in the hallway outside of courtroom 2. She arrived early for the trial each morning, bringing with her a freshly laundered and ironed shirt for her son to wear beneath his black vest. She would then bring the shirt home at night, rotating her washing and ironing between a single white shirt and single French blue one.

Seth's mother didn't enter the courtroom. She was on the defense's list as a possible witness but was never called to testify. The attendance of Seth's father, Joseph, was never noted by the papers.

One of the TV networks set up a powerful Wi-Fi hotspot in the building for the media to use during the trial. With her mobile device in her lap, Heather Mazzaglia sat on a vinyl-cushioned chair outside the clerk's office and did what thousands of other people around the country were doing: watched the live stream of the trial.

———————

Unlike Heather Mazzaglia, Kat's mother *did* testify. Denise McDonough got to court early and was speaking cordially with the witness advocate when Peter Hinckley arrived. The assistant attorney general thanked Denise for coming to help the prosecution and she said he was welcome. In an awkward attempt to make conversation, Hinckley reminded Denise that he was the prosecutor who'd put her daughter in jail. Denise later said she wasn't sure how she was supposed to react to the statement, so she just walked away to wait until she was called upon.

On the stand, Denise talked about how close she had been with her daughter and how that had changed when Kat ran away from home to be with Seth. She said Seth had gone to great lengths to keep Kat isolated from her family.

Lizzi's mother, Melissa Marriott, also testified. For weeks, she'd sat alongside her family in the gallery on mercilessly uncomfortable wooden benches. She spent much of that time working on a needlepoint, keeping her hands busy and her concentration on something other than the explicit testimony about her daughter's final minutes. The needlepoint was of a dolphin leaping from the water into a sky of many colors, symbolic of Lizzi's love of the ocean.

Now, as the state's second-to-last witness, her appearance was brief and transactional. She told the jury that, no, Lizzi had not been suicidal and, no, she didn't have any medical problems. No, Lizzi didn't have a history of seizures, her mother testified and, no, she didn't have family problems that would cause her to run away from home.

When asked if anyone had heard from Lizzi after the night of October 9, 2012, Melissa Marriott's voice cracked as she said, "No we have not."

The final witness was the state's deputy chief medical examiner, Jennie Duval. Although Duval hadn't been able to examine Lizzi's body, she provided medical context for the eyewitnesses' testimony. Duval said that if one were strangled by a rope, there would be visible ligature marks, just like the kind of marks Roberta and Paul had described seeing around Lizzi's neck.

Also, Duval testified, whether a victim is strangled or intentionally hanged, the neck and face will turn red or purple above the rope line, a discoloration that doesn't occur when one is smothered. In many cases, a victim of smothering can appear to have no external injuries at all.

After seventeen days of testimony and thirty witnesses, the state rested its case against Seth Mazzaglia.

———

The defense offered only a few witnesses. A medical examiner from Connecticut said Kat's testimony disproved the accusation of manual strangulation. He said that Kat had never claimed to see a "ligature furrow" on the neck.

(Ironically, Kat *had* told investigators she'd seen ligature marks on Lizzi's neck, but it wasn't until midway through the trial that the state realized it had never disclosed that fact to the defense. As a result of their discovery error, no mention of Kat's observations would be permitted.)

Defense investigator Lisa Greenwaldt testified to how she'd videotaped Kat's statement to the public defender. The jury again got to hear about Kat's unusual behavior as she described killing Lizzi by sitting on her face.

Under cross, Hinckley struck back, reminding Greenwaldt that she hadn't taped her very *first* meeting with Kat, suggesting the defense team had fed her information with leading questions. Greenwaldt's initial report indicated one of the public defenders had told Kat they believed "something of a more intimate nature" occurred in the apartment, and that was when Kat had offered her story about queening.

Hinckley said there were only a few handwritten notes from the first three-and-a-half-hour meeting with Kat and that Greenwaldt's final report wasn't prepared until eighteen months later.

————

The final act was scheduled for Wednesday, June 25, 2014.

AAG Peter Hinckley had given the opening argument, so as was custom, his cocounsel, Geoffrey Ward, would give the closing. Unlike Hinckley's oversized jacket, Ward's well-tailored suit hung comfortably on his shoulders. Above those shoulders, Ward's youthful face belied the oratory skill of a veteran litigator.

In a surprisingly passionate closing, Ward's first move

was an attempt to neutralize what he knew would be the defense's upcoming attack on their star witness. He reminded the panel of all of the sexual and psychological manipulation Seth had put Kat through.

"Those were real, genuine emotions that she showed when she testified. The crying and shaking . . . the *real* tears. You all saw them."

Seth, Ward said, had gone to great lengths to synchronize fake alibis, to point the finger at other people, and then try to do away with witnesses who could testify against him. He'd even tried to do away with Kat.

"He cares so little for her that he tells her to kill herself," Ward continued. "All of this is a glimpse into his twisted mind."

Ward recalled how dominant Seth Mazzaglia had been, how his every whim needed tending to.

"This defendant made clear if his sexual desires were not fulfilled, 'the Darkness' would get the better of him."

When Seth got upset that Kat would be gone for two weeks, Ward reminded the jury, he punished her by beating and sodomizing her. The punishment wouldn't stop until Kat could find him a sexual offering, and that's where Lizzi Marriott came in. But Lizzi did something no one ever did to the Master in his own home. She told him no.

"He was not in control of Lizzi, and he couldn't stand it. And he killed her for it."

Ward held up the black gloves Seth had worn. Lizzi's death was not the result of some tragic fetish accident or even a twisted snuff fantasy. The murder of Lizzi Marriott was the result of a temper tantrum by a stunted child who didn't get his way, a man so enraged by rejection that he raped Lizzi's lifeless corpse while shouting base insults at her.

"This case, above all else, is about the truth."

Pointing to Seth at the defense table, Geoffrey Ward said, "*He* is a cold-blooded killer. Give him the justice he has tried in so many ways, for so long, to avoid."

Despite the legal custom, defense attorney Melissa Davis did not deliver the closing for Seth's team. Joachim Barth, who'd given the opening statement nearly five weeks earlier, also took the opportunity to have the last word. As expected, his impassioned argument focused on Kat McDonough.

Barth described a young girl dying to get out of her parents' house, a girl who exploited Seth when she saw a chance to move in with him. Kat exaggerated stories, Barth said, like the one about her father having broken her nose, in order to get Seth's sympathy. It was Kat, not Seth, whose elaborate fantasy world permeated the couple's life, it was *she* who made him believe these personas could take over their bodies and change the future.

Barth told the jury that *Kat* was the one who'd sought out women online for kinky trysts. And they'd heard it from her own mouth, on video. They'd all seen Kat coldly explain how she'd smothered another human being for her own sexual gratification. It was *Kat*, Barth said, who'd gotten caught in lie after lie after lie.

"She has *got* to lie to protect herself."

Barth then asked the jury an expected rhetorical question: *What was at the heart of Kat's deception?* Her incredibly generous plea deal, he suggested, a deal so good that it would be just a matter of weeks before she was already eligible for parole.

"She has years of motivation. She has all the motivation of the beautiful things life has to offer."

———

On Thursday morning, June 26, 2014, the jurors returned to receive instructions from Judge Houran.

"Simply because a witness has taken the oath to tell the truth does not mean you have to accept the testimony as true," Houran warned, adding, "inconsistencies or contradictions in a witness's testimony do not necessarily mean you should not believe the witness."

He asked the jury to evaluate all the evidence with "care and caution" before he sent the panel of nine women and seven men to deliberate behind closed doors.

———

After eight hours of deliberation, the foreperson sent word on Friday morning that the jury had a question for Judge Houran about the conspiracy charge, one of two lesser charges against Seth. It was the third time they'd asked the court to clarify a matter of law since they began deliberating.

Almost immediately after receiving an answer from the judge about what comprises conspiracy, the jury sent word back they'd reached a verdict. It would be announced at one P.M., giving all interested parties time to assemble in the courtroom.

There were many more reporters waiting after lunch to get into courtroom 2 than had covered the trial day to day. There were also a great number of law enforcement officers from several agencies, all who'd either worked the investigation or helped conduct the search for Lizzi.

The jury's rapid verdict was the cause of much speculation; one of the sides clearly had captured the jury, and those assembled were genuinely split as to which had prevailed.

The murmuring subsided as the Marriott family entered the building and walked down the second-floor hallway for the last time. Bob Marriott was surrounded by his extended family, but Melissa was not in attendance. The presumption was that she couldn't bear to watch as the jury announced its decision.

The uncomfortable wooden benches were as packed as church pews on Christmas Eve. Seth entered in cuffs, escorted by several more deputies and bailiffs than usual. He sat down at the defense table, his leg almost immediately beginning to bounce as it had throughout the trial.

The virtual courtroom was also packed. Television stations in New Hampshire and Boston broke into their afternoon talk programming to cover the verdict live. With text message and e-mail bulletins announcing an imminent verdict, live streams were overloaded with viewers. At restaurants around New England, lunch-goers asked bartenders to change the channel so they could watch the end of the drama that had gripped the region for weeks.

After thanking the jury for its work, Judge Houran asked the court clerk to read the charges. Seth stood, and his attorneys, Joaquim Barth and Melissa Davis, placed their hands on his back as he rose from his seat.

"Madame foreperson, in the matter of *State v. Seth Mazzaglia*, the first charge: purposeful first-degree murder by strangulation. Do you find the defendant guilty or not guilty?"

The answer came back in a confident voice.

"Guilty."

"So say you all, members of the jury?"

A unanimous "yes."

The verdict meant an automatic sentence of life in prison without the possibility of parole.

Seth showed no emotion, standing still while the jury also found him guilty on the alternate first-degree murder charge—murder during the commission of a sexual assault—and charges of conspiring to falsify evidence and witnesses tampering. The only movement he made was after the verdict, when he offered his hands behind his back to the deputy for cuffing. He was to be taken away immediately, his formal sentencing to come at a later hearing.

Instead of being escorted back through the gallery and into the hallway, past the reporters and Lizzi's family, Seth Mazzaglia was walked by officers through a door at the front of the courtroom, next to the witness stand. Once he walked through it, he was effectively swallowed up into the state's penitentiary system.

————

After the jurors were dismissed, Bob Marriott lifted himself from the creaky wooden bench and stood silently, deep in reflection. His family and friends left him alone for a few moments before embracing him in relief and with comfort.

The attorneys began to gather their boxes of documents and pack up the other resources they'd wheeled into courtroom 2 a month and a half earlier. Prosecutors Peter Hinckley and Geoffrey Ward turned to the gallery, shaking hands and exchanging hugs with Lizzi's loved ones. Many of the police officers in the room joined them, waiting their turn to express relief and condolences.

The media had set up a shared microphone and halogen lights in empty courtroom 4. Working in New Hampshire, where every would-be president must campaign, local reporters are used to staging impromptu press conferences. While this scene had many of the same trappings, nothing but gloom accompanied this win. There were no real victors, only relief that the trial was over, even among the media, who'd spent weeks listening to unspeakable stories about abuse and a young woman's murder.

The defense team declined to comment and skipped the press conference. AAG Geoffrey Ward approached the microphone first, saying that he would not take any questions related to the prosecution because the defendant would be appealing, keeping the legal case alive until that process was complete. Surrounded by men in a variety of uniforms, Ward said their goal had been to "bring Lizzi home," and acknowledged that, sadly, they were unable to do that.

The prosecutors stood off to the side. The room fell to a hush, save the mechanical chorus of camera shutters, as the victim's family approached the microphone. Bob Marriott looked physically haggard, much older than he had at those candlelight vigils twenty months earlier.

Reading from a piece of paper, he began by thanking the members of law enforcement and the prosecution team for their work in ensuring Seth would never be able to hurt another woman. He said that surely there would have been other victims. His voice wavered then, setting off streams of tears from those around him, including from his sister, Becky Hanna, and her husband, Tony.

"Unfortunately, a trial, even with a conviction, cannot console us for the loss of Lizzi," he said. "We will always miss her and wonder what could have been."

As he spoke, various hands would rest on his shoulder, seeming to hold him up as he continued. For her parents, Lizzi Marriott had died twenty times a day, every day, in courtroom 2. He said, "This trial has been torturous for us. The truth of what happened to Lizzi is horrendous, and every time it has been told it has reinforced the despair that we feel." Still indignant at the suggestion that Lizzi was a willing participant in the sexual encounter that led to her death, he added, "Listening to the defense has been even worse."

Bob Marriott walked out of the room without looking back. The prosecutors and cops followed him through the door.

Cameramen and engineers began to gather their equipment and pull up the thousands of feet of cable that had been run throughout the courthouse and to satellite trucks in the parking lots. Reporters raced off to neutral corners to write stories for evening news deadlines. It was Friday, and come Monday, they could finally move on to other stories.

But few found it so easy to move on.

CHAPTER TWENTY-TWO

Until the Tides
Bring You Back to Me

From the state prison, Seth Mazzaglia spoke on the phone with his mother, Heather Mazzaglia, six weeks after his conviction. His legal troubles were still not over.

Seth had yet to be tried on the separate charge of soliciting Ryan Bachman's help in the planned escape from jail. When questioned by reporters on whether it was a waste of resources to move forward with the trial in light of Seth's murder conviction, Peter Hinckley argued that it wasn't, because the defendant had "committed the crime." (Seth would later plead guilty and put the matter to rest.)

He still hadn't been formally sentenced for Lizzi's death, but the outcome of his August 14, 2014, hearing wasn't in question. The judge had no discretion; the penalty for his conviction was an automatic life sentence without possibility of parole. Most of the hearing's time would be dedicated to victim impact statements from the Marriott family, a chance for them to directly address Seth about what he had done to Lizzi.

"I'm going to see if there's any way I can not attend," Seth told his mother.

He would ask his lawyers to file a motion allowing him to skip the hearing and be sentenced in absentia. There was no law that compelled him to be there.

"I already know what everyone's gonna say there, so why the hell do I have to be there? And it's a waste of my time," Seth complained.

Heather Mazzaglia sounded concerned.

"Well, it's for them," she said, referring to the Marriotts.

Seth became petulant.

"Yeah, well, I'm not feeling particularly gracious at the moment." He snorted. "If I had been found innocent of the big stuff like I should have been, and like I am, now then, it might be a different story. Then, then I might have some sympathy."

Heather Mazzaglia reminded her son that all he could do was regret his part in the crime, which he continued to claim was limited to his covering for Kat.

"Yeah, but I'm gonna have to sit there for an hour and a half listening to them yell and whine and bitch and moan and scream about how I'm a monster who killed someone when I'm not. That's what I'm literally gonna have to listen to for the whole time."

His mother tried again to express her displeasure, but Seth cut her off.

"It isn't gonna be, like, 'Oh, you took away our chance of burying her.' It's gonna be 'You're a monster,' and that's what it's gonna be over and over and over again."

Heather Mazzaglia empathized with the Marriotts. After all, she was losing her child too, albeit in a completely different way. She also was a victim of her son's actions, although she never characterized herself that way, at least not while speaking with him in prison. Instead, she tried to impart upon Seth the need to be gracious and to let the Marriotts have their day in court.

"They're in misery. They're in agony," she said. "Their daughter is lost. I would be the same if it were you. You have to sympathize with what they've lost."

Like a child who'd been scolded, Seth whined, "My preference would be not to attend the sentencing hearing."

"I think you have to be there to be sentenced," she said. "I think they have a right to confront you because the jury found you guilty."

———

Two days before the sentencing, the lawyers held a hearing on whether Seth could be compelled to attend his sentencing. Peter Hinckley argued it was important for the court, the public, and the victim's family that the defendant be in the courtroom. To prove Seth's objections were a matter of pride and not a matter of law, Hinckley read the transcript of the telephone call with his mother, which, like all calls from the state prison, had been recorded.

Forty-five minutes after the brief hearing ended, Judge Houran announced that the defense had withdrawn its motion. Seth would attend after all.

His attempt to avoid listening to the victim impact statements left the Marriotts livid.

Lizzi's mother, Melissa Marriott, said, "He's just a selfish coward and he really doesn't care about anybody else."

———

The sentencing was held in the same courtroom as the trial. On August 14, 2014, courtroom 2 was again packed with media, the Marriott family, and law enforcement officers from various agencies. Eight of the sixteen jurors and alternates from the trial were also in attendance.

When Seth Mazzaglia entered the courtroom, he wasn't wearing his trademark black vest. He was wearing an inmate's uniform. He looked unkempt, his hair greasy and mussed, as if he hadn't bothered to shower that morning.

From the podium in the well of the courtroom, Melissa Marriott looked at Seth and spoke to him evenly.

"Mr. Mazzaglia . . . I want you to know that I unequivocally hate you."

She called him a coward and said he "threw away" her daughter because Lizzi had the self-esteem he lacked.

Lizzi's uncle, Tony Hanna, testified that Seth had

brought nothing but darkness into the world. He inti-
mated that the sexual violence Seth so enjoyed inflicting
would be reciprocated behind bars.

Other relatives and friends, including Lizzi's girlfriend,
Bethany Atwood, spent two hours telling the court how
their lives had been forever changed because of what
happened on October 9, 2012.

The last to speak was Bob Marriott.

"I wish that good would triumph over evil," he said,
"but you are proof beyond any doubt how untrue that is."

Bob said he'd heard from other women, other ex-girl-
friends, whom Seth had victimized and controlled.

"I get sick to my stomach when I hear what you did.
You repulse me with your egocentric view. She said no to
you—*twice*—and for that denial you murdered her."

Propped on an easel in the court's well was a blown-up
photo of Lizzi. Bob pointed to it, calling it "Dad's Exhibit
One." The image was of his daughter on a sunny day. She
was smiling, cradling a frog in her hands, her nails painted
in bright shades of yellow and blue. Just like that Blanding's turtle she'd stopped to help across the street, Lizzi
had rescued this frog in the backyard. Bob said the photo
symbolized everything that Lizzi was: happy, caring, and
charitable. It was the opposite of everything in Seth Mazzaglia.

Bob picked up the photograph and held it up high for
the gallery to see. He slowly pivoted counterclockwise,
giving everyone in attendance a long look at his daughter's
image. It can be easy to forget the person at the center of

a trial when weeks are spent on forensics and immunity deals and tide charts and psychic personas. Bob Marriott wanted to make sure no one would forget his daughter.

The court recessed after the statements and before sentencing. Heather Mazzaglia asked the victim advocate if Lizzi's father would be willing speak with her. Bob and his son, Robert Marriott III, went into a side conference room and waited for her.

Seth's mother entered the room clutching a red Bible. She walked to Bob and fell into his arms, sobbing. He held the woman for what—to an Associated Press reporter looking on—seemed a long time. She pulled away and handed Bob a folded letter. She also gave Lizzi's brother a hug. Later, she repeated the scene with Melissa Marriott.

When a reporter asked what she told the Marriott family, Heather Mazzaglia said, "Only that I'm sorry."

At sentencing, Judge Steven Houran declared that Seth Mazzaglia would serve life in prison for the first-degree murder of Lizzi Marriott. Concurrently, he would serve seven to fifteen years for the conspiracy charges and pay an eight-thousand-dollar fine. The state also wanted Seth to pay about five thousand dollars in administrative fees and penalties, and another one thousand dollars to the Marriott family to reimburse them for counseling and mileage expenses to and from court.

Houran asked if Seth had anything he wanted to say. The man who once called himself Darkheart, his hands still shackled at his waist, stood.

He denied his guilt. "I did not rape and murder Elizabeth Marriott," Seth began. "However, I do understand the Marriott family's pain." He continued, "I did play a part in covering up her death, a mistake I tried to correct when investigators came to me and I showed them exactly where I left Lizzi's body. Unfortunately, they were unable to recover her and for that I am truly sorry. My heart goes out to the Marriott family and I am very sorry for their loss."

He sat after delivering his line. Seth Mazzaglia, with his BA in theater, had always played a good villain.

Denise McDonough did not attend Seth's sentencing, but her sister and father, the two people who'd backed her up when she'd confronted Seth at his apartment, did. They contemplated whether they should approach the Marriotts. They eventually did, but after introducing themselves, found they had no suitable words to impart. The Marriotts took their hands and said kindly, "We understand. We understand."

Afterward, Bob Marriott was asked if his opinion of Kat McDonough had evolved over the past few months. Her contribution to Seth's conviction was undeniable, but so was her role in Lizzi's murder.

"I have a lot of reason to very much dislike her and her involvement in what happened to my daughter," he said. "I also have a lot of sympathy for the situation she was in and what she was put through by that person we just sent to jail."

On November 6, 2014, just shy of her year-and-a-half minimum sentence, Kat McDonough had a parole hearing. The state parole board met at the men's prison in Concord, so Kat appeared by video link from the women's prison in Goffstown. The three-person panel was charged with evaluating her remorse, her behavior while incarcerated, and her likelihood to re-offend, among other considerations.

Bob and Melissa Marriott; Lizzi's uncle, Tony Hanna; and her grandmother were all in attendance. Denise and Peter McDonough also attended, though they were prohibited from taking part in the deliberations. Kat's parents were now officially separated, but their relationship with each other had improved greatly since the trial.

As the proceeding began, Parole Board Chairwoman Donna Sytek addressed Kat through the video monitor.

"It was a surprise to me that you were eligible at this point," she said, clearly aware of the notoriety surrounding this inmate. "You got the deal of the century," she added incredulously.

The board asked Bob Marriott if he wanted to speak. Less than three months had passed since Seth's sentencing, and it seemed his sympathy for Kat extended only so far.

"Kathryn McDonough is a despicable person," he said.

He explained how his daughter's murder had been the defining moment of his life. He'd cried every day for months, he said. His loss of control over life itself was completely consuming.

"You have failed at protecting your child" was how he described feeling. "You have no influence in the process to find justice. You are forced to experience the worst thing you can ever imagine."

He said it wasn't until July 2013 that the family had learned the full story, the depravity that had been inflicted upon Lizzi in her final moments. This was after Kat had made her plea deal and told authorities what she said had really happened inside the apartment. The Marriotts' anger was only amplified when they learned how little the law allowed for Seth's accomplice to be punished.

"The person who purposefully set up the circumstances that led to [Lizzi's] death hadn't done anything criminal," Bob said, his voice quivering with rage. "We lost our daughter and this is our consolation prize."

Bob said that he wanted Kat in jail for a very long time, but he had accepted that her plea deal was necessary in order to secure Seth's conviction. Even so, he told the parole board, he didn't think releasing Kat on the bottom end of her sentence was the right thing to do.

Kat, who should not have been expecting a pat on the back from Lizzi's family, cried softly while Bob Marriott spoke.

"I don't even know what to say," she said as he finished, reaching for a tissue.

"I wish you were here in person," said board member Mark Fulone, squinting at the video monitor. "I don't see any tears on your face."

Harkening back to Joachim Barth's devastating cross-examination of her, Kat looked thunderstruck at the accusation. Her mother, Denise, said she thought the tear comment was a cheap shot. Kat composed herself and replied, "I've had a lot of time to think about what a horrible, horrible thing it was. I allowed someone's life to end."

Sytek, a former New Hampshire speaker of the House of Representatives, took over the conversation. Kat's prison record was unremarkable. She had a minor violation for oversleeping, but no major infractions. Sytek was troubled that, of all the services provided at the prison, Kat had not taken the relationship-counseling course.

"It was that relationship," Sytek said of her relationship with Seth, "that resulted in this horrific crime."

But counseling was not a requirement of her sentence, and Kat seemed unaware that the program existed. Sytek pointed out that many female inmates found themselves incarcerated as a result of something going horribly wrong with their husbands or boyfriends.

When asked what her release plan was, Kat said she intended to move back home with her father. Fulone pointed out that she'd testified at trial her father had been emotionally abusive. Kat replied that things had changed. Peter McDonough now visited her regularly, she said. He was comfortable with his marriage being over. He was no longer taking out on his family any resentments he had about his life. Kat and her father had repaired much of what had broken.

The third board member, Jeff Brown, expressed skepticism about Kat staying in Portsmouth. Who on the Seacoast would hire her? How could she walk through Market Square without people recognizing her? How could she ensure her own safety? Though the board couldn't mandate that she leave the state on her release, they told her she should consider it.

"You're not someone who was just picked up for drugs. You were on the front page for over a year."

At the end of the hearing, Kat's request for early release was denied.

———

The play about Kat McDonough's life will not have a triumphant musical finale.

When Kat is eventually released, she will bear both the weight of her sins and the pain of her suffering. Denise McDonough worries about the many long, lonely years her daughter has yet to live. Will she find a new home, take a new name, seek her own second act? Will she return to the theater? Denise doesn't doubt it. In a wig or a corset or a princess dress, Kat will appear again on a stage and play whatever role she can get. And if she has learned anything, she will stick to the script.

———

The Marriotts created a scholarship in Lizzi's name, called the Intrepid Explorer Fund, to provide financial assistance to marine biology students who hope to continue Lizzi's mission to protect the ocean and its creatures.

The Atlantic White Shark Conservancy also honored Lizzi by naming a shark after her. The fourteen-foot female was tagged with a satellite tracker, and updates on her journey are posted online. "Lizzi the White Shark" is part of a larger study to unravel the mystery of how the species travel the Atlantic, and the data she provides may someday deepen our understanding of marine biology.

After the trial, Bob Marriott continued to visit Peirce Island, looking out over the rocks and talk to his daughter. But her mother could never do it. Despite all her happy memories of Lizzi at the beach, Melissa couldn't bear to look at the ocean again. Knowing her daughter was out there somewhere in its vast depths was too overwhelming. The Marriotts instead erected a marker for Lizzi next to a small body of water near their home in Massachusetts.

There is something cruelly poetic about a woman who lived for the ocean spending eternity there.

Like a tide coming in or a tide going out, sometimes the thought is poetic.

Sometimes the thought is just cruel.

We first heard the name Lizzi Marriott when everyone else in New England did, on October 12, 2012. Her face was all over the news, framed in the kind of breathless graphics it seems TV stations always roll when a beautiful coed goes missing.

The following days brought long shots of divers emerging from cold black waters, tense TV press conferences delivered by tight-lipped officials, and heartbreaking vigils full of tears and candlelight. There was a poster that became a fixture on bulletin boards and shop counters all over the state, as if Lizzi might be discovered wandering Concord's downtown or hiking in the White Mountains, the victim of some kind of innocent miscommunication.

As we followed the coverage and saw those posters

multiply, we suspected Lizzi had been the victim of something far worse. Everyone else in New England did too.

As true crime authors, we're often asked how we decide which cases to write about. The truth is that, while every murder is worth exploring on behalf of the victim, rare is the case that can fill the pages of a book, because in most, there is no before and there is no after; there is only the act itself and whatever punishment comes after it. But in the months following Lizzi Marriott's disappearance, it became clear that Seth Mazzaglia's arrest, followed by Kat McDonough's, pointed to a far more confounding narrative than the one law enforcement officials had laid out in the early days of the investigation.

It's not hard to fall in love with Lizzi Marriott and her family. Her father, Bob Marriott, maintains a Facebook page where he posts photos that reveal what a dazzling young woman she was. It seems no image of Lizzi exists in which she's not smiling, performing, or rescuing some wild creature in peril. Everyone who followed this case felt the Marriotts' loss very deeply. It was impossible not to. We corresponded with Bob Marriott for several months while working on this project, and it's clear that his pain hasn't diminished with the passage of time, and that he will never know why his daughter was taken away from those who loved her.

If there's one answer we do have to that impossible question, it's the one the jury handed down. Lizzi wasn't a victim because of her extraordinary openness and humanity or because she was "too trusting." She was a victim because Seth Mazzaglia orchestrated the events that ended her life.

We could not have anticipated the overwhelming complexity of Seth's fantasy world before we began researching this case. His story—that of an emotionally stunted loner whose adolescent notions about sex and power evolved into a longtime pattern of sexual violence—wasn't of particular interest to us. From the outset, it was clear that this would not be a book about Seth Mazzaglia, and although we knew his dark inner life would take up pages, it was never our central focus.

For us, it was Kat McDonough who emerged as the central and most confounding figure in this case. We may never know the full measure of her guilt or innocence, but we do know she wasn't the first woman Seth abused and pulled into his rage-fueled fantasies. And if not for Lizzi's murder and his conviction for it, Kat would probably not have been the last.

By all accounts, Kat was a typical seventeen-year-old when she met Seth. She attended high school, hung out with her friends, performed in plays, and—perhaps most typical of all—had a drama-filled relationship with her father.

But in the very short time she was with Seth, Kat evolved into a person who knowingly, perhaps willingly, pushed the defiled body of a friend into a tidal river in order to conceal a rape and murder. The questions around how that evolution happened were the ones we sought to answer. How did Kat's course change so radically in such a short period of time? Was she fully under the influence of an abuser? Or would digging into her story reveal a darkness that had been inside her all along?

As we attempted to unravel the complex investigation and legal maneuvers that came to define the public's perception of this case, we sometimes found ourselves investigating in circles or digging out of rabbit warrens that began with simple fact-checking phone calls. Much of this work helped us get closer to answering questions that continue to surround the guilty, but it also served to reveal something larger: While the truth is somewhat easy to prove, lies are nearly impossible to verify, and the gray area between the two is the most difficult to navigate of all.

Bob and Melissa Marriott ultimately chose not to contribute to this book. Although they were eager to share Lizzi's story before trial, the family has been disappointed with certain characterizations of Lizzi in the media and with depictions of the events surrounding her murder. We respected their decision and relied instead on information from previous interviews, Lizzi's own writings, and the public record in order to flesh out some details.

During our final correspondence, Bob did make two requests on behalf of his family. First, he wanted to raise awareness of the scholarship set up in Lizzi's name. He also asked, "Are you addressing domestic abuse at all? One thing that can come out of this is education about the cycle of abuse."

We believe this issue is a central theme in this story,

and we hope that readers come to know more about that cycle as they read this book.

————

At the time of this book's publication, Seth Mazzaglia's conviction is under appeal at the New Hampshire Supreme Court. Should the court vacate the verdict and order a new trial, he will be presumed innocent until a new jury weighs in on the crime.

There's one aspect of Seth's case that is no longer an open question. In 2015, New Hampshire Governor Maggie Hassan signed House Bill 225 into law. The bill, which had rare bipartisan support as it sailed through the state's House and Senate, makes it mandatory for defendants to appear in person during victim impact statements. It was drafted in direct response to Seth Mazzaglia's attempt to skip his own sentencing and his desire to avoid listening to Lizzi Marriott's family "yell and whine and bitch and moan and scream" about her murder.

ACKNOWLEDGMENTS

Because of Seth Mazzaglia's pending appeal, his legal case is still alive, and many of the usual sources, documents, and officials used in researching a story of this nature were not available, per New Hampshire law and legal code of conduct. This presented an enormous challenge; however, we would thank those who did work with us, either on background, on the record, or as not-for-attribution sources. This includes many relatives, friends, and acquaintances of the major figures in this story. Some of those people chose not to be identified out of respect for the families still dealing with the fallout from this tragedy. To those we've promised not to name, our gratitude is immeasurable.

For their invaluable contributions to our work, we would like to thank Carole Alfano, Jen Fansler, Laura

Mitchell, Christopher Orr, Kimberly Haas, and Emily Corwin. Without Denise McDonough's thoughtful participation, this story would lack many of the details we were able to include.

Neither Seth Mazzaglia nor Kat McDonough responded to our repeated requests for interviews. Heather Mazzaglia, through a family attorney, said she would not comment.

There are several people behind the scenes without whom our work as writers would never go further than our computer screens. They include our agent, Sharlene Martin at Martin Literary Management; our editor, Amanda Ng, as well as Lara Robbins, Jane Hammer, and the entire staff at Berkley Books.

Finally, we want to express our most heartfelt gratitude to our longtime editor, Shannon Jamieson-Vazquez. She has been a collaborator of the highest measure, possessing a keen eye and sharp pencil that we've relied on to guide our work. Over the years she's been our cheerleader, taskmaster, tinker, tailor, and marital referee—but most of all, we cherish her as a friend.